Sustainable Resource Development in the Third World

edited by
Douglas D. Southgate
and John F. Disinger

Routledge
Taylor & Francis Group
LONDON AND NEW YORK

First published 1987 by Westview Press

Published 2019 by Routledge
52 Vanderbilt Avenue, New York, NY 10017
2 Park Square, Milton Park, Abingdon, Oxon OX14 4RN

Routledge is an imprint of the Taylor & Francis Group, an informa business

Library of Congress Cataloging-in-Publication Data
Sustainable resource development in the Third World/
[edited by Douglas D. Southgate and John F. Disinger].
p. cm.—(Westview special studies in natural resources and energy management)
Includes index.
ISBN 0-8133-7522-3
1. Natural resources—Developing countries—Management.
2. Environmental policy—Developing countries. I. Southgate, Douglas Dewitt. II. Disinger, John F. III. Series.
HC59.7.S8826 1987
333.7'15'091724—dc19 **87-20137**
CIP

ISBN 13: 978-0-367-28932-4 (hbk)

ISBN 13: 978-0-367-30478-2 (pbk)

Sustainable Resource Development in the Third World

Published in cooperation with
the School of Natural Resources
of The Ohio State University

Contents

Part III
Case Studies

Tables and Figures

Tables

Figures

Acknowledgments

Special thanks and appreciation for their efforts in the staging of the symposium and the production of this volume are due to the following members of the staff of the School of Natural Resources at The Ohio State University: Craig B. Davis, Director; Judy A. Kauffeld, Editor; Sara Brenner, Janice J. Gorsuch, Marjorie Pless, Elizabeth A. Poeppelman, Jerri L. Shafer, and Mignonne A. Whitlow.

D.D.S.
J.F.D.

Preface

Over time, scientists, technologists, and resource managers in affluent countries have devised and institutionalized methodologies for exploiting and managing natural resources in their own environments with considerable success. In doing so, they have provided models, at least of development and affluence, that the less developed countries seek to employ.

Many mechanisms are currently used in the transfer of technology and its concomitants from the developed world to the developing world. Among the most successful are those promoting the open exchange of ideas and information between and among the key players from both worlds.

An international symposium involving both invited and contributed papers addressing the technological and institutional challenges of sustainable development of natural resources in the Third World was staged in September 1985 in Columbus, Ohio, co-sponsored by The Argonne National Laboratory of Argonne, Illinois, The Tropical Renewable Resources Program and the School of Natural Resources of The Ohio State University, and the United States Agency for International Development. This volume presents selected papers from the symposium.

Described in many papers are "success stories"; that is, approaches that have worked are examined. However, the authors have candidly and conscientiously provided complete treatments of their topics, indicating clearly the problems faced, false starts, and frustrations. In doing so, they offer useful suggestions for others to consider in developing their resource management strategies, along with evidence of many options which are better not employed, and many problems still in need of solution.

Douglas D. Southgate
John F. Disinger

1/ Introduction

Douglas D. Southgate

Throughout the developing world, renewable resources that are the bases for food and energy production are under severe strain. Land quality is deteriorating because of excessive grazing and cropping and because irrigation water is managed poorly. Firewood gathering, increasing agricultural competition for wooded land, and lax enforcement of reforestation laws have combined to create deforestation problems in many third world nations. The impacts of declining land quality, lost forests, and increased sedimentation of waterways are not confined to the countryside. As renewable resources deteriorate, urban residents face progressively higher food prices while paying more for hydroelectricity.

Concerned about the costs of environmental degradation, the governments of many countries have recently initiated projects intended to foster improved resource management or to ease human pressure on the environment. Erosion control has been encouraged on range and farmland upstream from reservoirs. The use of more fuel-efficient stoves has been promoted, where gathering of fuelwood is a primary cause of deforestation. To encourage tree conservation, innovation and adoption of improved nursery, harvesting, and milling technologies have been supported. Practically all of these initiatives have received financial support from donor agencies.

Some resources management projects have accomplished their objectives. Taken as a whole, however, efforts to conserve renewable resources in the developing world cannot be termed a major success. Even in countries where projects have been undertaken, it is difficult to show that the rates at which agricultural land is degraded, forests are lost, and water is polluted have been greatly reduced.

In part, the limited effectiveness of third world resource conservation projects reflects an inadequate understanding of tropical and subtropical environments. For example, those wishing to mount projects aimed at ameliorating sedimentation problems in reservoirs, waterways, and harbors find their efforts hampered by limited information about how erosion control at one site will affect sediment yield at some point downstream. Beyond such technical limitations, a variety of social and organizational constraints on renewable resource management present themselves in the Third World. In many countries, the primary agents of environmental change—small farmers and herders confined to marginal land—do not find resource conservation to be in their best interest, given prevailing market and institutional conditions. They are the ones, for instance, who suffer disproportionately from the credit shortages created by interest rate controls which prevail throughout the developing world. Denied access to formal financial markets, they must rely on informal markets, where interest rates are considerably higher. As a result, they are discouraged from investing in land improvement generally, and from adopting soil conservation practices specifically.

A variety of major impediments to improved resource management exists under the typical developing country tenure regime. For all intents and purposes, rangeland in much of the Third World is an open-access resource. Consequently, no individual has an incentive either to restrain his use of rangeland or to improve it. Furthermore, without a redefinition of property rights, a government's attempt to control erosion from rangeland (e.g., by sowing improved grass species) are bound to yield poor results as herders allow their animals to graze away all new growth.

Finally, there is a lack in much of the developing world of what may be termed an organizational infrastructure to implement conservation programs. Granted, networks of government and private organizations that now exist in the United States and other affluent countries do not always promote or accomplish the best possible use of resources. However, the absence of organizational infrastructure is a much more serious problem, particularly when an effort is being made to foster resource conservation in a crisis situation (e.g., when sedimentation is threatening to close off a multimillion-dollar dam complex).

Solution of the developing world's environmental problems requires simultaneous evaluation of the technical, social, and organizational aspects of those problems. This book contains observations on each. Most of the contributing authors focus on watershed management, broadly defined here to encompass both soil conservation and social forestry. In addition to this problem, renewable energy projects and threats to biological diversity are addressed. All chapters contain general insights into the assessment of environmental problems in the Third World and development of strategies for dealing with those problems.

Discussions in the next four chapters focus on the broad challenges facing individuals and agencies attempting to mount resource conservation projects and programs. In addition to outlining the dimensions of a world-wide social forestry program which would contribute in many ways to the welfare of rural poor and society as a whole, Gregersen and McGaughey identify five factors promoting implementation of an individual social forestry project. Referring to successful efforts in South Korea, Haiti, and elsewhere, they argue for (a) keeping technologies simple and adaptable to various environmental and social conditions, (b) keeping unit costs low so that relatively large numbers of people can be benefited, (c) taking a "systems approach" to social forestry and rural development, (d) insuring widespread participation by the local population, particularly including women, and (e) promoting effective financial and organizational support by governments and other groups.

In their chapter, Logan and Cooperband investigate the potential of agroforestry as a means of combatting soil erosion of the steeplands of the tropics and subtropics, addressing both "hard science" research needs and the necessity of people-related services. Next, a critical examination of the benefits of forestation is offered by Hamilton and Pearce. They caution that "over-selling" the impacts of tree-planting on rainfall, erosion, sedimentation, flooding, and water availability could lead to a backlash among governments and donor agencies against forestry and other conservation projects.

Closely related to the tendencies of some individuals to exaggerate the benefits of tree-planting has been the zeal with which others have over-promoted renewable energy technologies in developing countries. Kooi, who has become intimately familiar with this phenomenon while working in West Africa and elsewhere, denounces "uninformed boosterism" as a serious impediment within the cultures of affluent countries to renewable energy development in particular, and rural development in general.

Among the major recommendations made in chapters two through five is careful documentation of the economic and social impacts of resource conservation projects. Chapters six through eight address this task. In addition to outlining some fundamental vocabulary and techniques for economic evaluation, Southgate and Hitzhusen stress the need to pursue analysis at two levels. First, small farmers' and herders' incentives or disincentives to conserve resources under prevailing and alternative market and institutional conditions must be ascertained. Second, using the best information available about the external impacts of resource management decisions, the full social costs of a project must be compared to the full social benefits. The authors indicate the difficulties associated with accomplishing both tasks.

Hansen and Erbaugh offer a sociologist's perspective on small farmers' and herders' resource management decisions and on the factors influencing that group's participation in conservation projects. They contend that project success hinges on (a) the affected population's openness to change, particularly technological change, (b) the nature and degree of institutional change, (c) compatibility of the project with existing social organizations and customs, and (d) equitable distribution of project costs and benefits.

Serving as a counterpoint to much of the economic literature on third world environmental problems is Norgaard's chapter. He ascribes the shifting focus of that literature (first carrying capacity, then energy, and now genetic diversity) to the limitations of the prevailing economic paradigm. Contrasted to the "atomistic-mechanistic" world view of neoclassical economics is a coevolutionary world view, which Norgaard contends is a superior framework for conceptualizing environmental problems such as the threat to biological diversity, and for developing resource policy.

The remaining chapters in the book focus on individual resource conservation projects. Reading the case studies, one appreciates how heeding the advice offered in this book's early chapters and conducting sound social science analysis enhances the likelihood of project success. Kemph and Hernandez, drawing on their considerable experiences with a large-scale natural resource management effort in the Dominican Republic, comment forthrightly on the factors promoting and inhibiting the development and implementation of watershed management projects and nationwide conservation policy. Roth presents a general model for environmental education projects and discusses how that model has been applied in Barbados and the Dominican Republic. Developing a theme stressed by other contributors to this book, Barborak and Green indicate how enlisting the support of local populations has greatly facilitated efforts to protect threatened wildlands in several Latin American countries. They also note that non-governmental organizations can play a crucial role in conservation projects. Hyman, in his discussion of a project to encourage use of more fuel-efficient stoves in Kenya, shows that adopting technologies and information dissemination strategies to the existing cultural milieu is essential. The approach he describes contrasts sharply with the maladept efforts criticized so effectively by Kooi.

The concluding chapter is a highly personalized statement by Sunil Roy, a veteran public servant, which demonstrates his commitment to the concept and practice of sustainable development of natural resources as a necessary approach to the confrontation of world problems. His accounting of the situation in India, particularly as related to development efforts by representatives of the developed nations, affords an opportunity to ponder the global commonality of the institutional challenges facing those who would develop the resource base for the benefit of humankind.

Being based both on careful research and analysis and on first-hand experience, the case studies and more general chapters contained in this volume yield many insights to those charged with designing and implementing projects to encourage conservation of the Third World's fragile base of renewable natural resources.

Part I
Overview

2/ Social Forestry and Sustainable Development

Hans Gregersen
Stephen E. McGaughey

Social forestry is tree-related production for personal and local use. In many parts of the developing world, it is more acceptable technically—socially, culturally, and economically—than large-scale forestry and agroforestry. Social forestry technologies are simple, replicable, and low-risk, and unit costs can be kept in line. A holistic approach to land use is fostered, while local participation is both possible and necessary. But initiating social forestry can be costly. "Technological packages" are highly location-specific, community development institutions may be absent or ineffective, and foresters and extension agents may be unavailable or insufficiently trained. Nonetheless, there are success stories. Hans Gregersen and Stephen McGaughey highlight their common elements, identifying factors that impede the spread of social forestry and suggesting procedures that promote that practice.

Nature of the Problem[1]

The term "social forestry" is used here to refer to any tree- or forest-related production activity undertaken by rural inhabitants and local communities to supply forest-based goods and services mainly for their own use, but secondarily for local sale. It is forestry activity by poor rural people and includes such practices as agroforestry and small-scale tree farming.

At first glance, social forestry may seem far removed from current problems of less developed countries—poverty, malnutrition and food crises, debt and balance-of-payment problems, and energy shortages, among others. However, social forestry is an indispensable part of the necessary government response to several fundamental problems facing most LDCs: widespread rural poverty; food crises and declining agricultural productivity associated with poor land use, deforestation, erosion, and declining water availability; and energy shortages in rural areas, which in nearly all cases translate into fuelwood scarcity.

Social forestry provides the basis for increasing farm incomes and diversifying sources of income, while taking advantage of land that is not always well-suited for other purposes. The large-scale commercial counterpart to social forestry is industrial forestry, in which enterprises produce for commercial markets and end uses, i.e., timber for sawnwood and panels and fiber for pulp and paper. While industrial forestry absorbs substantial investment resources and covers large blocks of contiguous land, social forestry takes up small areas or is blended into existing crop and livestock production areas of farmers or communities whose present land base may be quite small.

There are many dimensions to resource management. Deforestation and poor land use by upland farmers in the Himalayas result in hundreds of millions of dollars worth of damages in the form of agricultural and flood losses. It is estimated that 50 percent of India's land area is subject to serious erosion and every year more than 600 million tons of topsoil are washed away (Anon., 1982). These types of problems are repeated in all regions of the Third World due to poor land use practices and deforestation upstream. Dam reservoirs in many LDCs are silting up many times faster than planned, with a growing cost in terms of agricultural and power benefits foregone. In the Sahel, poor land use has resulted in rapid desertification.

Social forestry activity widely integrated into land use improvement programs can reduce the severity of these problems and actually solve them in some cases. In addition to its land use improvement role through agroforestry practices, social forestry improves the lives of poor rural people through direct provision of food supplements, fruits and nuts, wood for local needs, shade, fibers and leaves. Social forestry generates new sources of income for farmers and rural communities and can help in the difficult process of people's transition from the desperate condition of rural subsistence to one of a better level of living.

About 100 million inhabitants in the Third World are cold today because they lack fuel to heat their homes. Many are hungry because they lack fuel to cook food so that it is digestible. Another one billion people face hardship and a rising threat of starvation in part because of growing fuelwood scarcity (FAO, 1981). In many areas of the Sahel, sustained fuelwood production capacity limits population growth more than does crop and livestock production capacity. For the rural poor worldwide, it is indeed fuelwood scarcity that is at the heart of their energy crisis.

Social forestry activity involving planting of fuelwood and multipurpose species in and around farms and villages by millions of local inhabitants is an economically feasible solution to the rural energy crisis in many countries, particularly if combined with programs to improve fuelwood conversion efficiency. While market-traded fuel substitutes may be available, they are not yet accessible to most rural poor because of their costs. Also, the process of urbanization, which has accelerated rapidly in Africa and is well advanced in Latin America, does not always relieve the energy problem, either because urban inhabitants continue using wood-based energy sources such as charcoal, or the resource costs of substituting urban energy detract from solving energy problems for rural inhabitants.

The depletion of forest capital—deforestation—has now become a major concern. However, in some regions the gap is widening between the problem and the national policies and programs meant to narrow it. For example, a recent statement of the World Resources Institute (1985) suggests that:

> Between 1980 and 2000, the annual fuelwood deficit will have grown from 407 to 925 million m^3. This amount, which is presently met by overcutting existing forests, is equivalent to the annual increment of wood from two hundred million hectares of fuelwood plantations. The current rate of tree planting in tropical countries is less than 2 million ha/yr or barely 1 percent of what is required.

The Challenge

The twin dramas of massive deforestation and the fuelwood crisis have drawn attention to social forestry opportunities. Also, the promotion of rural development programs and projects has provided, in part, a vehicle to integrate forestry with rural community development. However, in order to mobilize the necessary political resources and action to do something about the problems, evidence of positive opportunities to solve them is needed. The issues have to be recognized and solutions have to be sought, no matter how tentative and uncertain they may be. The present discussion attempts to summarize what has been learned from past experience and what priorities should be assigned in the future.

The existing knowledge of technically operable social forestry options now surpasses the understanding of how to achieve their wide acceptance by rural inhabitants. The main unanswered questions are institutional and deal with how to design, finance, implement and manage social forestry programs on a sufficiently large scale to make a difference for a large number of rural poor. There have been many successful isolated projects. However, in terms of the present dimensions of the problems—hundreds of millions of people without adequate fuelwood, millions of hectares of land being destroyed by flood, desertification and erosion, millions of malnourished people—pilot projects each benefiting 1,000 or 2,000 families are only a very small first element in instituting widespread sustainable land use systems in developing countries.

Thus the challenge facing governments today is how to develop systems that are technically, socially, culturally, and economically acceptable and that can be easily duplicated on a very large scale in most parts of the developing world. The poorest rural inhabitants of the world are guided first by their need for food, not by visions of what could be hoped for in the future. While food aid buys the starving poor only a few moments of respite, development of locally managed land use systems that increase sustained productivity of the earth creates the basis for permanent solutions to hunger in some parts of the world and for movement of large populations out of frightening conditions of subsistence. This fact has to be a central force in designing workable and effective land use improvement programs that appeal to the rural poor and meet their most urgent needs.

One might suggest rather naively that more public resources, research on appropriate technologies, and staff to implement projects will solve the problems and let the LDCs push ahead with social forestry programs. However, experience has shown that in this time of intense competition for public resources, one has to find workable solutions. Critical bottlenecks have to be identified and priorities for action and support clearly laid out. Some critical bottlenecks and first solutions will now be considered.

Lessons Learned from the Past

Social forestry is found in many forms. The most widely publicized social forestry practice is agroforestry, or the inclusion of trees and tree crops in farming systems integrated spatially or temporally with annual crops or livestock. Agroforestry is practiced throughout the world, from the kitchen gardens of Sri Lanka and Indonesia to intercropping by farmers of the Amazon. Shifting cultivation is, of course, one of the oldest and most widely practiced forms of agroforestry. However, it is extremely demanding in terms of land requirements per family. Many of the 200 or 250 million persons who practice it today will have to change to other forms of land use because of population pressures that are forcing shortened fallow periods and corresponding drastic declines in land productivity. A great deal has been written about agroforestry systems (Cf. MacDonald, 1982; Raintree, 1985). It holds promise in terms of increasing the land productivity in many areas. However, as Budowski (1981) suggests, it is not the answer to every problem and suffers from being oversold by its proponents in some instances.

Other types of social forestry include village plantations (woodlots) for fuel and other purposes and on-farm plantations for production of wood for home use or for local sale. In South Korea, a nationwide community fuelwood program resulted in hundreds of thousands of hectares being planted with multipurpose species in thousands of villages. In many cases the village woodlots were established on private land, with the landowner receiving 10 percent of the output (Gregersen, 1982). In a social forestry project in Gujarat (India), individual farmers plant trees and market the wood in cities. Seedlings and extension services are the main public inputs (World Resources Institute, 1985). Similarly, in Haiti, there is a successful program involving thousands of hillside farmers who plant trees provided through projects managed by private voluntary organizations (Murray, 1982; Conway, 1984). Over 13 million seedlings, about twice the amount initially targeted, have been planted (World Resources Institute, 1985).

Despite the magnitude of the worldwide fuelwood crisis, most farmers who plant trees do so for multiple purposes and not just to meet their own fuelwood needs. Reviews of some twenty studies of farmer motivations for tree planting confirm this point (Spears, 1985; FAO, 1985). Other purposes include poles, fodder, fruits and nuts, shade, and fencing. Fuel is a by-product in some cases. At the same time, the informal (and therefore unrecorded) tree-related activity of rural landholders is often widespread, according to available evidence (Cf. Mnzava, 1983). A study in Kenya found that 76 percent of all households in the Kakamega

District planted trees or directly seeded on their land and about 38 percent had a small nursery with from just a few to several thousand trees. An estimated 50 million seedlings per year were produced by farmers (van Gelder and Kerkhof, 1984). Wiersum and Veer (1983) found that a great deal of unrecorded fuelwood production by farmers takes place in the Ilocos region of the Philippines.

Early organized social forestry projects were isolated efforts, inspired and promoted by a few individuals. There was little experience to draw on, other than on-site observation and the advice of local inhabitants. Since the first formal social forestry projects in the early 1970s, experience and results of monitoring have accumulated; generalizations have been drawn and guidelines developed for future projects. However, as other critical reviews of experience accumulate, it is evident that social forestry production is much more complex to organize and is more situation-specific than originally thought. Thus Arnold (1984) has concluded that:

> Generalization concerning availability of land, length of production period and possession of relevant knowledge and skills as constraints to participatory tree growing are proving to apply only in some instances. A more precise, situation-specific approach to participatory tree growing is therefore needed.

A similar feature has been well-known for crop and livestock research and forms a basis for the geographic distribution of international agricultural research centers, whose main functions are basic research on crop varieties and livestock and the management of germplasm banks. International coordination and stable financing of forestry research is presently almost non-existent, so that the design of an international social forestry research network would have to account for this location-specific feature of social forestry.

Keeping this limitation on social forestry systems in mind, certain factors are keys to the success of past social forestry efforts. While they may not be extant in all successful programs, their incorporation into future projects will certainly increase the likelihood of widespread positive impacts. The success factors are grouped into five general guidelines, as follows:

1. Technologies developed and used should be simple and have high probabilities of successful implementation under varying environmental conditions and levels of management skill;
2. Unit costs should be kept low so that large numbers of farmers can be benefited by the limited resources available through external aid channels;
3. Programs and projects should take a holistic or systems approach to social forestry and rural development, which considers the interaction of all land uses and specifically integrates agriculture and forestry elements;
4. Programs must have effective and widespread local participation, including that of women who often have the major role to play in

tree-related activity—e.g., fuelwood collection, tree planting and tending, gathering of fruits and nuts;

5. Finally, projects must be supported effectively by governmental funds and institutions, as well as nongovernmental ones. Government resources should be made available to forestry and other development institutions and beneficiaries through appropriate financing mechanisms (grants, loans, tax incentives, etc.), accompanied by permanent support for research, extension and training. The lack of any one of these elements may be the source of substantial project failure and beneficiary frustration.

Simple, Replicable, Low-Risk Technologies

The expectations and technical ability of the local, rural inhabitant should be kept in mind when designing technical packages for social forestry. The simpler the design and the more closely it follows existing practice, the more likely that the technology will be widely adopted. Even more importantly, the chosen technical packages should function under a variety of agroclimatic conditions and for farmers with widely varying skills and levels of management experience. Since low-income farmers are risk-averse, as has been shown in traditional agricultural crop and livestock systems, the development of social forestry will usually face initial resistance in incorporating new adherents—farmers are more concerned with feeding their families this year than obtaining fuelwood two, three or five years from now.

Two conclusions can be drawn at this point. First, there are good arguments for early establishment and support of national research and development that introduce local considerations into forestry species selection and project design. In the case of the previously mentioned community fuelwood project in Korea, there was a conscious search for species that survive varying environmental conditions and diverse planting approaches. The search for maximum yield was tempered by a desire to find low-risk technologies (species and planting methods) with wide local applications.

Second, lack of comprehension of tree planting and management methods is a sure way to subject new technologies to rejection by local populations because of the appearance of large risk elements. Straightforward, simple technologies, with clear, understandable instructions and clear statements of the benefits to be derived from their application have a much better chance of being accepted by local populations. Simplicity and clear instructions were two ingredients in the success of the Haiti forestry outreach program that has involved more than 20,000 farmers.

Keeping Program Unit Costs Low (per output or per beneficiary)

No matter how clearly successful a pilot project appears, if it involves substantial public outlays of resources per beneficiary it will not be a viable project model for solving the social forestry problems for a large region or country. Social forestry projects that have planting costs of US $800 or more per hectare are not viable ones for solving the Third World's fuelwood problems. New low-cost alternatives have to be found and applied. Many variations on the low-cost social forestry package involving free seedlings and extension assistance need to be tried. The outreach forestry program in Haiti provides an excellent example of what can be accomplished with relatively few resources, active project designers and managers, and local farmers having a profit motive (Timberlake, 1983).

Taking a Holistic Approach to Land Use

A very effective way to introduce social forestry packages into rural areas is to integrate them with agriculture and local community development activity. In point of fact, if one observes rural communities in Asia, Africa or Latin America, the use of trees and local forests are a part of local culture, from religious ceremonies to shelter, implement handles, fuel for cooking, and fodder for animals. In Nigeria and other parts of Africa, leaves are an essential ingredient for the cook; in Korea and the Amazon, certain trees have ceremonial functions; in the Majjia Valley of Niger, trees protect crops against wind and help in the maintenance of soil moisture for agriculture; in Costa Rica, trees are used as living fences, which provide fuel and control animal movement; in Colombia, farm tool handles are made from local woods; in Peru, forests protect wildlife, which provide 80 percent or more of the protein in the diets of some local people. While there are other examples, the point has been made: trees are an essential ingredient in the lives of the rural poor of the Third World and affect most community activities.

In some regions, detailed studies of the role of the forest and trees in rural life have been made. Thus Singh, Pandey, and Tiwari (1984) analyzed energy balances in some typical middle mountain Himalayan villages and found that "i) the agro-ecosystems are centers of massive energy consumption and their viability depends on the supply of energy from the forest, and ii) adequate livelihoods from farming alone are not possible."

As mentioned earlier, farmers plant trees for multiple purposes, including food and protection of crops. They have many functions that relate to their own food needs, fodder for their cattle, and products for sale. While trees do compete (but not always) with agriculture for scarce farm land, they can also complement agricultural activity, actually raising agricultural productivity while providing wood products. This is the case, for example, in the Majjia Valley of Niger, where the windbreak function of trees has raised agricultural productivity in bordering fields by as much as 23 percent due to the higher moisture retained in the soils (Bognetteau-Verlinden, 1980). Other studies show similar results (Gulick, 1984). Some highly productive and sustainable intercropping systems have been developed by rural people over time, such as in the kitchen gardens of Sri Lanka and Indonesia. The term "three dimensional farming" (Douglas, Hart and

Ranganathan, 1982) is appropriate, since such systems essentially reach up with the trees to increase the total use and productivity of a small farm area.

There are other reasons for linking social forestry activity to agriculture and food in a community systems context. In many parts of the world, fuelwood scarcity is intimately tied in with declining agricultural productivity. The two have to be explicitly linked in order to provide the proper motivation and response by political leaders, who understandably have a stronger interest in food than in trees. Denuding upland watersheds for fuelwood results in erosion and soil loss, followed shortly by declines in agricultural productivity. When woodfuels are no longer available, or are difficult to reach, rural people then turn to crop residues and animal dung for fuel, materials which should be going back into the soil to maintain its productivity. Indeed, this was one of the factors which encouraged the Koreans to press ahead rapidly with their fuelwood program in the community and agricultural development context. On a global scale, food grain production losses due to dung burning are estimated to be around 20 million tons per year.

Food security in Africa, and also in Latin America and Asia, has become a major question of concern for governments and international agencies. In recent years, because of well-known debt and balance-of-payment problems, rapidly growing urban populations (especially of the poor with new food consumption demands), widespread rural poverty, and malnutrition have made it more difficult for some societies to meet minimum food requirements. Until recent years it has been thought that forestry could not contribute to the resolution of this problem. But it is clear that social forestry, especially agroforestry, has an important function in rural areas to stabilize and improve family consumption and help sustain livestock. Thus, governments do not always have to choose between short-term food needs and forestry programs; rather, the latter can contribute significantly to the farmer's goals by protecting the agricultural land and water base and supplying food and fodder, and increasing cash income.

Local Participation

It is now well recognized that active and effective local beneficiary participation is a major factor in the success of social forestry programs (Arnold, 1984; Noronha, 1982; World Bank, 1980). Without it, such programs are frequently doomed to failure, especially given the purposes and outputs of social forestry. As discussed earlier, in some successful cases (e.g., Korea, Kenya, Philippines, and India) a tradition of local participation in forestry activity is already well accepted and practiced. The role of outside intervention (government, community, organization) in such cases is merely to facilitate further spread of social forestry activity. In other cases, a program may initiate activity in communities, with the objective of increasing its acceptance as benefits are demonstrated to other local communities (Mnzava, 1983; Arnold, 1984).

Two questions are posed here: What constrains rural inhabitants from becoming more actively involved in social forestry activity? And, how can outside efforts expand local participation?

There are three elements that shape the success of local participation in social forestry programs—technical silvicultural knowledge, resource scarcity, and incentives. The first can be thought of as the issue of how technical forestry knowledge is obtained and transferred to the local communities; the second as the extent of the resource constraints, whether they be land or inputs of financing; and the third as the various elements that provide economic and financial encouragement for the local population to undertake social forestry investments. Each of the three constraints will be examined briefly.

Lack of knowledge by beneficiaries about how to plant and manage trees either as pure stands or as part of an integrated agroforestry system has to be assessed at two levels. First, adequate research and local testing will have to be done by the project coordinator to select the proper tree species. Secondly, the knowledge that is obtained will have to be made available to farmers through extension, training, publicity, and other education programs. For example, effective extension efforts, using large numbers of local people with ties to the community, is considered a major factor in the success of the Haitian outreach program. The local trainers had been organized by a private voluntary organization, which was directing the particular project.

The second major factor—resource scarcity—refers to the resource constraints that limit a local community's ability to participate in a social forestry program. In some cases, the most severe problem is that people lack access to land on which to plant trees. Programs in West Bengal have solved this problem by providing land for the landless on which to plant trees (Spears, 1983). The land remains in government ownership, but the output goes to the planter. In Korea, the government required landowners with steep idle lands to let villagers plant the land in exchange for 10 percent of the harvest. New land settlement programs in the Amazon provide another approach for the landless, if they are encouraged to adopt environmentally sustainable farming systems.

The third element—incentives—is the basis for stimulating an increase in beneficiary participation in social forestry projects. Often one is able to enhance incentives for individual farmer or cooperative participation by setting up active cash markets for the goods that are being produced (e.g., Gujarat, India). Other incentives may be in the form of direct or indirect financial gains to the beneficiaries (Cf. Gregersen and McGaughey, 1985; Gregersen, 1984).

Financial incentives have been used with great success by several countries in promoting large-scale industrial forestry (e.g., Chile, Brazil) and national social forestry programs (e.g., Korea). The greater part of public resources and direct subsidies have gone to industrial forestry in these countries. But more recently, with the attention given to social forestry, international institutions have begun to consider how to design financial incentives for small-scale forestry investments. This can be done in two ways—making loans to cooperatives and individuals for tree planting (often in conjunction with agricultural loans), or by the provision of grants or subsidies of different kinds. Grants can take many forms, including input cost sharing, free or low-cost marketing services, loan guarantees, free government research and extension, among others.

In some cases, it turns out that lack of beneficiary interest is due to the fact that government is involved in a program and the local inhabitants do not trust it (Cf. Palin, 1984; Noronha, 1982). Local inhabitants often do not think that they actually will get the benefits from tree planting (Hoskins, 1979). Resistance to government arises from the tradition that forest services are protectors of the forest and thus have a reputation as policemen, not as supporters of local productive forest activity. In point of fact, many forest services still maintain not only that reputation, but also that philosophy. For this reason, there is an increasing interest in and emphasis on setting up social forestry projects through independent nongovernmental groups such as private voluntary organizations.

Institutions for Project Execution and Finance

The eventual success and wide acceptance by the rural population of social forestry will depend ultimately on the ability of a number of public and private institutions to design the technology, transfer the resources, and administer the programs continuously for long periods of time. While there are no easy formulas for institutional design, certain elements that guide the role of private and public groups are becoming clear, mainly from experience with small-scale social forestry programs. A first principle is that one does not always have to depend solely on the efficiency of a central forestry organization to institute social forestry. The national organization may need to assume the responsibility, especially for developing the technological packages that will form the basis for specific regional social forestry projects. The presence of a very strong national forestry organization has not always been essential for the success of certain industrial forestry programs (e.g., Brazil). However, since the technological packages for social forestry programs may be more complex and even more location-specific than industrial forestry, certainly some minimum research and extension services will have to be supplied nationally. But because social forestry will have to benefit large numbers of low-income farmers, more creative institutional arrangements will have to be sought.

It is for this reason that non-government organizations (NGOs) often can provide a valuable service by administering projects in the areas in which they already are established and have grassroots support. This is a major factor in the success of the Haiti project discussed earlier. NGOs also have a very good track record in a number of African countries. Weber's (1982) review of social forestry projects in CILES countries points to the success of NGOs in the Sahelian region. Weber states that "the common denominator of success is the way projects have been administered in the field, how the local population was approached, and how project activities are being carried out so that local interests are stimulated and respected." NGOs are particularly strong in mobilizing local interests in areas in which they already are established.

Regardless of how effective NGOs are in administering projects, government involvement and commitment, at least at the policy level, is necessary. Spears (1981) states that "...whatever agricultural crop or livestock or forest plantation crop combinations are envisaged, the capacity of governments to ensure adequate support services and inputs will be a decisive factor in determining whether a particular farming system is sustainable." This point is borne out in the case of the successful Korean community fuelwood program, where government support in terms of logistics, extension services, seedling availability, timeliness of research, and financial support were identified as essential factors in success (Gregersen, 1982).

With regard to land tenure institutions, governments can play a role in determining success of programs. For example, Arnold (1984) points out that "the success of community forestry in the middle hills in Nepal stems from a willingness by that government to turn over state land to groups of local people to manage as village forests." The case of land allocation to landless poor in West Bengal has been mentioned earlier. Although there was no direct transfer of land title, there was a transfer of use rights. In the case of a successful smallholder wood production program on Mindanao (associated with pulpwood production for a major pulp mill), a willingness of government to relax the initial requirement that farmers had to provide evidence of title helped to insure success (FAO, 1979).

In many cases, particularly those involving communal property or commons, central and regional governments have little authority. Local institutions must be called upon to make appropriate land use and other decisions which affect the eventual distribution of benefits, e.g., fuelwood. Frequently, there is no effective community level organization to manage lands, and even if there is, there may be divergences of interest within the community as to how benefits and costs should be distributed (Noronha, 1980; Arnold, 1984). Strong local leadership is a factor in resolving conflicts.

A major institutional problem is how to make financing available for social forestry projects. There are many financing options open for the project authority. One approach would be for the government to provide most of the inputs free-of-charge to the producers, including tools, seedlings, fertilizers, and even wage costs. While this is an apparently simple solution, it may place a heavy burden on the project authority to provide services beyond its own capacity to administer. Another approach is for the government to provide cash payments to the beneficiary, but this may be accompanied by substantial "leakage" of funds for other purposes. Another scheme is to provide short- and long-term credit separately or through a functioning crop-livestock credit program. Social forestry programs are not likely to operate effectively without some degree of government subsidization, either by reducing the credit costs or improving the loan terms to the beneficiary or by granting some direct subsidies.

Conclusions

Rural man's adjustment to his environment over the centuries has evolved a complex, low-risk agriculture and forestry culture. Elements of this are called social forestry by today's foresters, because poor rural inhabitants can utilize trees for viable economic advantage. Modern man is able systematically to improve local social forestry conditions by introducing species that provide multiple outputs, including those for resource (water and soil) protection, food, fiber and fuel. As foresters have accumulated knowledge on how social forestry works, it has become possible to expand participation to a larger rural population, especially those dependent upon marginal land resources.

Initial optimism of foresters, environmentalists, and rural development specialists has given way to a more realistic view of implementing social forestry on a large scale. Several elements work against easy massive replication of social forestry. The technological package (tree species and management program) is highly location-specific. The community development institutions that can mobilize large numbers of beneficiaries are not always present. There are not now large numbers of professional foresters and rural extension agents with sufficient knowledge. All these factors add up to fairly high project costs at the beginning.

But also there is encouragement to be found in the examination of the recent record. Several countries have been able to mount successful national social forestry programs—Korea, the Philippines, India, among others. In other countries, individual pilot projects have found workable solutions.

Some particularly crucial project success elements have recently surfaced. First, it is probably not possible to think of large-scale social forestry without public subsidies to the beneficiaries. For this reason there needs to be much more analysis of optimal subsidy packages, which combine direct and indirect payments with credits and free public services. Secondly, it is becoming clear that for social forestry to produce higher farm incomes, secure local markets for forest products must be encouraged. Thus, researchers and project directors will have to devise appropriate financial mechanisms, find secure cash markets for local produce, and establish private and public institutions with a stake in local rural development.

Finally, international financing and technical assistance agencies have still not done enough to finance social forestry (either as separate projects or as activities in larger projects). These agencies should examine their loan conditions to ascertain if they are compatible with social forestry, and determine whether adjustments need to be made in interest rates and grace, disbursement and repayment periods. If these adjustments are not made, it will be necessary for government financial authorities to compensate for these conditions with larger national financial incentives for local social forestry.

NOTE

1. The introduction to this paper is adapted from a draft manuscript on social forestry policy issues and initiatives being prepared by Professor Gregersen for the World Bank's Economic Development Institute.

References

Anonymous. 1982. How conservation practices saved a village on the edge of disaster. *Ceres*, September-October, pp. 5-6.

Arnold, J.E.M. 1984. Forestation for Local Community Development. In: *Proceedings of the International Symposium on Strategies and Designs for Afforestation, Reforestation, and Tree Planting*, K.F. Wiersum (ed). Agricultural University, Wageningen, Netherlands. pp. 48-62.

Arnold, J.E.M. 1983. Community Forestry and Meeting Fuelwood Needs. Submitted to the British Association Symposium, *Replenishing the World's Forests*. 7 pp.

Arnold, J.E.M. 1983. Economic Considerations in Agroforestry Projects. *Agroforestry Systems*, 1:299-311.

Bognetteau-Verlinden, E. 1980. *Study on Impact of Windbreaks in Majjia Valley, Niger*. CARE/Niger Forest Service.

Budowski, G. 1981. Applicability of Agroforestry Systems. Paper presented at *International Workshop on Agroforestry in the African Humid Tropics*, IITA, Ibadan, Nigeria, April 26-May 1, 1981. 12 pp. (See MacDonald, 1982).

Conway, F.J. 1984. *Social Science Research in Forestry Project Design: A Case Study*. USAID/S&T/RD. 5 pp.

Douglass, J., R.A. de J. Hart, and G.S. Ranganathan. 1982. *Forest Farming, Prosperity for India*. Dehra Dun, India: Natraj Publishers. pp. 1-34.

Food and Agriculture Organization of the United Nations. 1985. *Tree Growing by Rural People: Review Draft*. Prepared for the Seventh FAO/SIDA Expert Consultation on Forestry for Local Community Development. FAO, Rome. 133 pp.

Food and Agriculture Organization of the United Nations. 1981. Map of Fuelwood Situation in the Developing Countries: At a Scale of 1:25,000,000.

Food and Agriculture Organization of the United Nations. 1979. Forestry Paper 17, Supplement 1, Case Study No. 1, Philippine smallholder tree-farming project. FAO, Rome.

Gregersen, H.M. 1984. Strategies and Designs for Afforestation, Reforestation and Tree Planting. In: *Proceedings of International Symposium*, K.F. Wiersum (ed.). Agricultural University, Wageningen, Netherlands, 19-23 Sept. 432 pp.

Gregersen, H.M. 1982. Village forestry development in the Republic of Korea—A case study. *Forestry for Local Community Development Programme Series*, Food and Agriculture Organization of the United Nations, Rome.

Gregersen, H.M., and S.E. McGaughey. 1985. *Improving Policies and Financing Mechanisms for Forestry Development*. Economic and Social Development Department, Inter-American Development Bank, Washington, D.C. 63 pp. + appendices.

Gulick, F.A. 1984. *Increasing Agricultural Food Production through Selected Tree Planting Techniques*. Bureau for Africa, USAID, Washington, D.C. 148 pp.

Hoskins, M.W. 1979. *Community Participation in African Fuelwood Production, Transformation and Utilization*. Workshop on Fuelwood and Other Renewable Fuels in Africa, Paris. Overseas Development Council/USAID, Washington, D.C.

MacDonald, L.H. (ed.). 1982. *Agro-Forestry in the African Humid Tropics*. Proceedings of Workshop in Ibadan, Nigeria. United Nations University, Tokyo, Japan. 163 pp.

Mnzava, E.M. 1983. *Tree Planting in Tanzania: A Voice From Villagers*. Forest Division, Dar Es Salaam. SIDA. 88 pp.

Murray, G.F. 1982. *Cash-Cropping Agroforestry: An Anthropological Approach to Agricultural Development in Rural Haiti*. Presented at the Wingspread Conference on Haiti: Present State and Future Prospects. Racine, WI: Pan American Development Foundation. 36 pp.

Noronha, R. 1982. Seeing people for the trees: social issues in forestry. Prepared for the USAID Conference on Forestry and Development in Asia, Bangalore, April 1982.

Noronha, R. 1980. Village woodlots: Are they a solution? Prepared for the Panel on the Introduction and Diffusion of Renewable Energy Technologies, National Academy of Sciences, Washington, D.C.

Palin, D.J. 1984. Institutional Arrangements for Forestation. In: *Proceedings of International Symposium*, K.F. Wiersum (ed.). Agricultural University, Wageningen, Netherlands, 19-23 Sept. pp. 312-330.

Raintree, J.B. 1985. *Agroforestry, Tropical Land Use and Tenure*. Background paper for International Consultative Workshop on Tenure Issues in Agroforestry, 27-31 May 1985. Nairobi. 52 pp.

Singh, J.S., U. Pandey, and A.K. Tiwari. 1984. Men and forests: A Central Himalayan case study. *Ambio*, 13(2):80-87.

Spears, J. 1985. Personal Communication.

Spears, J. 1983. Replenishing the World's Forests: Tropical Reforestation: An Achievable Goal? *Commonw. For. Rev.* 62(3): 201-217.

Spears, J. 1981. Small Farmers—Or the Tropical Forest Ecosystem? A review of sustainable land use systems from tropical forest areas. In: *Tropical Forests: Utilization and Conservation*, F. Mergen (ed.). Yale School of Forestry and Environmental Studies. New Haven, CT. pp. 14-47.

Timberlake, L. 1983. Easy cut, easy grow. *Earthwatch*, No. 14. Nov. 14. p. 7.

van Gelder, Berry, and Paul Kerkhof. 1984. The agroforestry survey in Kakemega District. Kenya Woodfuel Development Programme, Working Paper No. 3. October. Beijer Institute, Nairobi.

Weber, F. 1982. *Review of CILSS Forestry Sector Program Analysis Papers*. (USDA/OICD/TAD/WW) (AID/USDA/USFS). Forestry Support Program. 40 pp. + appendix.

Wiersum, K.F., and C.P. Veer. 1983. Loan Financing of Small-holder Treefarming in Ilocos, a Comment. *Agroforestry Systems*, 1:361-365.

World Bank. 1980. *Sociological Aspects of Forestry Project Design*. Agriculture and Rural Development Department, Central Projects Staff, World Bank, AGR Technical Note No. 3. 100 pp.

World Resources Institute. 1985. *The World's Tropical Forests: A Call for Accelerated Action*. World Resources Institute, Washington, D.C. Draft, June 21. 90 pp.

3/ Soil Erosion on Cultivated Steeplands of the Humid Tropics and Subtropics

Terry J. Logan
Leslie R. Cooperband

"For numerous political, social, and economic reasons," small farmers in third world countries have no alternative to cultivating environmentally fragile lands, including fields that are steeply sloped. Terry Logan and Leslie Cooperband cite evidence strongly suggesting that adopting agroforestry—"an agricultural technology that incorporates trees into annual and perennial cropping systems"—would greatly reduce the heavy soil erosion that frequently occurs when small farmers colonize hillsides. Much remains to be learned about agroforestry to enhance its economic attraction to hillside farmers and to increase its value as an erosion control measure. Several areas of scientific research and infrastructure development needed to promote the use and effectiveness of agroforestry are identified in this paper.

Introduction

Soil erosion has long been considered a major impediment to sustained agricultural production throughout the world. This is especially true for the less developed countries (LDCs) of the tropics and subtropics, which depend on agriculture to feed burgeoning populations and to earn foreign exchange. Water erosion can be particularly severe in these areas because of high annual rainfall and frequency of high-intensity storms (Lal and Russell, 1981; Greenland and Lal, 1976). Lands once protected by tropical forests and savannahs have been cleared to grow rice, maize, edible beans, cassava, and other crops that provide little protection from the elements (Lal and Greenland, 1979).

Soil erosion problems have become especially severe in the humid tropical and subtropical steeplands of Africa, Asia, Latin America, and the Caribbean. Consistent with conventional definitions, these are lands with a slope exceeding 20 percent, lying within 23° of the equator, that receive more than 1200 mm of precipitation a year, on average (Greenland, 1977). In recent decades, the original inhabitants of those areas have shortened fallow cycles of traditional shifting cultivation systems, largely because of increasing population density

(Sanchez, 1976; El Swaify et al., 1982). Complementing this trend, small farmers who are not indigenous to steeplands have colonized those areas as population has grown. Because prime agricultural land has been used for high-value plantation crops, cities have expanded into surrounding agricultural lands, and agricultural colonization has been stimulated both by infrastructure development (e.g., road construction) and by land tenure laws that reward deforestation.

In recent years, considerable work has been done on traditional and modern cropping systems in the humid tropics and subtropics. In the lowland tropics and subtropics, the major concerns have been nutrient loss through leaching and high acidity (Sanchez, 1976) as well as soil structure degradation. The latter results from organic matter decomposition and soil surface exposure to high temperatures and water evaporation. In the steepland tropics and subtropics, on the other hand, the major concerns for sustained agricultural production have been soil erosion with the associated loss of rooting depth, water holding capacity, and nutrient supply (Lal and Greenland, 1979).

Examined in this paper are the extent, causes, consequences, and control of accelerated soil erosion in steeplands of the tropics and subtropics, with particular emphasis on small farmer cultivation of annual crops. These various aspects of soil erosion are described briefly and then illustrated using the factors of the Universal Soil Loss Equation (USLE) developed by Wischmeier and Smith (1978). A discussion of agroforestry as a means to combat soil erosion follows. Throughout the paper, recommendations for research and development are made for steepland soil erosion in general and agroforestry in particular.

Small Farmer Cultivation on Humid Tropical and Subtropical Steeplands

The most recent estimate of arable land in the world is 1.5 billion hectares (ha), which is slightly more than 10 percent of total global land area—13.1 billion hectares (Dudal, 1980, 1981). Five billion hectares, or 38 percent of total land, is in the humid tropics and subtropics. Norman (1979) estimates that about 3 billion hectares in the tropics and subtropics have climatic and soil conditions potentially suitable for cropping. Steeplands would account for a significant but unknown percentage of this total.

Cultivation of steeplands in the humid tropics and subtropics is practiced almost exclusively by poor farmers on holdings of less than 5 ha (Sheng, 1982). Many of these areas, as in the Andes of Peru and the terraced paddy ricelands of the Phillipines, are ancient (Cox and Atkins, 1979); others such as the Himalayan foothills of India and Nepal are of more recent origin and the result of population growth.

Some humid tropical and subtropical steeplands have been used for long periods. In some cases like the pre-Colombian Andes, present populations have not maintained the engineering works, such as terraces and irrigation canals, required for sustained production. In many other areas, crop production in humid tropical and subtropical steeplands is more primitive and shifting cultivation is commonly practiced. Among mountain tribesmen of tropical and subtropical Asia,

Africa, South and Central America, and parts of the Caribbean, very small holdings (usually less than 0.5 ha) are cleared, burned, and cropped with minimal subsequent cultivation for two to three years, followed by abandonment. Many of these peoples have low population densities and some maintain a nomadic existence.

As populations have increased in the 20th century, there has been a steady conversion of native vegetation (forest, scrub savannah, and grasslands) to annual and perennial crop production, including tree species like banana, plantain, and coffee. Virgin forests have also been converted to pasture for cattle and small livestock. In many cases, shifting cultivation is still the dominant farming system, with cultivated cropping for two to three years followed by fallows of up to 10 years. As population pressures have increased, however, fallow periods have declined. In addition, land conversion from native vegetation has increased.

Subsistence farming on tropical and subtropical steeplands can be classified into two major categories: those primarily involving annual and perennial crops, and those maintaining ruminant animals (cattle and goats) on unimproved pasture. In many cases, the farmer is not producing exclusively for subsistence but may also be growing cash crops such as tobacco, dry beans, cabbage, onions, and potatoes (as in the Cordillera of the Dominican Republic) for market in the urban centers or even for export.

In a few areas, the Venezuelan Andes for example, small farmers have shifted entirely from subsistence agriculture to intensive vegetable production. This system utilizes large inputs of irrigation, fertilizer, and pesticides (Cooperband, 1986). From an economic perspective, it has become difficult to promote soil-conserving land uses like pasture or agroforestry because the economic status of small farmers has been elevated irreversibly.

The most serious increases in soil erosion are observed, however, where trees and savannah are cleared for subsistence crop production. These include annual grains and pulses (upland rice, maize, sorghum, and dry beans); perennial grains (pidgeon peas); root crops (cassava, potatoes, cocoyam), and sweet potato; and occasionally tree species such as bananas, plantain, coffee, and mango. Because of low fertility and generally shallow soils, cropping densities in steepland farming are low and farmers commonly practice clean cultivation (i.e., complete burial of crop residues by plowing, and hand weed control). In some areas such as the central highlands of the Dominican Republic Cordillera, weed and crop residues are collected and burned. This results in low percentage ground cover throughout the year with obvious consequences for soil erosion. This practice, in turn, results in losses in plant nutrients and soil organic matter, which are essential to subsistence farmers who use little or no fertilizer. The resulting low crop yields contribute to the problem of low soil cover and further increase the potential for soil erosion. In a study of rainfall erosion in the Dominican Republic, Veloz and Logan (1986) found that fertilizer alone (500 kg/ha/crop of 12-24-12 fertilizer) decreased erosion by approximately 50 percent in a groundnut, dry beans, maize, and pidgeon pea mixed cropping system on a 30 percent slope with clean cultivation. The reduction in erosion was attributed to an early and more profuse development of vegetative soil cover.

An Illustration Using the Universal Soil Loss Equation

Soil erosion has troubled man throughout the ages. Ancient terraces in Asia and Central and South America attest to early attempts to sustain crop production in the face of severe erosion. However, the systematic study of water erosion dates only to the Dust Bowl in the central U.S. in the 1930s. This disaster gave rise to the U.S. soil conservation movement and to the development of regional research stations for the study of erosion and erosion control. Several of these sites have been operating continuously since that time and provide detailed information on water erosion and its control in temperate regions. Similar programs have existed during the same general period in Europe.

The study of tropical and subtropical erosion has more recent origins. Lowdermilk (1953), in his highly influential publication based on his observations in the Middle East and China, raised the issue of global erosion and the problems that this would pose for future populations. Others (e.g. Hudson, 1971) recognized early the difficulties of extrapolating experiences from temperate regions to the humid tropics. Researchers like these were responsible for some of the first erosion studies in the tropics themselves. Since the early 1970s, these efforts have expanded greatly with the work of Lal and associates at the International Institute of Tropical Agriculture (IITA) in Nigeria (Greenland and Lal, 1977; Lal and Greenland 1979; Lal and Russell, 1981; Lal et al., 1986). Four international conferences on soil erosion have been held in the last decade.

Research on water erosion in the tropics has been influenced greatly by U.S. and European studies, particularly those conducted by Wischmeier and his associates (Wischmeier and Smith, 1978). Although developed for conditions in the Central U.S., there have been numerous attempts to extend their methodology to the tropics and subtropics (see Greenland and Lal, 1977; El-Swaify et al., 1982).

Wischmeier and his colleagues (Wischmeier and Smith, 1978) recognized that the impacts of several factors influencing long-term soil loss from water erosion could be expressed as the Universal Soil Loss Equation:

$$A = RKLSCP$$

where A is the long-term annual soil loss (metric tons/hectare/year); R is the erosion-producing rainfall or rainfall erosivity; K is the inherent susceptibility of the soil to rainfall erosion, or erodibility; L and S are slope length and slope steepness, respectively; and C and P account for land cover and the effects of conservation practices (such as terraces), respectively. Although researchers in the tropics have found difficulties in using the USLE directly, it nevertheless correctly identifies the primary factors contributing to rainfall erosion. These factors will be discussed within the perspective of small farmer subsistence agriculture in the steepland tropics and subtropics, not because we believe that the USLE is the best way to describe the erosion process, but because it provides a useful framework for discussion of those factors most causative in water erosion.

Rainfall Erosivity

Rainfall causes soil erosion through two major mechanical processes: soil detachment by raindrop impact and overland flow (runoff), and removal of suspended soil particles (sediment) by runoff. Wischmeier (1959) found that erosion caused by individual storms was proportional to the product of total storm energy and the maximum 30-minute intensity, *EI*. Tropical storms are characterized by much higher intensities than those in temperate regions (Lal, 1977). Hudson (1971), for instance, found that cumulative kinetic energy of storms with intensities exceeding 2.5 cm/hr was a better index of rainfall erosivity for Zimbabwe in Central Africa than Wischmeier's *EI*. Lal (1977) has found that the best correlation with soil loss for tropical regions is with total rainfall amount and peak storm intensity, *AI*.

In addition to the uncertainties in quantifying the physical effects of rainfall on soil erosion, obtaining the minimal rainfall data required to calculate erosivity indices is difficult. The large networks of meteorological stations found in developed countries do not exist in most LDCs. Especially serious is the lack of climatological data for the more remote and inaccessible steeplands of the tropics and subtropics. Where stations have been installed, the period of record is usually short and the quality of the data poor. Quite often, only total storm rainfall data, and not intensities, are available. The need for intensive rainfall monitoring is a particular problem in mountainous areas where total rainfall and intensity can change markedly over short distances as a function of altitude and wind direction.

Soil Erodibility

In the USLE, soil erodibility (*K*) is defined as the amount of soil loss per unit of *EI* (Wischmeier and Smith, 1978). It is a quantitative parameter measured in the field on "standard" plots where other factors in the equation are held to fixed, arbitrary conditions. These conditions, chosen originally because they were typical of those used in the original field studies in the U.S., are slope length of 22.1 meters, slope steepness of 9 percent, and soil tilled up and down the slope and kept bare with periodic tillage.

The original erosion plots on which *K* values were determined used natural rainfall over a period of many years. This is an expensive undertaking even for countries like the U.S. In order to extend the range of soils over which *K* values could be determined, standard plots were subjected to storms of fixed intensity and duration by means of various rainfall simulators (El-Swaify, 1977). Extrapolation to soils on which *K* values were not directly measured was achieved by correlating soil erodibility with those soil factors found to be most related to soil erosion susceptibility. For the continental U.S., these were found to be: content of silt and very fine sand particle sizes, soil structure, water permeability, and organic matter content. These were combined in a nomograph (Wischmeier and Smith, 1978) from which the *K* value could be read.

El-Swaify and co-workers (El-Swaify, 1977; El-Swaify et al., 1982) used a rainfall simulator to determine relative erodibilities of major soil groups in Hawaii. Based on U.S. soil taxonomic subgroups (Soil Conservation Service, 1975), they found that relative erodibilities were sufficiently variable to prevent easy classification on the basis of soil taxonomy. However, they felt that there was some agreement between their work and others (see El-Swaify et al., 1982) which showed that the Oxisols, heavy clay Vertisols, and weakly aggregated Alfisols possess low, moderate, and high erodibilities, respectively. The Ultisols, with which the Oxisols are primarily associated, were found to have low erodibilities in Hawaii and Puerto Rico but covered a wide range from "extremely high" to "extremely low" in Central America and Venezuela (El-Swaify et al., 1982).

El-Swaify et al. (1982) have shown that erodibilities of tropical soils may involve factors other than those used in the USLE nomograph (Wischmeier and Smith, 1978). Of particular concern are the higher contents of iron and aluminum oxides and the more dispersed nature of organic matter in tropical soils, materials which are known to be involved in the stabilization of soil aggregates against water dispersion. Likewise, El-Swaify et al. (1982), caution against using textural classes in the USLE nomograph for tropical soils, such as the Ultisols and Oxisols. Soil texture is determined by differential sedimentation of different particle sizes following dispersion of the soil to destroy aggregates. False textural values can be obtained for soils like the Oxisols and Ultisols if the iron oxides which bind aggregates in these soils are not completely removed by chemical extraction.

Soil erodibilities have also been shown to vary over times as short as a growing season. Romkens (1985) emphasized the importance of determining K over long periods of time in order to integrate the variable effects. This, however, requires a major commitment of financial resources to long-term studies compared to the less expensive and quicker rainfall simulator method; these kinds of resources are not readily available in LDCs.

An additional factor that appears to be particularly significant for the Oxisols is the potential effect of soil fertility management on soil erodibility. Tama and El-Swaify (1978) have shown that soil dispersibility is related to the degree to which soil pH deviates from the inherent pH of the point of zero charge (PZC) of soil minerals as a result of particle-to-particle charge repulsion. Liming Oxisols which have PZCs in the range of 4-6 to near neutral pHs could result in increased soil erodibility. This paper's senior author and C. Castro, an Ohio State University doctoral student, are presently studying this phenomenon on two Oxisols in southern Brazil. Their field plots have been limed to give a pH range of 4 to 7.5 and they are measuring soil detachment as an index of soil erodibility.

Erodibility is an inherent soil property. Its use in soil erosion assessment at the farm or watershed level requires some knowledge of landscape soil variability. In the steeplands of the tropics and subtropics, soil variation is great. Changes in topography and active geologic erosion give rise to highly variable conditions for soil formation. While the highly weathered Oxisols and Ultisols are well represented in the steeplands, quite often steepland soils are less weathered. Active geologic processes continuously expose fresh parent material through vulcanism, erosion, and sedimentation. To develop an accurate assessment of soil variability in steepland areas, soil mapping must be conducted on a scale that is unrealistic for most LDCs. Soil mapping in these countries is rarely done at a scale more detailed than 1:250,000, which is considerably less than the 1:15,840 scale used in the U.S. for county soil surveys. The FAO world soils map is only available at a scale of 1:5,000,000. This lack of basic soils information represents, in the view of the authors, one of the major impediments to watershed management in tropical and subtropical steeplands.

Slope Length and Slope Steepness

The USLE calculates the slope length factor (*L*) as equal to $(\lambda/22.1)^m$, where λ is the slope length in meters and m is a coefficient with values of 0.3, 0.4, and 0.5, with the higher values representing steeper slopes. The value of 22.1 in the expression is the standard plot length in meters (Wischmeier and Smith, 1978). As these authors indicate, modeling the slope length/erosion process suggests that values of m greater than 0.5 may be appropriate for slopes exceeding 10 percent. However, there are insufficient data to develop these coefficients with confidence. This is problematic in steeplands, which we have defined as those with slopes greater than 20 percent, inasmuch as lands with slopes of 50 percent or more are commonly cultivated.

Because of the highly dissected nature of mountainous landscapes, slope lengths are short and complex. In many areas, uniform slopes rarely exceed 50 m and there may be several slope segments in the overall slope. Foster and Wischmeier (1974) proposed a procedure for calculating the slope length from analysis of individual slope segments. Castro and Zobeck (1986) have recently described a procedure to determine slope segments from soil survey data. Although these procedures help to overcome the errors in attributing single simple uniform slopes to complex landscapes, a more appropriate approach is to use distributed runoff and erosion models to account for deposition (Beasley and Huggins, 1982). This, however, requires extensive and detailed data and usually involves calibration to local conditions.

The USLE calculates the slope steepness factor (*S*) as equal to $65.41 \sin^2 \theta + 4.56 \sin \theta + 0.065$, where θ is the angle of slope (Wischmeier and Smith, 1978). Wischmeier and Smith indicate that percent slope is $100 \tan \theta$ rather than the sine function used. However, substitution of the sine for the tan function does not affect the calculation of the slope steepness effect on soil loss for slopes as high as 20 percent. Beyond this range, the predictive power of the S factor is unknown, so direct field research must be conducted to provide reliable data on the effects on soil erosion of slopes exceeding 20 percent.

Few erosion plot studies have been conducted with slopes approaching those found in the steeplands. Dangler et al. (1976), found a linear increase in soil loss with slope steepness for slopes between three and 18 percent. Aina et al. (1976), used slopes of one to 15 percent in their studies of cropland erosion in Nigeria. In the same experiment, Lal (1977) found the same effect on soil loss with cultivation from a 10 to 15 percent slope range as from a slope range of one to

10 percent. On the other hand, Gumbs et al. (1985) measured erosion from slopes of 11, 22, and 52 percent in Trinidad using conventional tillage on the 11 and 22 percent slopes and no-till on the 22 and 52 percent slopes. Surprisingly, there was no slope effect on either runoff or erosion within a given tillage treatment. Veloz and Logan (1986) have been studying erosion with different tillage and soil conservation practices on a 30 percent slope in the Cordillera Central of the Dominican Republic. However, slope itself is not a variable in the experiment.

Cover and Crop Management

The effect of cropping on soil loss is primarily due to soil cover, or the degree of land surface protection from raindrop impact and runoff erosion. Plant canopy coverage of the land surface protects against raindrop impact, but not against runoff. The cover and crop management factor of the USLE (*C*) is the combined effects of soil cover and plant canopy summed over some period, such as crop season, a year, or a crop rotation. For major temperate-region crops, *C* factors are tabulated in the USLE Manual (Wischmeier and Smith, 1978). In addition, the USDA Soil Conservation Service in Puerto Rico gives values for crops in the Caribbean area. Factors for tropical regions are also provided by Lal (1977), Roose (1977), and El-Swaify et al. (1982).

The cropping practices of small subsistence farmers are usually complex and do not lend themselves to easy categorization. A mixture of annual and perennial crops is commonly planted in the same field. Growth rates vary with the crop, making soil cover and plant canopy development complex. A major need in conservation planning is to determine *C* factors at the local level for specific cropping practices. These are easily obtained by frequent measurements of ground and canopy cover using simple techniques such as the string-knot method for estimating percent soil cover (Laflen et al., 1981).

Crop residue conservation is a major component of crop management for erosion control. There is an increasingly large body of evidence from temperate and tropical regions indicating that maintaining more than 50 percent residue cover can reduce soil loss by as much as 90 percent (Aina et al., 1976; Lal, 1977; Veloz and Logan, 1986). Lesser but significant reductions have been obtained by others (Benatti et al., 1977 as cited by El-Swaify et al., 1982). However, Gumbs et al. (1985) found little effect of residue on soil loss.

Several of the studies reported above reveal that residue cover also significantly reduces runoff, although the effect is not as great as erosion reduction. The significance for the shallow steepland soils is that reduced runoff and decreased evaporation from residue cover may be benefiting crop production by increasing soil moisture. Such a benefit is far more apparent to the farmer than is reduced soil loss. This could be utilized to encourage residue management.

Residue cover can be achieved by two methods: *in situ* conservation of crop residues, and hand placement of off-site plant material like crop and animal residues, sugarcane bagasse, banana leaves, and branches of fast-growing tree species. Residue management for the tropics has recently been discussed by

Wilson and Lal (1986). Clean tillage is a time-honored farm practice around the world and is the only option available to small subsistence farmers. Chemical weed control is unavailable, unacceptable, or financially prohibitive. Small farmers are also inclined to burn crop residues because incorporating residues by hand or with animal power is difficult. This makes adopting *in situ* residue management highly unlikely unless chemical weed control is made more readily available or is subsidized. In addition, it can only succeed if the farmer is able to rationalize, in terms of sustained crop yields, the short- and long-term benefits of residue management. These include rooting depth preservation, water holding capacity, and inherent fertility. In most cases, small farmers cannot see these relationships. In a recent survey of small steepland farmers in the Dominican Republic (Morillo, 1986), most respondents were unfamiliar with the term and even the concept of "erosion." They were aware, however, that their soils got "tired," so that they eventually abandoned them to brush.

Soil Conservation Practices

In contrast to crop and residue management practices that have the primary objective of protecting the soil surface from raindrop impact and runoff scour, soil conservation practices (terraces, hillside ditches, and other measures which constitute the P factor in the USLE) are designed to reduce runoff velocity by reducing slope length and steepness. They are also designed to protect concentrated runoff channels from gully erosion. Whereas crop and residue management practices require major changes in crop cultivation, conservation practices are primarily structural and allow the farmer to avoid a switch in crop management. However, installing them is expensive, requiring significant technical inputs. Also, conservation practices must be maintained to be effective. We are not aware of any extensive LDC small farmer soil conservation program that was not the result of significant government intervention in the form of subsidies (e.g., food for work) or direct cash payments and technical assistance.

El-Swaify et al. (1982) point out the need for slope length and gradient control on cultivated lands with steep slopes. Sheng (Sheng and Stennett, 1975, as cited by El-Swaify et al., 1982; Sheng, 1982) has described a number of slope control practices that are appropriate for mountainous areas. These include bench terraces, hillside ditches, individual basins, orchard terraces, miniconvertible terraces, and hexagons. To these can be added other cross-slope practices like rock walls, grass barriers, and combinations of grass barriers and hillside ditches (Veloz, 1984). Veloz and Logan (1986), in an evaluation of several of these practices on a 30 percent slope in the Dominican Republic, found that a combination of hillside ditches and grass strips reduced erosion more than hillside ditches alone. Grass strips were found to be more effective than rock walls. None of these practices were as effective as no-till, however, which reduced runoff and erosion by more than 90 percent.

A major impediment to using terraces on humid tropical and subtropical steeplands is the very shallow soils that are encountered in these areas, often less than 0.5 m to bedrock. In these instances, hillside ditches and other cross-slope practices may be more appropriate. However, Sheng (1982) points out that grass strips are not effective on slopes greater than 17-18 percent and hillside ditches do nothing for slopes greater than 25 percent.

Research and Development Needs

In the preceeding discussion, we described efforts in the last decade or so to develop a fundamental understanding of water erosion processes in the humid tropics and subtropics. These efforts are continuing at international centers like IITA and in individual countries and will, in the future, improve our ability to predict and to control water erosion in these environments. However, only a few of the studies cited above have been conducted under conditions faced by small subsistence farmers in the steeplands of the tropics and subtropics. These conditions are unique and will require specific attention by researchers before our knowledge of how they affect erosion is adequate to the task of proscribing erosion control measures. Some specific needs are identified below:

1. Precipitation monitoring networks are needed in the steeplands for the accurate determination of rainfall erosivities.
2. Surveys of steepland soils are needed at scales of 1:50,000 or smaller to provide meaningful data on properties affecting water erosion.
3. The soil erodibility (*K*) factor is not constant for a given soil, especially with the Oxisols. The seasonal effects of climatic and cultural factors on soil erodibility should be studied for subsistence farming systems.
4. Soil surface protection through in situ residue management or placement of off-site residues has been shown to be highly effective in reducing runoff and water erosion. These practices, however, usually require substantial herbicide use, which is expensive for the subsistence farmer. It also requires safety precautions with which farmers are often unfamiliar. Research is needed, therefore, on alternative practices which provide some residue cover but minimize herbicide use.
5. On very steep slopes, those exceeding 25-30 percent, no single crop management or conservation practice is effective in reducing erosion to tolerable levels. Combinations of practices such as residue management, cross-slope barriers, hillside ditches, and agroforestry are needed if farmers are to sustain crop production on these soils. Long-term research is needed on the erosion control potential for very steep slopes of various combinations of practices that are appropriate for small subsistence farmers.
6. Steepland soils are often characterized by shallow rooting depths and low water-holding capacities. Research is needed on the effects of residue cover, organic matter amendments, canopy

shading and other practices on water infiltration, evaporation, and soil moisture storage.

7. Until recently, international research and development agencies have devoted less attention to the problems associated with steepland farming than they have to the problems of developing tropical and subtropical lowlands. Despite this, there have been steepland studies in Asia, Central and South America, and the Caribbean. The findings of this research need to be more effectively disseminated. In addition, greater resources need to be allocated for continued efforts in steepland small farmer research.

Numerous technologies are available for combating soil erosion on tropical steeplands. These generally employ two approaches: engineering and ecological. Engineering approaches, including bench terraces, rock walls, and hillside ditches, require high initial capital, high labor inputs, and a certain level of technical skill. Ecological approaches utilize theoretical principles like diversity, stability, and equilibrium to encourage more sustainable agricultural systems. These might include stratifying cropping systems to minimize erosive effects of raindrop impact.

Unfortunately, many of these fundamental ecological principles have not been applied to agricultural systems and tested in any rigorous, systematic fashion. Many assumptions about the ecology of agricultural systems are based on research using relatively undisturbed ecosystems. Despite such "shortcomings," the discipline of agroecology has finally come of age. Although much of agroecological research is theoretical or basic in nature, certain hypotheses are being tested in applied contexts. One such case is agroforestry, an ecological approach to controlling soil erosion.

Agroforestry: A Means to Sustainable Agriculture on Tropical Steeplands

Agroforestry has been defined in numerous ways. Simply stated, it is an agricultural technology that incorporates trees into annual and perennial cropping systems. The overall intent of agroforestry systems is to promote positive interactions among trees and crops to obtain better crop yields and to sustain production using the limited resources available on a small farm (Mergen, 1986). Agroforestry has long been utilized at the subsistence level by indigenous peoples. Only recently has it been scientifically described and analyzed. With this current surge of scientific interest, agroforestry has also become a viable option for LDC small farmers who need to improve and to sustain production without using high-input technologies.

For numerous political, social, and economic reasons, LDC small farmers are concentrated in steeplands where soil fertility is low and on other marginal land. Recognizing that relocation of these individuals and their families is unlikely, researchers, extensionists, and farmers in certain LDCs have been developing agricultural systems, like agroforestry, that utilize low inputs and appear to be agronomically, ecologically, and economically sustainable. In the discussion below, we will explore past and current examples of agroforestry systems, address why agroforestry is attractive for steeplands and what possible obstacles may impede implementing agroforestry in these areas, and investigate future research and extension needs with respect to agroforestry on steeplands.

Past and Current Agroforestry Systems

As stated earlier, agroforestry has been practiced for hundreds of years by agricultural communities worldwide. Traditional forms still in practice include taungya agriculture in Africa, Mexico's Lacandon Indian mixed cropping systems, and the home gardens of New Guinea, Java, and other Southeast Asian cultures. Within these types of agroforestry, there is a deliberate use of trees for fodder, fuelwood, and fruit-bearing (Lundgren and Nair, 1985). These systems, however, are relics of an age of low population densities and cultures for which sustained but low-level production was sufficient to meet community food requirements. There is currently significant pressure to abandon traditional forms for more modern agricultural technologies.

In addition to traditional forms, there are also unintentional uses of trees in agriculture that can be classified as agroforestry. In many rural communities trees and shrubs are used for fence posts, living barriers, shade, and ad hoc fruit bearers (mango, papaya, banana, citrus). Trees like guayaba and various palms like peach palm are allowed to regenerate naturally in pastures because they provide shade and supplemental forage for livestock (Lagemann and Heuveldop, 1983). In the steeplands of Central America, farmers plant their coffee and cacao under shade trees like *Erythrina poeppigiana*, *Cedrela odorata*, and *Cordia aliodora* (Mergen, 1986). In most cases, these trees are selectively left standing when the rest of the forest vegetation is cleared for cultivation.

During the past five to eight years, scientists at the Centro Agronomico Tropical de Investigacion y Ensenanza (CATIE) in Costa Rica, IITA (Nigeria), and the agricultural experiment station at Yurimaguas, Peru, administered by the Peruvian government and North Carolina State University, have been conducting research on agroforestry systems and addressing certain fundamental adoption and extension issues. CATIE researchers, for example, are doing much work with leguminous tree species (*Erythrina poeppigiana*, *Gliricidia sepium*, *Inga* spp., *Leucaena leucocephala*) in combination with coffee, cacao (*Theobroma cacao*), and annual crops (corn, cassava, etc.). They also have an interesting project in which legume trees are cultivated as fodder for penned small ruminants (goats primarily). The legume tree biomass is produced on-farm by growing the trees either as small plantations or intercropped with food crops. The goats are contained in wooden pens and fed high-quality legume tree stems and leaves. They have been bred to live only on high quality forage and cannot subsist on low-grade native pasture (Dr. German Sanchez, CATIE, personal communication). This type of system seems highly appropriate for steeplands on which goats and other livestock are major sources of environmental degradation. Additional benefits are derived from the legume trees, the nitrogen fixing abilities of which enhance soil fertility.

At IITA and Yurimaguas, the first investigations into the possibilities for utilizing alley cropping techniques on problem soils have been conducted. Alley cropping is a form of traditional agroforestry in which food crops are grown in alleys or rows formed by trees or woody shrubs (Wilson et al., 1986). Trees or shrubs are cut back when crops are planted and maintained as short hedge rows (two to three meters high) during cropping. The leaves and stems are added to the soil as either green manure or mulch. Most alley cropping systems use leguminous trees. Residues from these trees have a C:N ratio low enough to decompose rapidly without nutrient immobilization by soil microorganisms. According to Wilson et al. (1986), planting trees with food crops is advantageous because trees have deep roots that absorb soil moisture from the lower soil strata and restore mineral nutrients to the surface soil. The shade they provide reduces soil temperatures and evaporation as well as creating favorable microclimates for beneficial soil organisms (e.g., earthworms). Current research at Yurimaguas, however, indicates that crop rows grown closest to the trees produce smaller plants with presumably lower yields (Cheryl Palm, North Carolina State University, personal communication). These types of tree/crop interactions are currently being investigated. Other Yurimaguas research activities include determining the nutrient properties, mulch capabilities, and decomposition rates of various legume trees in combination with rice and corn. As yet, this type of research has not been applied to steeplands.

A third agroforestry system utilizes silvopastoral principles. This is the deliberate combination of trees and pasture. The concept itself is quite ancient; attempts to maximize the benefits derived from such an association are recent, however. Anecdotal evidence reveals that livestock preferentially graze in patches where trees were formerly located (Miguel Ayarza, North Carolina State University, personal communication). Ayarza hypothesizes that extensive root dieback upon tree removal creates microsites of high nutrient availability. This high nutrient availability, in turn, promotes better plant growth, which is somehow recognized by grazing livestock. If this hypothesis is correct (it has not been tested yet), the same type of phenomenon would occur, to a lesser extent, when pasture trees are periodically coppiced. Trees in pasture, aside from the obvious benefits to animals (shade, additional forage), may be instrumental in combating soil erosion and maintaining healthy soil physical properties, especially on steeplands. Research in these areas is only in its infancy.

Agroforestry's Attractiveness for Steepland Agriculture

It is difficult to dispute claims that cultivating steeplands promotes soil erosion and degrades the physical, chemical, and biological properties of soils. Soil erodibility, although dependent on inherent soil characteristics, is a dynamic property (Lal, 1984). It is readily altered by changes in structural stability, organic matter content, and biotic activity. Because these factors can be manipulated, soil erodibility can be either aggravated or diminished. Raindrop impact, which is the prime instigator of soil erosion, can be lessened by maintaining continuous cover throughout the year (Lal, 1984). Agricultural systems that provide the following features will reduce soil erosion and sustain crop production:

1. prevent soil detachment by raindrop impact,
2. improve structural stability of the soil surface as well as its water retention and transmission properties, and
3. reduce runoff rate and velocity by providing appropriate surface drainage systems which channel water properly and increase infiltration.

Cropping systems with multiple canopy structures or those with continuous cover can provide such features. As noted by Greenland and Lal (1977), forestry systems are best suited to achieve such goals, but perennial tree crops or even pasture can be effective as well. In steepland rural communities, where the need to produce food outweighs the ecological benefits derived from maintaining forested hillsides, perennial tree crops or agroforestry systems appear to be the best solutions for soil erosion and land degradation.

There are ecological as well as socio-economic justifications for implementing agroforestry practices on steeplands. The ecological and agronomic factors will be explored first. In discussing the conservation role of trees, soil conservation is meant to encompass soil erosion control as well as the improvement of the physical, chemical, and biological properties of soils (Lundgren and Nair, 1985). According to studies conducted by Nair at IITA, incorporating woody perennials into the agricultural landscape can improve soil fertility, increase soil organic matter content, and increase soil water permeability, water holding capacity, and infiltration rates. Soil fertility can be enhanced by continuous additions of residues, including tree roots and stem/leaf mulches. This, in turn, increases the organic matter content of the soil, which can moderate soil reaction extremes and consequent nutrient availability/release patterns. Trees planted along slope contours stabilize other conservation structures (rock walls, grass strips, hillside ditches), decrease runoff, and provide fodder, fuelwood, lumber, or food.

From a socio-economic perspective, agroforestry is attractive for marginal areas like steeplands. For political and economic reasons, steepland rural communities do not receive the same levels of infrastructure or capital inputs as do urban areas or more productive flatlands. In many cases, small hillside farmers lack land titles and do not have access to credit to purchase agricultural inputs (fertilizer, pesticides, irrigation tubing, etc.). Even if they had capital to purchase these inputs, poor roads make distribution of such items very difficult. Given these conditions, steepland rural communities need agricultural systems that require low input levels and produce sustainable yields. In addition to sustained food crop yields, these communities must produce fodder, fuel, and shelter materials from a limited geographical area (Lundgren and Nair, 1985). In this sense, an integrated system like agroforestry seems ideal.

Despite the apparent advantages of agroforestry systems for steeplands, there are several obstacles or constraints to farmer adoption and/or implementation. The benefits derived from planting tree crops are not immediate. In most cases, farmers must wait three to five years before the first harvest can be made.

Although they will be able to harvest the annual crops within one growing season, farmers will still be required to adopt a long-term mindset. This shift from short-term to long-term thinking will be required of extensionists, development planners, and politicians as well.

In certain communities, traditional farming practices will have to be altered if agroforestry practices are implemented. A case in point is the Dominican Republic. Although trees are an integral component of the Dominican agricultural landscape, farmers seldom use trees in any systematic way. There is no precedence, for example, of using legume tree leaves or stems as animal fodder or mulch. In fact, many Dominican farmers remove all residues from their fields before, during, and after cultivation. Given the need for cultural change, however slight, there is bound to be resistance until the practices are proven economically and socially acceptable.

A third impediment to agroforestry adoption revolves around the controversy of sustained production versus increased yields. Agroforestry systems, on the whole, will not increase crop yields like high input, monoculture systems. Their strength lies in sustaining moderate yield levels for longer periods without exhausting the natural resource base. If agroforestry is to be accepted as a viable option for steepland agriculture, farmers, extensionists, and governmental officials will have to concur that the benefits from longer but lower yield systems outweigh those from short-term, high-yield systems. Until this conversion occurs on a fairly large scale, implementation of agroforestry will proceed rather slowly.

Future Research and Extension Needs

Although the arguments in favor of agroforestry on steeplands are encouraging, many of the ecological and agronomic justifications are based on anecdotal or circumstantial evidence. Little empirical data exist regarding the role and use of tree crops in land use systems in general and soil conservation in particular (Lundgren and Nair, 1985). Among research needs are the following: a) appropriate woody species for given agricultural settings, b) the most appropriate ways of incorporating tree crops into other farm production components, c) the most efficient management schemes to optimize benefits, and d) maximizing tree crop benefits in the context of soil conservation activities.

In addition to these macro-level research needs, little is known about perennial/annual crop interactions or how soil chemical, physical, and biological properties are affected by perennial/annual crop associations. How, for example, is annual crop productivity affected by shade, root competition, water stress, and nutrient competition (Mergen, 1986)? If different plant associations modify microclimatic conditions, would physiological responses be altered as well? With respect to plant/soil interactions, knowledge gaps exist regarding nutrient release and availability in soils where trees and annuals are associated. Modification of soil physical properties, like soil structure, water holding capacity, and rooting depth, also need further investigation. Finally, the realm of interactions among soil macro- and microfauna, tree crops, annual crops, and soil has barely been explored.

These are just several recommendations for research in agroforestry that cover deficits in ecological and agronomic fields. Economic analysis of agroforestry systems is also needed. If they are not profitable, then they will not be adopted or sustained no matter how ecologically or agronomically sound they are.

References

Aina, P.O., R. Lal, and G.S. Taylor. 1976. Soil and crop management in relation to soil erosion in the rainforest region of Western Nigeria. Proc. National Soil Erosion Conf.. Lafayette, IN. Purdue University.

Beasley, D.B., and L.F. Huggins. 1982. ANSWERS users manual. EPA-905/ 9-82-001. USEPA Great Lakes Natl. Prg. Office, Chicago, Ill.

Benatti, R. Jr., J. Bertoni, and C.A. Moreira. 1977. Perdas por erosao emplantio directo e convencional de milho em dois solos de Sao Paulo. Revista Brasil. de Ciencia do Solo, Brasileira, Brasil. pp. 121-123.

Castro, C., and T.M. Zobeck. 1986. Evaluation of the topographic factor (LS) from the Universal Soil Loss Equation on irregular slopes. *J. Soil Water Conser.* 41:113-116.

Cooperband, L. 1986. Conservacion del suelo en la agricultura de ladera. In Primer Seminario Internacional de Conservacion de Tierras y Aguas. Secretaria de Estado de Agricultura, Santo Domingo, Repub. Dominicana.

Cox, G.W., and M.D. Atkins. 1979. Agricultural Ecology. An analysis of world food production systems. San Francisco, CA: W.H. Freeman and Co., 721 pp.

Dangler, E.W., S.A. El-Swaify, L.R. Ahuja, and A.P. Barnett. 1976. Erodibility of selected Hawaii soils by rainfall simulation. USDA-ARS W-35 Report. U. Hawaii, Honolulu, Hawaii.

Dudal, R. 1980. Soil-related constraints to agricultural development in the tropics. In: *Soil-related constraints to food production in the tropics.* Los Banos, Phillipines. IRRI and Cornell University. pp. 23-37.

Dudal, R. 1981. An evaluation of conservation needs. In: *Soil Conservation,* R.P.C. Morgan (ed.). Problems and Prospects. John Wiley and Sons, Chichester, U.K. pp. 3-12.

El-Swaify, S.A. 1977. Susceptibilities of certain tropical soils to erosion by water. In: *Soil Conser. and Mgt in the Humid Tropics,* D.J. Greenland and R. Lal (ed.). John Wiley and Sons, Chichester, U.K. pp. 71-77.

El-Swaify, S.A., E.W. Dangler, and C.L. Armstrong. 1982. Soil erosion by water in the tropics. University of Hawaii, Honolulu, Hawaii. 173 pp.

Foster, G.R., and W.H. Wischmeier. 1974. Evaluating irregular slopes for soil loss prediction. Trans. ASAE. 17:305-309.

Greenland, D.J., and R. Lal. 1977. Soil erosion in the humid tropics: The need for action and the need for research. In: *Soil Cons. and Mgt in the Humid Tropics,* D.J. Greenland and R. Lal (ed.). John Wiley and Sons, Chichester, U.K. pp. 261-265.

Greenland, D.J., and R. Lal. 1977. *Soil Conservation and Management in the Humid Tropics.* John Wiley and Sons, Chichester, U.K. 283 pp.

Greenland, D.J. 1977. The magnitude and importance of the problem. In: *Soil Conservation and Management in the Humid Tropics,* D.J. Greenland and R. Lal (ed.). John Wiley and Sons, Chichester, U.K. pp. 3-7.

Gumbs, F.A., J.I. Lindsay, M. Nasir, and Angella Mohammed. 1985. Soil erosion studies in the northern mountain range, Trinidad, under different crop and soil management. In: *Soil Erosion and Conservation,* S.A. El-Swaify et al. (ed.). Soil Conservation Soc. of Amer., Ankeny, IA. pp. 90-98.

Hudson, N. 1971. *Soil conservation*. Cornell University Press, Ithaca, NY.

Huxley, P.A. 1986. The prediction of biological productivity and sustainability of tree-crop mixtures. Trop. Agric., 63:68-70.

Laflen, J.M., M. Amemiya, and E.A. Hintz. 1981. Measuring crop residue cover. *J. Soil Water Conserv.* 36:341-343.

Lagemann, J., and J. Heuveldop. 1983. Characterization and evaluation of agroforestry systems: The case of Acosta-Puriscal, Costa Rica. Agroforestry Systems. 1:101-115.

Lal, R. 1977. Analysis of factors affecting rainfall erosivity and soil erodibility. In: *Soil Conservation and Management in the Humid Tropics,* D.J. Greenland and R. Lal (ed.). John Wiley and Sons, Chichester, U.K. pp. 49-56.

Lal, R. 1984. Soil erosion from tropical arable lands and its control. *Adv. Agron.* 37:183-248.

Lal, R., P.A. Sanchez, and R.W. Cummings, Jr. 1986. Land Clearing and Development in the Tropics. Rotterdam, Netherlands: A.A. Balkema Publishers, 450 pp.

Lal, R., and D.J. Greenland. 1979. *Soil Physical Properties and Crop Production in the Tropics*. John Wiley and Sons, Chichester, U.K. 551 pp.

Lal, R., and E.W. Russell. 1981. *Tropical Agricultural Hydrology*. John Wiley and Sons, Chichester, U.K. 482 pp.

Lowdermilk, W.C. 1953. Conquest of the land through seven thousand years. USDA-SCS Agric. Inform. Bull. 99.

Lundgren, B., and P.K.R. Nair. 1985. Agroforestry for soil conservation. In: *Soil Erosion and Conservation,* S.A. El-Swaify et al. (ed.). Soil Conser. Soc. Amer., Ankeny, IA. pp. 703-717.

Mergen, F. 1986. Agroforestry—an overview and recommendations for possible improvements. *Trop. Agric.* 63:76-80.

Morillo, A.G. 1986. An evaluation of small hillside farmers' knowledge of and attitudes toward environmental conservation resulting from the environmental workshops. M.S. Thesis. The Ohio State Univ. Columbus, OH, 133 pp.

Norman, J.T. 1979. *Annual Cropping Systems in the Tropics. An Introduction*. University Presses of Florida, Gainesville, FL. 276 pp.

Romkens, M.J.M. 1985. The soil erodibility factor: A perspective. In: *Soil Erosion and Conservation,* S.A. El-Swaify et al. (ed.). Soil Conserv. Society of America, Ankeny, IA. pp. 445-461.

Roose, E.J. 1977. Application of the Universal Soil Loss Equation of Wischmeier and Smith in West Africa. In: *Soil Conservation and Management in the Humid Tropics,* D.J. Greenland and R. Lal (ed.). John Wiley and Sons, Chichester, UK. pp. 177-187.

Sanchez, P.A. 1976. *Properties and Management of Soils in the Tropics*. John Wiley and Sons, New York, NY. 618 pp.

Sheng, T.C. 1982. Erosion problems associated with cultivation in humid tropical hilly regions. In: *Soil Erosion and Conservation in the Tropics*. Amer. Soc. Agron., Madison, WI. pp. 27-39.

Sheng, T.C., and H.R. Stennett. 1975. Forestry development and watershed management in the upland regions—Jamaica. FAO Working Document SF/JAM 505. FAO-UNDP, Rome, Italy.

Soil Conservation Service. 1975. Soil taxonomy: A basic system of soil classification for making and interpreting soil surveys. USDA-SCS Handbook No. 436, Washington, DC.

Soil Conservation Service. 1980. Universal Soil Loss Equation. Caribbean Area. Technical Notes. San Juan, Puerto Rico. USDA-SCS. 63 pp.

Tama, K. and S.A. El-Swaify. 1978. Charge, colloidal, and structural stability relationships in oxidic soils. In: *Modification of Soil Structure*, W.W. Emerson et al., (ed.). John Wiley and Sons, Chichester, U.K. pp. 41-52.

Veloz, R.A. 1984. Design and installation of runoff erosion plots in the Dominican Republic. M.S. Thesis. The Ohio State University, Columbus, OH. 117 pp.

Veloz, R.A., and T.J. Logan. 1986. Erosion control for cultivated steeplands in the Dominican Republic. Amer. Soc. Agron., Madison, WI: Agronomy Abstracts.

Wilson, G.F., B.T. Kang, and K. Mulongoy. 1986. Alley cropping: Trees as sources of green-manure and mulch in the tropics. *Biol. Agric. and Hort.* 3:251-267.

Wilson, G.F., and R. Lal. 1986. New concepts for post-clearing land management in the tropics. In: *Land Clearing and Development in the Tropics*, R. Lal et al. (ed.). A.A. Balkema Publishers, Rotterdam, Holland. pp. 371-381.

Wischmeier, W.H. 1959. A rainfall erosion index for a universal soil-loss equation. Soil Sci. Soc. Amer. Proc. 23:246-249.

Wischmeier, W.H., and D.D. Smith. 1978. Predicting rainfall erosion losses—a guide to conservation planning. USDA Agriculture Handbook No. 537. 58 pp.

4/ What Are the Soil and Water Benefits of Planting Trees in Developing Country Watersheds?

Lawrence S. Hamilton
Andrew J. Pearce

Although forestry projects yield important benefits, planting trees is not the sole and sufficient solution to all land and watershed management problems. Lawrence Hamilton and Andrew Pearce present an annotated primer of the unwarranted assumptions regarding the benefits of third world afforestation. They caution that raising unrealistic expectations about those benefits, either purposefully or by default, is ultimately self-defeating for resource planners and managers.

Introduction

Will the years 1985-1995 be "The Decade of Forestation" in the tropics? Millions of hectares will undoubtedly be planted, forming a major component of national forestry department and private organization programs. Forestation[1] objectives will include meeting fuelwood and biomass energy needs, establishing community forests, rehabilitating degraded watersheds, increasing soil stability within agricultural lands, and meeting domestic and export commercial wood needs as natural forests are further reduced in extent.

The Food and Agriculture Organization of the United Nations (FAO) estimates that the current rate of tropical plantation establishment is 1.1 million hectares per year, and claims that this rate needs to be greatly increased. In 1981, the U.N. Energy Conference called for an increase in the worldwide annual rate of planting for fuelwood from 0.5 million hectares to 2.5 million hectares. China announced a few years ago bold plans for forestation of 25-30 percent of its total land area. Both the 1985 FAO Action Program in Tropical Forestry and the World Resources Institute (WRI) 1985 Accelerated Action Plan call for greatly increased forestation. The latter calls for a five-year investment totalling U.S. $1886 million in 56 developing countries for fuelwood and agroforestry alone, mostly devoted to tree planting. The WRI plan also proposed large investments in the industrial forestry and watershed land use sectors, both having large components of forestation (WRI, 1985).

A host of benefits will be claimed for these forestation programs, whether intended for watershed rehabilitation alone or as part of multipurpose programs. Trees and forests do indeed have many benefits and products, many of them related to water and soil conservation. Some of the benefits widely claimed can be achieved, some can only be achieved under specific circumstances, some are questionable, and some are demonstrably false or incompatible with other claimed benefits. Project planners, foresters, and others involved in development must strive for greater accuracy and logic in their claims for benefits from forestation.

It is time to disavow the "trees-are-a-panacea-for-all-land-and-water-ills" stance and become more realistic about what forests will and will not do for watershed protection. There are important reasons for forestation in development projects, but foresters and planners risk "backlash" from disappointed publics and clients in the future if frequently claimed benefits relating to rainfall, soil erosion, sedimentation, floods, and water availability are not forthcoming, and forthcoming promptly.

Forestation and Rainfall

It has been claimed that forestation will increase rainfall (World Water, 1981). What does research have to offer on this topic? Some Russian work cited and summarized by Shpak (1968) showed approximately 10 percent more rain in forest areas as opposed to adjacent open areas. Shpak goes on, however, to point out precipitation measuring problems that invariably allow forest gauges to catch more rain. He concludes that "the considerable increase (found by some authors)... is usually overstated... the problem of the effect of forest on precipitation remains open at present." In this context, it is worthwhile to note that the error range for typical point measurements of rainfall is around $\pm$ 3 to 5 percent. For whole-catchment averages, rainfall precision is never likely to be better than $\pm$ 5 percent. An early study in the United States following large-scale "deforestation" by smelter fume injury showed small (14 percent) but significantly greater precipitation in the forest area compared with the denuded area (Hursch, 1948). A subsequent analysis of those experimental procedures by Lee (1978), however, indicated that when catch differences (mainly from wind effects) are accounted for, the differences were less than 0.5 percent and were much smaller than measurement error. In the tropics, Bernard (1953) found no evidence of any influence of forests on rainfall for the one-million-square-kilometer Central Congo Basin. He speculated, however, that forest clearing, by increasing the heat reflectance, might introduce some instability into weather patterns.

For most hydrometeorological situations in Asia and the Pacific, it is more likely that Pereira's 1973 summary is still valid: "There is no corresponding evidence as to any effects of forests on the occurrence of rainfall" (Pereira, 1973). We probably need little or no more research on this—except perhaps in the Amazon Basin—where Salati et al. (1983) have suggested that forest clearing of areas between one and 100 kilometers in diameter may significantly reduce rainfall immediately downwind. This thesis is appealing, but as yet there is little evidence to support it. Nor is there substantial evidence that following large-scale forestation (for example, in North Island, New Zealand) there has been an increase in rainfall due to the tree planting.

There is one exception. In restricted physiographic and climatic situations (for example in coastal fog belts or at high elevations characterized by very frequent or persistent clouds) forests can capture atmospheric aerosols (Zadroga, 1981). This so-called "occult" precipitation is added to the effective moisture received by the area and, where the necessary conditions are exceptionally persistent, may represent a substantial percentage of the total precipitation. Shuttleworth (1977) shows that rates of capture are very low, implying that wind-driven cloud or fog must persist for several thousands of hours per year for occult precipitation to amount to several hundred mm/year. In Hawaii, occult precipitation on a single, open-grown tree represented an increase of 760 mm above a nonforested 2,600 mm of rainfall (Ekern, 1964). This increase in total precipitation for a single tree or a row will be greater than that for a closed forest stand because of the mutual sheltering effects of the trees. Denuded areas in similar elevational/climatic situations could have occult precipitation restored through forestation—especially by belts of trees through which wind-driven cloud can move. Further research with different tree architecture and spacing may be warranted if specific forestation plans are proposed in the limited tropical areas which have the necessary climate and topography. This is especially the case in dry coastal environments with frequent fog.

FORESTATION AND EROSION

Popular wisdom insists that planting trees will prevent erosion and that removing trees, *per se*, results in drastic erosion leading to land degradation. Trees, particularly trees in forest stands, do indeed reduce the amount of erosion. Thus conventional wisdom broadly coincides with proven effects. For instance, soil erosion under dense natural humid and seasonally humid tropical forest is often less than one ton per hectare (ha) per year (UNESCO/UNEP/FAO, 1978). Nonetheless, substantial surface erosion can occur in undisturbed forest (Lal, 1983), as can landslips and debris avalanches on steep forested slopes (Lin, 1984). There are also many actively rising mountain ranges that have erosion rates as high as 10 mm per year (>200 tons per ha) under natural high forest vegetation. In these dynamic tectonic regions, no vegetative cover can greatly restrain the natural rate of erosion and tree planting will have limited effect over time. Data on natural uplift and erosion rates are needed before percentage reductions in erosion rate can be even crudely estimated for forestation activity.

For a given situation, however, forest ecosystems are safest from the accelerated erosion standpoint because human activity is generally less than in other kinds of land-use systems. Moreover, following forestation of open land, there is generally a reduction in (but not prevention of) erosion. To be more precise, it is also necessary to separate three classes of erosion: (a) surface (sheetwash and rills), (b) gully, and (c) mass wasting (landslips, slumps, debris flows, etc.).

Surface Erosion

Surface erosion under humid tropical primary forest is generally more severe than in humid temperate forests, because of more frequent and intense rains, less litter, thinner humic horizons, and less ground vegetation on the soil surface (Birot, 1968). Dietrich et al. (1982), for example, found sediment yields from primary forest in Panama to be 6 tons/ha/year, resulting mainly from extensive surface runoff. In woodland or non-evergreen closed forest, rates of erosion are probably comparable between tropic and temperate zones, with similar rainfall regimes. If understory vegetation in forests is not grazed nor the litter burned, erosion rates are generally very low.

Simply putting trees or forests on the land does not eliminate surface erosion. Bell (1973) reported significant erosion problems in pure *Tectona grandis* plantations in Trinidad, and similar problems have been reported in El Salvador and Thailand (Kunkle, 1983) and in Java (Coster, 1938) where there is little or no understory vegetation and/or litter is removed. Brunig et al. (1975) reported annual erosion rates on moderate slopes for undisturbed natural forest, teak plantations widely spaced with mixed understory, and dense teak plantations with no understory as 0.2-10, 2-10, and 20-160 tons/ha, respectively. Understory and/or litter retention and management are vital to minimize surface erosion.

Advocates of forestation sometimes cite the benefits of having a tree canopy interposed between the falling rain and the bare soil to reduce splash erosion (detachment of particles by raindrop impact, and then movement). Actually, splash erosion can be greater on bare soil surfaces under trees because drop sizes are larger. Coalescing raindrops on large-leaved species (such as teak) falling from a high canopy may be more damaging to the soil than the unintercepted rain itself. For instance, *Albizza falcataria* with a canopy height of 20 m yielded raindrops with an erosive energy equal to that of rain in the open. But for *Anthocephalus chinensis* with its large leaves at only 10 m canopy height, erosive energy was 50 percent greater than for rain in the open (Lembaga Ekologi, 1980). Similar findings were reported from the evergreen temperate (small-leaved) rainforest by Mosley (1982).

Repeated results of surface erosion studies in forests have shown that it is the leaf litter, humic horizons, and low understory that impart erosion protection (for example, Wiersum, 1985). If these are removed for fodder and/or fuel, or if livestock are turned in to graze, the presence of trees alone will not minimize surface erosion on slopes. It is common practice for Nepalese hill farm families to gather litter under forest plantations (or natural forests) for livestock bedding and fuel. This practice increases the risk of surface erosion, the reduction of which was one of the reasons for the forestation enterprise. Recognition of this problem has led the Nepal-Australia Community Forestry Project to the practice of frequent prunings to make these products available as fuel and bedding, while retaining the annual leaf or needle fall on the ground surface (L.S. Hamilton, pers. obs.). A hazard has developed in the Philippines, where leaves under plantations of mahogany, teak, and gmelina are gathered to make mosquito-repellent coils, poultry feed, and fertilizer (Yao and Nañagas, 1983). Wiersum (1984) has synthesized much of the research literature on erosion under various forest and tree crop systems and presented an interesting table of averages (lumping all data, even though derived from different slopes and soils; Table 4-1). Note that as soon as the litter is removed, by cultivation or weeding or burning, the erosion rate increases substantially.

Introducing trees into a cropping system (agroforestry), whether shifting agriculture or sedentary agriculture, has been suggested as a desirable watershed management practice. It should be recognized that from the surface erosion standpoint, the trees will only give reductions if the cropping practices maintain a complete leaf litter, mulch, or vegetative cover on the soil. Good soil conservation farming (or grazing) must prevail if an agroforestry system is to achieve erosion reduction benefits.

Another aspect concerning trees and erosion merits some attention. A hazard arises in connection with soil disturbance associated with preparing the site for forestation, and with subsequent cultivation to reduce competition in the early establishment phase. In the drier parts of tropical Asia and the Pacific, competing vegetation may not be a concern; thus the hand-planting and lack of subsequent cultivation bring no erosion problems. But experience in moist areas of Queensland (Australia) and Nigeria has shown that site preparation pays off in terms of increased survival and growth. Even in the Fiji dry zone, Bell and Evo (1982) suggest that the Fiji Pine Commission employ cultivation prior to and during the establishment of eucalypt energy plantations. Researchers in Australia have developed a set of planting site preparation guidelines for tropical Queensland based on erosion studies conducted since 1974 (Cassells et al., 1982). Contour row-ploughing has been found most satisfactory in erodible soils (Cassells, pers. com.). Fast-growing, nitrogen-fixing trees would seem to offer advantages in requiring little weeding because of growth rate, and encouraging protective ground cover due to nitrogen fixation.

In tropical areas with a dry season, fire can be an important factor in watershed management. Fire is often used as a land management tool by grazers or shifting cultivators using grassland fallow. Fire can "escape" into the adjacent plantation or be deliberately introduced to secure a usufructuary or tenurial advantage. The major watershed-behavior effect of fire is the removal of the litter and near-ground vegetative cover that protects the soil from surface erosion (Hamilton, 1983). Water-repellency of topsoil may also be induced (Rice, 1982; Wells, 1981). Very hot and prolonged fires, especially when repeated, may also reduce the organic content of the soil and reduce structural stability. Dry ravel may be an important and rapid erosion process for short periods after fires (Rice, 1982). Hot, prolonged fires may also kill the trees completely, thus initiating loss of root strength. Frequent fires may keep a forested site in a continually eroding condition. In Pakistan, frequently burned stands of *Pinus roxburghii* were reported to exhibit as much erosion as unterraced croplands (Raeder-Roitzsch and Masur, 1968). In planted forests, particularly those consisting of conifers, eucalypts or *Casuarina*, fire is a major hazard. If a program of watershed

Table 4-1. Erosion in Various Tropical Moist Forest and Tree Crop Systems (*ton/ha/year*)

	Minimal	Median	Maximal
Multistoried tree gardens (4 locations, 4 observations)	0.01	0.06	0.14
Shifting cultivation, fallow period (6 locations, 14 observations)	0.05	0.15	7.40
Natural forests (18 locations, 27 observations)	0.03	0.30	6.16
Forest plantation, undisturbed (14 locations, 20 observations)	0.02	0.58	6.20
Tree crops with cover crop/mulch (9 locations, 17 observations)	0.10	0.75	5.60
Shifting cultivation, cropping period (7 locations, 22 observations)	0.40	2.78	70.05
Taungya cultivation (2 locations, 6 observations)	0.63	5.23	17.37
Tree crops, clean-weeded (10 locations, 17 observations)	1.20	47.60	192.90
Forest plantations, burned/litter removed (7 locations, 7 observations)	5.92	53.40	104.80

From: Wiersum (1984)

rehabilitation involves forestation, there may be local customary users of the land who would prefer not to find trees occupying the land, for they seldom are beneficiaries when the forests are harvested. Their support must be obtained before commencing a tree-planting program, or fire may be a continual problem. Programs of social or community forestry have been successfully adopted in many countries (FAO et al., 1984).

Gully Erosion

Once gullies have developed through some inappropriate land use practice, their stabilization for watershed rehabilitation is important but difficult. In an advanced state, gullies are usually undergoing complex erosional processes of headcutting, slumping, or other mass failure, and surface erosion. The important remedial action is to protect the surface with vegetation, litter, and root system networks as rapidly as possible, to alter the flow of water away from the gully headwall, and to reduce undercutting of gully headwalls and sidewalls. Trees have a major role to play here, especially fast-growing species, though they may be combined with grasses, herbaceous material, or shrubs. Gully stabilization may even require reshaping or minor structural measures, especially at the gully heads. Gully stabilization and rehabilitation with productive vegetation is a complex technical activity, and may require more than forestry expertise to do well permanently. This is especially true in non-humid areas with a rainfall regime of high intensity storms and difficulties in getting vegetation established due to lack of soil moisture. Weber and Hoskins (1983) presented various structural methods that can be carried out manually with local materials in Africa, and Crouch et al. (1984) have documented techniques using small but more sophisticated weirs for gully control in Australia.

Mass Erosion

In watershed planning and management, slopes which are prone to mass erosion merit special attention as "critical areas." Megahan and King (1985) have made suggestions for identifying areas of high hazard. Land use allocations and management policies for landslide-prone areas should be based on the degree of climatic, topographic, and soil-properties hazard. In the case of deep-seated slide hazards, this is indicated simply by whether or not slides occur in the area (i.e., "hazardous" or "not hazardous"). Forestation or deforestation has little or no influence on these hazardous areas. For shallow slides, the degree of hazard can be broadly assessed, and stratified, for different levels of care. One set of criteria for hazard rating is based on storm rainfall intensity and duration and on slope gradient and shape. Megahan and King summarized the literature and suggested that shallow landslips are limited to slopes greater than 45 to 55 percent, with a maximum frequency of occurrence at about 70 percent. Landslips also are correlated with slope concavities and convergences that concentrate water. Sidle et al. (1985) also reviewed a range of methods for predicting landslide occurrences and locations.

Sites prone to shallow landslips are given greater stability by tree roots. Tree roots impart additional shear strength to the soil. The greatest proportional increase in strength is when soils are saturated and high pore pressures have reduced or eliminated frictional components of strength. O'Loughlin (1984) documented that between 5 and 10 years after establishment of *Pinus radiata* plantations on erosion-prone sites, root development began to increase substantially the slope resistance to shallow failures. However, he found that forestation was not generally effective in containing retrogressive slumping around headwalls of actively eroding gullies and large landslides.

Where land is already cleared and under some kind of cropping or grazing regime, the introduction of trees in an agroforestry land-use system can improve the stability of areas prone to shallow slips. Rows of trees on the contour with alley cropping or grazing would appear to offer the best arrangement in utilizing both the strength of tree roots and the "fence" function of trapping any surface wash from uphill, thus gradually creating a series of natural terraces. A good example of such a practice, developed spontaneously over time by traditional hill people, may be found in Cebu in the Philippines (Vergara, 1984). Here, on slopes ranging up to 80 percent, rows of *Leucaena leucocephala* have been established as producers of stemwood for fuel, leaves for inter-row mulch and soil amendment, and nitrogen through fixation by this fast-growing legume. Soil shear strength can also be imparted by roots of many fruit trees that may be used in an agroforestry system.

Forestation and Sedimentation

Increased sediment in streams, lakes, and reservoirs and discharge into seas can harm or kill valuable aquatic life (including fisheries, mangrove, and coral reef resources), impair water quality for domestic uses, irrigation, and industrial processes, reduce reservoir capacity for important flood, hydropower, and irrigation storage, shorten the useful life of hydroelectric turbines and water pumps, interfere with navigation, and aggrade river channels, thus aggravating flooding. Most of these unwanted effects of sediment are in the downstream portions of watersheds where the greater part of the wealth, political power, and population of a drainage basin usually reside. The links between upstream land erosion and downstream sediment problems have been recognized by these affected people, and there are increasing levels of action being called for to reduce harmful sedimentation through better upland watershed management. Attention is being currently given to benefit/cost assessments of the erosion/sedimentation interaction in major water resource development projects (see, for instance, Fleming [1982], and Dixon and Easter [1986]).

It has been claimed that the mere presence of forests can eliminate stream sediment problems (waters flow crystal clear), and that restoring forest cover will completely rectify serious sediment problems in a watershed. The presence of forests, by their effects in reducing erosion, can indeed have a beneficial impact on sediment output in regions where natural erosion rates and sediment yields are not great. Streambank erosion, streambed degradation, and remobilization of temporarily stored sediment are, however, normal processes, and much sediment that causes mischief derives from these sources. Nonetheless, man-made land erosion contributes substantially to sediment loading of many streams. Identifying the extent and significance of man-induced erosion and sedimentation is generally difficult and time-consuming.

Hardjono (1980) reported on reforestation benefits in Indonesia, from subwatersheds planted with *Pinus merkusii*, *Tectona grandis*, *Swietenia macrophyla*, and *Eucalyptus alba*. He found sediment yields from forested areas to be one third of those from an agricultural watershed. Even introducing trees into grazing or cropping land in a well-managed agroforestry system can have important sediment reduction effects (Hamilton, 1983). Having forests downslope of an area undergoing surface erosion can also trap the sediment and store it either temporarily or permanently. Under long-fallow, patchwork-mosaic, shifting agricultural systems, there is usually brushland or forest downslope of a cropped area which may be experiencing some surface erosion (Hamilton, 1983). It is this feature that causes traditional stable shifting cultivation systems to be relatively benign as far as sediment in streams is concerned. The increasing and extensive change from shifting to "shiftless" (short- or no-fallow) slash-and-burn agriculture on steep slopes, on the other hand, can markedly increase sediment yield.

This downslope sediment-trapping effect highlights the importance of streamside buffer strips of undisturbed forest. The effectiveness of streamside buffers has been documented for tropical Australia by Gilmour et al. (1982) on sites where substantial overland flow occurs due to an impeding layer at about 20 cm. Observations of serious stream sediment problems in South Africa following logging led Bosch and Hewlett (1980) to develop strong recommendations and planning design aids for what they termed "streamside management zones." These streamside forest areas can also reduce streambank erosion by helping to stabilize banks. Forestation of streamside areas is important in watershed rehabilitation even though some loss of water may occur due to increased evapotranspiration.

The sediment-trapping and storing processes highlight another major problem having to do with watershed rehabilitation measures to reduce sediment loads. It is extremely difficult to predict when the reduction of erosion by forestation will show up as less sediment in a reservoir—capturing a benefit to which money value can be assigned. Megahan (1981) has described the storages in the erosion/sedimentation processes and depicted them as in Figure 4-1. The sediment showing up in a stream after one storm event may have come from temporary storage where soil eroded over a number of years has been deposited. Thus the full effect of soil erosion reduction measures through a practice such as forestation may not show up for many years, even decades, in terms of a realizable downstream benefit in sediment reduction (Hamilton and Pearce, 1986).

Burning of plantations can result in dramatic increases in sediment production and in the relative importance of sediment-producing and sediment-transporting processes (Rice, 1982). Increased dry ravel can transport much sediment to stream channels within a few hours of fire passage (Rice, 1982). The impact of burning depends on the fire intensity, duration, and frequency, on the occurrence of major storms following the burn, and on the rate of revegetation. One of the most dramatic reports was based on a major wildfire in Australia's temperate Snowy Mountains (Working Group on the Influence of Man on the Hydrologic Cycle, 1972). Suspended sediment content at a flow of 60-80 m^3 per second was increased 100 times in comparison with pre-fire conditions. It was estimated that the total sediment load in one of the creeks draining a burned catchment was 1000 times greater than it was before the fire. Under humid tropical conditions, where the regrowth of vegetation is more rapid, such large

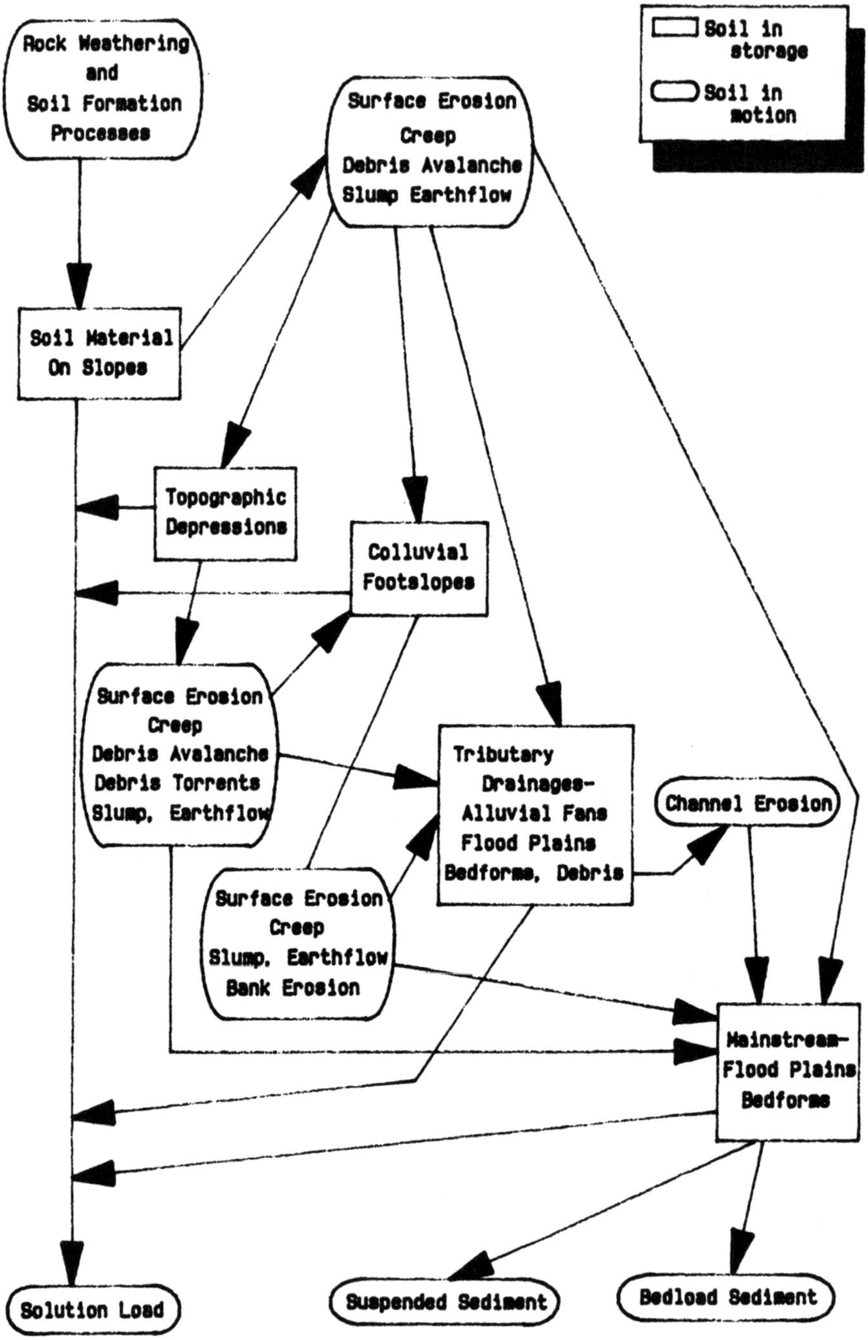

Figure 4-1. Erosion/Sedimentation Processes in a Watershed (Megahan, 1981).

increases in sediment load are not as likely after burning. Much also depends on how soon a major storm event occurs after a fire (Boughton, 1970).

In summary, there is good evidence that forests have an important beneficial role to play in reducing the downstream social and economic costs of unwanted sediment when natural erosion rates are not extreme. The question of when such benefits are realizable, and their quantification even with "ballpark" changes in sediment delivery ratios, remains unanswered in many places. Techniques for minimizing sediment production, even under forest land uses such as logging, are known and can be implemented where control over loggers is possible. Even where such control is minimal, post-logging rehabilitation is relatively cheap, easy, and beneficial if done early after logging. It is prudent to plan and lay out the extraction routes at the time of plantation establishment using conservation guidelines, and to use these as access roads for planting and subsequent silviculture.

Forestation and Floods

There is a widespread belief that forest cover in upland watersheds will prevent floods downstream in major rivers. This belief is also translated to "floods are caused by forest cutting, and flood damage can be eliminated by large-scale reforestation or afforestation of upland catchments." For instance, monsoonal floods in the Ganges and the Indus (which have always occurred) have been attributed to tree cutting in the uplands (World Water, 1981). Recently, the European Environmental Bureau (1982), writing about tropical forests, stated that "forests guard against flooding," including major floods on large rivers, not just in small storms or on small streams emanating from the forest in the upper watershed. A statement by Openshaw (1974) that "the principal cause of the recent floods in the Indian sub-continent was the removal of tree cover in the catchment areas for fuelwood," also referred to calamitous floods on large river systems. In the Philippines, following the great Agusan flood of 1981, the state minister in a newspaper interview placed "30 percent of the blame on logging of headwater forests," even though "flooding is an annual event, and major floods are expected about every 20 years" (Corvera, 1981). In the same newspaper article, a top official in the Philippine Bureau of Forest Development was interviewed about the measures necessary to control logging and encourage reforestation in order to avoid such catastrophic flooding. Sharp and Sharp (1982) claim that "overlogging is now officially recognized as the cause of the July 1981 severe flooding of the Yangtze" in China.

Are people looking for a scapegoat so that they do not have to consider that floods have always occurred, and can ignore that in actuality damage is increasing because of greater flood plain occupancy, greater channel constriction and alteration by human structures, and more roads, ditches, and non-absorbing surfaces speeding water on its way downhill? Are they equating forest cutting with large-scale forest clearing followed by conversion to a subsequent abusive land use which denudes, degrades, compacts, and gullies the area so that precipitation is largely transformed into rapid surface runoff and then into sediment-laden stormflow? Are these popular concerns about forest cutting and floods valid, or are they misinterpretations of research findings?

Findings from paired small-watershed research in which one watershed has been logged do indeed usually (but not always) show greater stormflow volumes, higher peakflows, and sometimes earlier peaks in streams emanating from the logged area (Douglass and Swank, 1975; Reinhart et al., 1963). These changes are invariably greatest (up to threefold increases) in very small storms, and diminish rapidly in percentage terms with increasing storm size (e.g. Pierce et al., 1970; Harr et al., 1975; Pearce et al., 1980). In very large storms, such as those which produce floods, changes in volume and peak discharge from cutover areas are usually less than 10 percent (Hewlett and Helvey, 1970). Flooding may be increased close to the cutover area, but as the water is routed down a major river basin, this effect is quickly reduced to insignificance amid other processes of overriding importance, such as the nature and intensity of the precipitation, the direction the storm moves across the basin, the size and morphometry of the basin, and the channel geometry and storage characteristics of the major river. Hewlett (1982) has recently examined the evidence worldwide from forest watershed research and reported that there is no cause-effect relationship between forest cutting in the headwaters and floods in the lower basin. Even if a whole basin were under a forest harvesting regime, normally it would not be logged off all in one year. Those portions that are logged rather quickly return to a prelogging hydrologic regime as the forest regenerates and full canopy is restored, even though it is young growth. Often a substantial part of this stormflow/peakflow effect on small basins is due to poorly located and designed roads, skid trails, and log landings, all of which speed water off-site. Thus, proper conservation logging will generally reduce, but not eliminate, effects on upstream flooding. Major floods occur because too much precipitation falls in too short a time, or over too long a time. In either case, the rainfall exceeds the capacity of the soil mantle to store it and the stream channel to convey it. Damaging major floods are not due to cutting of forests. It is important to note in this context that under natural conditions, streamflow levels exceed the "bank-full" capacity of perennial stream channels once in 1-1/2 to 3 years on average (Leopold et al., 1964).

The previous discussion has referred to the impacts of forest harvesting on floods, not on the effects of forest harvesting followed by conversion to agriculture or grazing and subsequent degradation by misuse. Such degraded areas, possibly encompassing whole river basins, may indeed aggravate flooding and be one of the causes of increased and serious flood damage. However, controlled grazing or agriculture under a sound soil and water conservation regime should no more cause floods than careful forest harvesting does. One cannot observe the well-designed and well-maintained rice terraces on steep slopes in Java, Bali, or Nepal with their fine water control effects, and claim that disappearance of the former forest is causing floods. Yet it must be recognized that such good soil and water conservation is not commonly practiced in the current land-hungry conversion of forests to agriculture in much of the hill country of developing nations.

Articles that have been written showing correlations between the reduction in forest cover in a basin over time and the increasing frequency and extent of flooding in the lower basin are not proof of cause and effect. These are simply empirical correlations, and similar correlations could be found associated with the increased mileage of roads, the increased number of children in the basin, or the decrease in number of tigers. Such studies often do not provide information on secular change in rainfall or rainfall patterns, or ignore such data even when they are available (e.g., Gentry and Lopez-Parodi, 1980; cf. Nordin and Meade, 1982).

Foresters and watershed planners must be clear about forest cutting, stormflows, and downstream floods. They must not raise false expectations about flood control being achieved through forestation activities. Tree planting will have minor or negligible effects in reducing major flooding from infrequent major storms or monsoonal type rainfall. It is true that local upstream flood peaks may be delayed or reduced, and storm flow volumes will probably be reduced in small storms. These are important upstream benefits. However, once the soil water storage capacity is saturated, all the water reaching the ground surface will quickly become stormflow. Thus on shallow soils, or soils with shallow impeding layers to percolation, the effects of forests may be very small in any kind of prolonged rain, or in high intensity storms. There may be many valid reasons for tree planting on such sites, but anticipated elimination of flood damage should not be one of them.

There is one indirect way in which forest planting may contribute to reducing downstream flood severity. Sediment reduces the ability of dams to impound floodwater, and raises the river bed, and thus sediment can aggravate normal floods. If we can, through forestation, slow down erosion processes and reduce sediment supply to streams, we may eventually have an effect on the extent of flooding by restoring stream channels to their former capacity for storing and conveying floodwaters and reduce the rate of loss of flood storage capacity in reservoirs.

Forests and Water Availability

There is a widespread belief that logging of tropical forest watersheds has caused wells, springs, streams, and even major rivers to cease flowing, at least during the dry season (Eckholm, 1976; Sharp and Sharp, 1982), and that tree planting will restore the reliability of streams. This is because of a supposed "sponge" effect of the tree roots, forest litter, and soil. It is claimed that the roots soak up water in the wet periods and release it slowly and evenly in the dry season to maintain water supplies (Spears, 1982; Myers, 1983). Roots may be more appropriately labelled a "pump" rather than a "sponge." They certainly do not release water in the dry season, but rather remove it from the soil in order that the trees may transpire and grow. The forest soil and litter do have a higher storage capacity than less organic-rich soils, but most of this water is used to sustain plant growth, rather than sustain streamflow. Moreover, the interception losses on forest canopies in short or low intensity rains in the dry season may be proportionately quite large, reducing dry-season recharge of soil water.

Forestation of upland watersheds has sometimes been advocated partially on the grounds that it will induce greater dry-season stream flows, raise groundwater well levels, and restore the reliability of springs (World Bank, 1978). The Chipko movement leader claims "tree planting, particularly of broad-leaved varieties, creates water" (World Water, 1981). In most respects, putting forests on open land produces the opposite hydrologic effects to cutting them down. All paired-catchment cutting experiments have shown greater low flow in streams following cutting until closed-canopy regrowth occupies the site (Bosch and Hewlett, 1982). Most well-conducted experiments have shown that forestation has reduced streamflow year-round (Banks and Kromhout, 1963; Van Lill et al., 1980). For instance, Mathur et al. (1976) in India, reported water yield decreases of 28 percent following establishment of eucalypts. The Fiji Pine Commission's planting in their dry zone grassland has resulted in serious reductions in total yield, and dry-season reductions of 65 percent (Kammer and Raj, 1979). Lowering of groundwater levels has usually followed forestation (Holmes and Wronski, 1982). It is currently reported that in several parts of China, planting of *Populus* is being used to improve areas where the water table is too close to the surface for growth of annual crops.

On deep soils, forests lose more water in evapotranspiration than do other types of vegetation, so that there is less water available for streamflow. One might speculate that increased evapotranspiration loss due to tree planting would be more than compensated for on compacted and degraded areas by having their infiltration rate and capacity improved. The infiltration rate, however, is often not limiting, except in very high intensity storms. In prolonged rainfall, soil storage capacity may be exceeded no matter how many trees are on the soil surface. There are no experimental results showing such greater recharge benefits to wells and springs, and to the base flow that supplies dry season streamflow. There are, however, many anecdotal reports of renewed springs and more reliable dry-season flows following forestation, though none of these to our knowledge has been verified by research. We do need information from paired catchments where, for example, badly overgrazed eroded hills are successfully forested and are compared with an untreated similar control catchment. Popular wisdom and a great deal of professional judgment argues for better recharge and possibly increased flow in these circumstances. Most of the research from which evidence is now available has been conducted in circumstances of less-severely degraded land. Until supporting results are forthcoming, and the range of necessary conditions can be specified, however, watershed project planners or managers and foresters should carefully eschew claiming such benefits.

Summary

There are many excellent reasons for reforesting or afforesting upland watershed lands. As part of sustainable development, the clarion call to embark on large-scale tree planting programs makes good sense. As a strategy to establish "wood factories" to meet needs for fuel, timber, and other wood products, these programs are very much needed. Such actions may relieve some of the pressures on the remaining bits of natural forest, so that adequate systems of biosphere reserves, national parks, and protected areas can be established as part of the development process. As a rehabilitation device to make degraded, unproductive lands produce a useful crop, and to rebuild productivity gradually, tree planting is well proven (though the economics may be questionable on the poor sites).

Once a leaf-litter or understory has been established, forest plantations are normally very protective against surface erosion. Once a surface root network develops, and downward striking roots penetrate into any consolidated layer, greater resistance to some types of mass erosion ensues. Since most plantations are established with the intent of subsequent harvest, it is important to remember that disturbance of the litter and understory ground cover or death of the roots will reduce these protective functions.

It is necessary, however, in justifying or advocating forestation projects, that unrealizable claims of some other benefits not be made. Tree planting alone has not been shown to increase local rainfall, to prevent floods, to increase the flow of streams and springs, or to raise well levels. Only where plantations could capture frequent occult fog or cloud precipitation can any increase in stream or groundwater yields be expected on the basis of present evidence. It is possible that on degraded sites, forestation could increase infiltration capacity and recharge to an extent which more than compensates for increased evapotranspiration loss. But there is no experimental evidence for this effect.

Problems in achieving sustainable development and conservation of soil and water resources in the tropics are legion enough without being plagued by misunderstanding, myth, and misinterpretation. Semantic fuzziness adds to the difficulties. Words or phrases such as "deforestation," "drought," "flood prevention," and "runoff" usually need to be defined or avoided in favor of more precise words or phrases. The consequences of imprecision may be seen in fruitless disagreement between interest groups, propaganda instead of education, bad policymaking because of a shaky scientific base, or even good policymaking but for the wrong reasons. Perhaps foresters have acquiesced in silence to the use of some misinterpretations and misunderstandings because the arguments or rhetoric being used were aimed at protecting forest resources or at establishing new forests, surely actions worthy of nations and statesmen. But, if we close the existing forests to human use and reservoirs still silt up, and when we have reclothed deforested basins with planted forest and we still have floods, and if on top of that the streams still dry up or dry up even more rapidly, then there will be a well-deserved backlash. The credibility of watershed management and planning professionals will be rightly called into serious question and decades of progress toward better and more rational land use could be lost.

NOTE

1. The term "forestation" is used as suggested by the international symposium, "Let There Be Forest," held at Wageningen in 1983. It includes the activities of afforestation, reforestation, and tree planting outside of forests such as in windbreaks, on farm bunds, or in agroforestry.

References

Banks, C.H., and C. Kromhout. 1963. The effect of afforestation with *Pinus radiata* on summer baseflow and total annual discharge from Jonkershoek catchments. *Forestry in South Africa*, 3:43-65.

Bell, T.I.W. 1973. Erosion in the Trinidad teak plantations. *Commonwealth Forestry Review*, 52:223-233.

Bell, T.I.W., and T. Evo. 1982. Energy plantations in the Fiji dry zone. Fiji Pine Research Paper 10. Suva and Lautoka.

Bernard, A.E. 1953. L'evapotranspiration annuelle de la foret equatoriale congolaise et son influence sur la pluviosite. *Comptes Rendus*, IUFRO Congress, Rome, pp. 201-204.

Birot, P. 1968. *The Cycle of Erosion in Different Climates*. London: B.T. Botsford.

Bishop, D.M., and M.E. Stevens. 1964. Landslides on logged areas in Southeast Alaska. USDA Forest Service Research Paper NOR-1.

Bosch, J.M., and J.D. Hewlett. 1980. Sediment control in South African forests and mountain catchments. *South African Forestry*, 115:50-55.

Bosch, J.M., and J.D. Hewlett. 1982. A review of catchment experiments to determine the effect of vegetation changes on water yield and evapotranspiration. *Journal of Hydrology*, 55:3-23.

Boughton, W.C. 1970. Effects of land management on quantity and quality of available water: A review. Australian Water Resources Council Research Project 68/2, Report 120. Manly Vale: University of New South Wales.

Brunig, E.F., M. von Buch, J. Heuveldop, and K.F. Panzer. 1975. Stratification of the tropical moist forest for land use planning. *Plant Research and Development*, 2:21-44.

Cassells, D.S., D.A. Gilmour, and P. Gordon. 1982. The impact of plantation forestry on stream sedimentation in tropical and sub-tropical Queensland—an initial assessment. In: *Resources—Efficient Use and Conservation*, pp. 138-142. National Conference Publication 8218. Barton: Institution of Engineers, Australia.

Corvera, A. 1981. What caused the great Agusan flood? *Weekend*, March 1, pp. 12-13.

Coster, C. 1938. Surficial runoff and erosion in Java. *Tectona*, 31:613-728.

Crouch, R.J., R.A. Henry, W.J. O'Brien, and V.G. Sherlock. 1984. Small weirs for gully control. *Journal Soil and Water Conservation New South Wales*, 40(2):88-93.

Dietrich, W.E., D.M. Windsor, and T. Dunne. 1982. Geology, climate and hydrology of Barro Colorado Island. In: *The Ecology of a Tropical Forest*,

E.G. Leigh, A.S. Rand, and D.M. Windsor (eds.), pp. 21-46. Washington: Smithsonian Institution Press.

Dissmeyer, G.E., and G.R. Foster. 1980. A guide for predictive sheet and rill erosion on forest land. USDA Forest Service Technical Publication SA-TP11. Washington.

Dixon, J.A., and K.W. Easter. 1986. Economic analysis at the watershed level. In: *Watershed Resources Management: An Integrated Framework with Studies in Asia and the Pacific*, K.W. Easter, J.A. Dixon, and M.M. Hufschmidt (eds.), pp. 53-70. Boulder, Westview Press.

Douglass, J.E., and W.T. Swank. 1975. Effects of management practices on water quality and quantity. USDA Forest Service General Technical Report NE-13:1, Upper Darby.

Eckholm, E. 1976. *Losing Ground*. New York: W.W. Norton.

Ekern, P.C. 1964. Direct interception of cloud water on Lanaihale, Hawaii. *Proceedings Soil Science Society of America*, 28:417-21.

European Environmental Bureau. 1982. The environmental importance of tropical moist forests. *Deforestation and Development Newsletter*, June 1982, pp. 1-7.

FAO (RAPA), EWEAPI, and UNDP. 1984. *Community Forests: Some Aspects*. Proceedings of a workshop sponsored by UNDP, East-West Environment and Policy Institute, and FAO. Bangkok: FAO Regional Office.

Fleming, W.M. 1982. Environmental and economic impacts of watershed conservation on a major reservoir project in Ecuador. In: *Economic Approaches to Natural Resource and Environmental Quality Analysis*, M. Hufschmidt, and E. Hyman (eds.), pp. 292-299. Dublin: Tycooly.

Gentry, A.H., and J. Lopez-Parodi. 1980. Deforestation and increased flooding of the upper Amazon. *Science*, 210:1354-1356.

Gilmour, D.A., D.S. Cassells, and M. Bonell. 1982. Hydrological research in the tropical rainforests of north Queensland: Some implications for land use management. In: *Proceedings First National Symposium on Forest Hydrology*, E. O'Loughlin and L. Bren (eds.), pp. 145-152. Barton: Institution of Engineers, Australia.

Hamilton, L.S. (with P.N. King). 1983. *Tropical Forested Watersheds: Hydrologic and Soils Response to Major Uses or Conversions*. Boulder: Westview Press.

Hamilton, L.S., and A.J. Pearce. 1986. Biophysical aspects in watershed management. In: *Watershed Resources Management: An Integrated Framework with Studies from Asia and the Pacific*, K.W. Easter, J.A. Dixon, and M.M. Hufschmidt (eds.), pp. 33-51. Boulder: Westview Press.

Hardjono, H.W. 1980. The effect of permanent vegetation and its distribution on streamflow of three sub-watersheds in Central Java. Paper at Seminar on Hydrology and Watershed Management, Surakarta, 5 June.

Harr, R.D., W.C. Harper, J.T. Krygier, and F.S. Hsieh. 1975. Changes in storm hydrographs after road building and clearcutting in Oregon Coast Range. *Water Resources Research*, 11:436-444.

Hewlett, J.D. 1982. Forests and floods in the light of recent investigation. *Proceedings Canadian Hydrological Symposium*, June 14-15, pp. 543-560. Fredericton.

Hewlett, J.D., and J.D. Helvey. 1970. Effects of forest clearfelling on the storm hydrograph. *Water Resources Research*, 6:768-782.

Holmes, J.W., and E.B. Wronski. 1982. On the water harvest from afforested catchments. In: *Proceedings First National Symposium on Forest Hydrology*, E. O'Loughlin and L. Bren (eds.), pp. 1-6. Barton: Institution of Engineers, Australia.

Hursch, C.R. 1948. Local climate in the Copper Basin of Tennessee as modified by the removal of vegetation. USDA Circular 774, Washington.

Kammer, R., and Raj. 1979. Preliminary estimates of minimum flows in Varaciva Creek and the effect of afforestation on water resources. Fiji Public Works Department Technical Note 79/1. Suva.

Kunkle, S.H. 1983. Forestry support for agriculture through watershed management, windbreaks, and other conservation actions. *Proceedings Eighth World Forestry Congress*, Vol. 3, pp. 113-138. Jakarta: Indonesia Directorate of Forestry.

Lal, R. 1983. Soil erosion in the humid tropics with particular reference to agricultural land development and soil management. In: *Hydrology of Humid Tropical Regions*, R. Keller (ed.), pp. 221-239. International Association of Hydrological Sciences Publication No. 140. Wallingford.

Lee, R. 1978. *Forest Microclimatology*. New York: Columbia University Press.

Lembaga Ekologi. 1980. Report on study of vegetation and erosion in the Jatiluhur catchment, 1980. Bandung: Institute of Ecology.

Leopold, L.B., M.G. Wolman, and J.P. Miller. 1964. *Fluvial Processes in Geomorphology*. San Francisco: Freeman.

Lin, Y.L. 1984. Status of forest hydrology research in Taiwan. In: *Country Papers on Status of Watershed Forest Influence Research in Asia and the Pacific*, L. Hamilton, M. Bonell, and E. Mercer (eds.), pp. 238-296. East-West Center Working Paper, Honolulu.

Mathur, H. N., Rambabu, P. Joshie, and B. Singh. 1976. Effect of clearfelling and reforestation on runoff and peak rates in small watersheds. *Indian Forester*, 102:219-226.

Megahan, W.F. 1981. Effects of silvicultural practices on erosion and sedimentation in the interior West: A case for sediment budgeting. In: *Interior West Watershed Management*, D.M. Baumgartner (ed), pp. 169-181. Pullman: Washington State University.

Megahan, W. F., and P.N. King. 1985. Identification of critical areas on forest lands for control of nonpoint sources of pollution. *Environmental Management*, 9(1):7-18.

Mosley, M.P. 1982. The effect of a New Zealand beech forest canopy on the kinetic energy of water drops and on surface erosion. *Earth Surface Processes and Landforms*, 7(2):103-107.

Myers, N. 1983. Tropical moist forests: Over-exploited and under-utilized? *Forest Ecology and Management*, 6(1):59-79.

Nordin, C.F., and R.H. Meade. 1982. Deforestation and increased flooding of the upper Amazon. *Science*, 215:426-427.

O'Loughlin, C. 1984. Effectiveness of introduced forest vegetation for protection against landslides and erosion in New Zealand's steeplands. In: *Proceedings*

Symposium on Effects of Forest Land Use on Erosion and Slope Stability. C. O'Loughlin and A. Pearce (eds.), pp. 275-280. Honolulu: East-West Center.

Openshaw, K. 1974. Woodfuels in the developing world. *New Scientist*, January, pp. 271-272.

Pearce, A.J., L.K. Rowe, and C.L. O'Loughlin. 1980. Effects of clearfelling and slashburning on water yield and storm hydrographs in evergreen mixed forests in western New Zealand. *International Association of Hydrological Sciences Publication*, 130:119-127. Washington: IAHS.

Pereira, H.C. 1973. *Land Use on Water Resources in Temperate and Tropical Climates*. London: Cambridge University Press.

Pierce, R.S., J.W. Hornbeck, G.E. Likens, and F.H. Bormann. 1970. Effects of elimination of vegetation on streamflow quantity and quality. *Proceedings Symposium on the Results of Representative and Experimental Basins*, International Association of Hydrological Sciences Publication 96:311-328. Washington, IAHS.

Raeder-Roitzsch, J.E., and A. Masur. 1968. Some hydrological relationships of natural vegetation in the chir pine belt of Pakistan. *Proceedings First Pakistan Watershed Management Conference*, November, pp. 345-360. Peshawar: Pakistan Forest Institute.

Reinhart, K.G., A.R. Eschner, and G.R. Trimble, Jr. 1963. Effect on streamflow of four forest practices, in the mountains of West Virginia. U.S. Forest Service Research Paper NE-1, Upper Darby.

Rice, R.M. 1982. Sedimentation in the Chapparal: How do you handle unusual events? In: USDA Forest Service, General Technical Report. PNW—141: 39-49.

Salati, E., T.E. Lovejoy, and P.B. Vose. 1983. Precipitation and water recycling in tropical rain forests with special reference to the Amazon Basin. *The Environmentalist*, 3(1):67-72.

Sharp, D., and T. Sharp. 1982. The desertification of Asia. *Asia 2000*, 1(4): 40-42.

Shpak, I.S. 1968. Effect of forest on water balance components of drainage basins. Kiev, pp. 137-43. Academy of Sciences of the Ukraine SSR. (Translated from Russian, 1971. Israel Program for Scientific Translations, Jerusalem.)

Shuttleworth, W.J. 1977. The exchange of wind-driven fog and mist between vegetation and the atmosphere. *Boundary-layer Meteorology*, 12:463-489.

Sidle, R.C., A.J. Pearce, and C.L. O'Loughlin. 1985. Hillside stability and land use. American Geophysical Union, Water Resources Monograph No. 11. Washington: AGU.

Spears, J. 1982. Rehabilitating watersheds. *Finance and Development*, 19(1): 30-33.

UNESCO/UNEP/FAO. 1978. *Tropical Forest Ecosystems*. Natural Resources Research XIV. Paris: UNESCO.

Van Lill, W.S., F.J. Kruger, and D.B. Van Wyk. 1980. The effect of afforestation with *Eucalyptus grandis* (Hill ex maiden) and *Pinus patula* (Schlect. et Cham.) on streamflow from experimental catchments at Mokobulaan, Transvaal. *Hydrology*, 48:107-118.

Vergara, N.T. 1984. Appropriate use of steep slopes for stable agriculture and agroforestry. In: *Proceedings Symposium on Effects of Forest Land Use on Erosion and Slope Stability*, C. O'Loughlin and A. Pearce (eds.), p. 309. Honolulu: East-West Center.

Weber, F., and M. Hoskins. 1983. *Soil Conservation Technical Sheets*. Moscow: University of Idaho.

Wells, W.G. 1981. Some effect of brushfires on erosion processes in coastal Southern California. In: *Erosion and Sediment Transport in Pacific Rim Steeplands*, T. Davies and A. Pearce (eds.). IAHS-AISH Pub. No. 132, pp. 305-342. Washington: IAHS.

Wiersum, K.F. 1984. Surface erosion under various tropical agroforestry systems. In: *Proceedings Symposium on Effects of Forest Land Use on Erosion and Slope Stability*. C. O'Loughlin and A. Pearce (eds.), pp. 231-239. Honolulu: East-West Center.

Wiersum, K.F. 1985. Effects of various vegetation layers in an *Acacia auriculiformis* forest plantation on surface erosion in Java, Indonesia. In: *Proceedings Second International Conference on Soil Erosion and Conservation*, S. El-Swaify, W.C. Moldenhauer, and A. Lo (eds.), pp. 79-89. Ankeny: Soil Conservation Society of America.

Working Group on the Influence of Man on the Hydrological Cycle. 1972. Influence of man on the hydrologic cycle: Guide to policies for the safe development of land and water resources. In: *Status and Trends of Research in Hydrology*, pp. 31-70. Paris: UNESCO.

World Bank. 1978. *Forestry Sector Policy Paper*. Washington: World Bank.

World Resources Institute. 1985. The world's tropical forests—A call for accelerated action. Draft Report released at IX World Forestry Congress. Washington: WRI.

World Water. 1981. How trees can combat droughts and floods. *World Water*, 4(10):18, October.

Yao, C.E., and F.V. Nañagas. 1983. Litter fall commercialization: a threat to Cebu reforestation. *Canopy International*, 9(8):6-7.

Zadroga, F. 1981. The hydrological importance of a montane cloud forest area of Costa Rica. In: *Tropical Agricultural Hydrology*, R. Lal and R. Russell (eds.), pp. 59-73. New York: John Wiley and Sons.

5/ Renewable Energy Projects In Developing Countries: Contributing to Success and Failure

Clarence F. Kooi

When problems inhibiting development in the Third World are discussed, attention is typically focused on the inadequacies of the developing countries—deficiencies in resource base, poverty, lack of education, inadequate infrastructures, and insufficient or inadequate technologies. Clarence Kooi points out that a number of problems hindering development in the Third World originate in the affluent countries—fashion, misunderstanding (or non-acceptance) of local priorities, unreasonable expectations relative to useful life and maintenance of technologies, misunderstandings of the labor-intensiveness appropriate to a local culture, use of ineffective "low technologies," and attempts to use technologies inappropriate, for whatever reasons, to tasks at hand. Kooi draws on his experience with renewable energy projects in Western Africa to discuss the latter set of problems.

Introduction

Sustainable development of natural resources in the Third World implies, among other things, the development of indigenous energy resources, including solar, wind, biomass, and other renewable resources. In contrast to their funding decisions in past years, donor agencies no longer favor alternative energy projects. Consequently, the effort to develop indigenous energy resources has, to a large extent, ended.

In West Africa, the results of this change are far less important than one would have expected from the magnitude of the effort. My objective in this paper is to discuss the reasons for this lack of success of past projects. Perhaps some of the lessons can be applied to future programs of renewable energy development in developing countries.

Much has been written concerning the problems of energy technology development and of transferring those technologies to the Third World. There are social, cultural, and religious barriers to consider. Rural populations are usually illiterate. They do not have the necessary technical skills, nor do they have the required managerial capabilities. Rural populations in developing countries are strongly risk-averse. In addition, the infrastructure needed to support a technological development is weak, incomplete, or non-existent.

I propose to present another set of problems which hinder development projects—those which are characteristic of the developed rather than the developing country. My discussion will be limited to public and government organizations involved in development work, but much of it will apply to private organizations as well. It is based primarily on experience in the sixteen countries of the Economic Community of West African States, Lesotho, and Haiti.

Barriers to the Development of Renewable Energies

Fashion

Fashion is a major barrier. When renewable energies are in fashion, money flows freely. Consequently, some of it is wasted. When they are out of fashion, the very best projects go begging for support. Shortly after the 1973 oil crisis, the governments of the United States and of many other industrialized countries mandated substantial sums of money for renewable energy development in third world countries. The absorptive capacity wasn't there. Many people of doubtful qualifications and unrealistic expectations came to assist with the consumption of this money and to espouse their concepts of renewable energy development in third world countries. Many bad projects were inaugurated. What were the properties of these projects which predisposed them to success or failure?

Local Priorities

Local populations have their priorities. In rural Sahel, these priorities are obtaining food and water reliably and without the limitations imposed by near total reliance on human labor. Yet the major emphasis in energy by most development agencies during the last five years has been to satisfy fuelwood needs. An elderly man mending fish nets in a village on the banks of the Bani river in Mali asked our group, which was inspecting a cooking stove project, why we didn't give them something they needed rather than the mud stoves we were installing. A village chief in a nearby village stated that his priority was "farming implements," agricultural production in much of West Africa being limited by lack of available labor during peak seasons. Water is almost always afforded a high priority. The rural energy survey funded by USAID in Mali in 1982 concluded that energy for water and food production was assigned a higher priority by the local population than energy for cooking. For success, it is essential that the energy project address something which is a high local priority.

There are renewable energy projects which failed, partially at least, because they satisfied the donor's rather than the recipient's priority criteria. Others have succeeded in spite of a low donor priority because they responded to the recipient's needs. Among the latter are the photovoltaic systems, usually including water pumps, which many donor personnel claim do not respond to the needs of true development, labelling them "inappropriate," "high technology," and "gold plated." Yet in West Africa they are the most successful renewable energy devices. This can be attributed to, among other things, their responsiveness to a high priority local need.

Design and Construction

The physical design and construction of the system or device must be such that it works properly and has a reasonable life span without the need for excessive repair and maintenance. This seems to be such an elementary idea that it hardly needs saying. Yet there have been numerous renewable energy devices built in West Africa that never worked, others whose outputs were far too small to justify their costs, and others that needed repairs so frequently as to be useless. There are several reasons for such occurrences. First, an attempt was made to make a labor-intensive device based on the postulate that labor is cheap and plentiful. This was, however, sometimes applied excessively and sometimes in situations were the postulate was not valid. Second, good engineering and construction practice was not followed. Third, project management was poor. Fourth, inadequate (or no) provision was made for service and spare parts. Fifth, the builders did not take proper account of the physical conditions of the site; for example, windmills were built in locations where wind speeds were too low.

Labor Intensity

It was thought that the devices and systems must be labor-intensive. This pervasive notion is imbedded in the United States foreign assistance legislation (Committee on Foreign Relations, 1983). Yet it is often false, and, indeed, has contributed to the failure of several energy projects in West Africa.

At a pyrolitic converter that I visited in Ghana, a man was assigned to watch a thermometer and to signal an excessive temperature. When his attention waned, the wall of a reactor unit tended to burn through. A thermostat would have been much cheaper and it would have eliminated much repair work and down time.

The village people at a biogas installation in Senegal told me it was shut down because it was planting season and they didn't have the time to collect dung and tend the digester.

Hand water pumping can be even more onerous than usual during peak seasons. Unlike fuelwood, water cannot be stockpiled during the off-season.

Being "labor intensive" can often lead to operating costs that are considerably higher than one would have if a "non-labor-intensive" solution had been chosen. Wages may be low, but labor costs can still be higher than the costs of an automatic or machine solution. This is particularly true if one uses a reasonable shadow wage to reflect the scarcity of labor during peak seasons. Rural people in West Africa have scheduled their activities to fit the agricultural peak work seasons. They construct and repair houses, stockpile wood, and accomplish similar tasks during the off season; there is considerable off-seasonal labor migration to the cities. One would like an energy system that would be seasonally labor intensive.

Engineering and Construction

Good engineering and good construction practices are essential to success. This principle has been widely ignored, especially by the "low technology" school, during the past decade when renewable energies and "appropriate technologies" were the fashion. The adherents to this school distrusted "technicians," the term applied to people trained in the sciences and engineering. They distrusted machines with too many metal parts and preferred those to be rusty. Bamboo bearings were preferred to metal bearings, even if the latter were available on the local market. A rustic appearance was highly valued. Sound design principles and construction principles were not applied; indeed, they were sometimes not known. Consequently, many machines had low outputs and frequent breakdowns; in fact, many never worked at all.

I have records of a windmill in Mali which, during the three-month period covered by the records, broke down six times and required repairs, had to have repair and modification work to correct for faulty operation another six times, required eight trips to town to buy materials and do welding, and was out of action about half of the three-month period. Most renewable energy devices do not receive such attention and are permanently out of action after only a few breakdowns.

Many low technology devices built in West Africa were designed to use local materials, local skills and local resources, but good design, engineering and construction practices were absent.

Useful Output

Above all, a machine must work and produce a useful output. Failures of energy devices have been attributed to economic or social factors when, in fact, the device never worked, or never produced a product. The pyrolytic converter mentioned above is an example. A developing country can ill afford the cost of ignoring standard engineering and construction practice which is the product of hundreds of years of experience. It is to be hoped that donors will no longer entrust technical development projects to members of the low technology school. It has been a prescription for failure and a waste of money.

But it is not that simple. Some very competent work toward development of appropriate technologies has failed. The most notable instance in the domain of renewable energies is the solar pump designed and originally built at the University of Dakar, starting some twenty years ago. It used the heat from flat-plate solar collectors to drive a Rankine cycle piston engine. The idea was to use well-known technologies and local construction and materials as much as possible. Although these pumps were widely distributed, especially in Africa, most of them are no longer in operation.

These pumps had two major problems. The ratio of cost to output was too high and the operating life of the collectors was too short. The first problem is inherent in the fundamentally low efficiency of low temperature heat engines, which implies large collector areas and large amounts of materials—concrete, iron and glass. The second problem is a consequence of the use of local materials and labor for the construction of the collectors. The quality was simply too low. The collector of a pump which I saw in Mali in 1978 was being rebuilt after only two years of operation due to the poor quality of local construction and to corrosion. This second problem will gradually be solved as the skills of the local design and construction people increase. The first can only be resolved by replacing the collector by one which uses less expensive materials, such as has been done in Israel where the solar pond (water, salt, and plastic) replaces the standard collector (glass and metal).

The history of this solar pump teaches not only the lesson of quality construction but, equally important, that *the cost of a system or device must be justified by its output.* There is a standard and well-known way of determining this. It is the calculation of the net present value (NPV) of all the cash flows over the life of the system. Its companion is the calculation of the internal rate of return (IRR), which measures the return on the investment. These are not perfect tools. Environmental and social benefits or costs are hard to quantify, applicable discount rates are difficult to determine, and shadow prices (often reflecting social costs and benefits) must usually be guesses. They can, nevertheless, often give a clear indication of the economic viability of the system or device.

Only a few renewable energy projects in Africa were ever subjected to such analysis. I routinely ask builders of windmills what their costs are and how much water they expect to pump. They can usually supply cost information but never (with two exceptions) the quantity of water expected. Consequently, they cannot do an NPV-IRR calculation to compare the proposed technology to a conventional method, such as diesel or hand pumping. If this had been done, most of the windmills in West Africa would never have been installed. The wind speeds, with a few exceptions, are too low and the quantity of water pumped is too small to justify the cost of the windmill.

It is generally true that the initial cost of a renewable energy device is higher than that of a competing conventional energy device. The lower operating costs are expected to compensate for the higher initial cost. The NPV-IRR calculation shows whether the compensation is sufficiently great to make the renewable energy device the better choice. During the 1970s, a belief existed in the donor organizations that inexpensive renewable energy technologies that were produced locally, culturally acceptable, environmentally benign, and, implicitly, with a good output, were possible. Neither the low cost nor the good output materialized (in the same device). When the cost was low, the output was low and the device functioned poorly or not at all. When the output was good and the device worked reliably, its cost was high.

Unrealistic Assumptions

The belief that "energy technologies which are environmentally acceptable, require minimum capital investment, are most acceptable to and affordable by the people using them, are simple and inexpensive to use and maintain, and are transferable from one region of the world to another" (Committee on Foreign Relations, 1983) was a major contributor to the large number of unrealistic if not impossible renewable energy projects undertaken in developing countries. This unrealistic belief has been one of the greatest hindrances to the development of sustainable energies in developing countries. On three occasions, people have complained to me that the engineers at the solar energy laboratory in Bamako were not working on such devices. Those people and many others in the development agencies will have to accept reality. Such renewable energy devices do not exist! The development of renewable energies in the third world countries requires adherence to the possible and rejection of the impossible. Limited resources should not be allocated to pursuit of this chimera.

Project Management

Insufficient attention has been paid to proper project management. The problems came primarily in two forms. The project design included too many participating organizations. A project to build a single solar pump in Senegal involved four organizations in the country, one in Europe, and two in the United States. That was just too complex for a project of that size. There was no place that I could identify where the central responsibility for project execution lay. Things were done wrong, late, or not at all. The project failed for several reasons but poor design with respect to management appeared to be the principal one.

The second part of the problem was a consequence of the type of management personnel assigned by the donor organization to renewable energy projects. Almost without exception, these individuals had no management experience and seldom had technical experience or training. This resulted in seriously slipped schedules and, in fact, many essential things never being done at all. The lack of technical capacity was reflected primarily in the unrealistic expectations mentioned earlier and a lack of appreciation of the work of technical people.

Service and Repair

Usually no provision was made for service and supply of spare parts. This was probably a result of the assumption that the technology was to be locally maintainable with local materials and labor. Since such devices did not materialize, spare parts and skilled service became necessary. The results of their presence or absence was striking. In one windmill project in Senegal, funding for service had been budgeted but the funds were not released. Consequently, all windmills were out of operation within a year. In another windmill project in the same region, spare parts were made available, a schedule of inspection and maintenance was observed, and all windmills operated satisfactorily.

Timeframes for Success

Development and establishment of renewable energy technology in a developing country takes time, perhaps ten to twenty years. Yet projects sponsored by developed countries are seldom longer than four years. This impatience for quick results is another barrier to development. It is worth mentioning that many religious organizations do not suffer from this defect. They are in there for the long haul and they are the ones who have the best record in the renewable energy field in Africa. The secular organizations could well follow their example.

Conclusions

I have reviewed some of the problems encountered during the development of renewable energies in West Africa. They were consequences of the behavior of the people of the donor countries. We could well describe them as cultural barriers to development. Indeed, a great deal of this behavior originates in the alternate life style anti-establishment (and, ipso facto, anti-technological) culture so prevalent during the 1960s and 1970s in the developed countries. Cultural and social barriers to development or transfer of technology are commonly imputed to the people of the developing countries. These cannot be ignored. But it is time to take a good look at some of our own cultural barriers.

We should not be using the developing countries as a proving ground for our unproven concepts of alternate routes to development and transfer of technology. We should instead go back to proven procedures, sound science and engineering, sound economics, and attention to our own, as well as developing countries', cultural barriers to development.

Reference

Committee on Foreign Relations, Committee on Foreign Affairs, U.S. Senate and U.S. House of Representatives. 1983. Legislation on foreign relations through 1982. Joint Committee print, Volume I, p. 25, Sec. 106B and Sec. 107. Washington, DC.

Part II
Social Science Analysis

6/ Economic Analysis of Renewable Resource Conservation in the Third World

Douglas D. Southgate
Fredrick J. Hitzhusen

Economic analysis of natural resource development projects in third world countries is difficult. Estimates of the environmental impacts of such projects are imprecise. In addition, placing economic values on those impacts is not easy due to limited knowledge of the interactions between natural and social systems. In addition to reviewing the issues that arise when undertaking a benefit-cost analysis of a natural resource development project, Douglas Southgate and Frederick Hitzhusen stress the need to consider the full range of market and institutional forces influencing natural resource use when evaluating a specific project.

Introduction

During the late 1970s and early 1980s, projects to arrest environmental degradation were initiated in many developing countries. Where forests were being lost because of fuelwood gathering, efforts were made to establish fuelwood plantations, to promote use of more efficient stoves, or to introduce alternative energy technologies. In the watersheds of existing and planned dams threatened by sedimentation, adoption of erosion control measures was encouraged.

Project analysis is invariably a complex task, given the distortions induced by regulations, administered prices, and an over-valued currency. These distortions are present in practically every developing country's economy. In addition, analysis of a natural resource development project, whether it be conducted in the Third World or in an affluent country, presents special challenges to an economist since a large share of such a project's outputs are externalities (off-site impacts). Rarely is it easy, for example, to estimate all the external benefits (e.g., erosion control and reduced flood sedimentation) associated with establishing a forest. For another example, although environmental degradation promotes rural-to-urban migration and other costly social adjustments, it is difficult to quantify the social costs avoided because environmental quality is maintained.

A central feature of the typical third world natural resource development project is an investment undertaken either to ease an environmental constraint on economic development or to ameliorate a symptom of declining environmental quality. Accordingly, issues that must be addressed in order to employ the standard conceptual framework developed for analysis of investment projects (Gittinger, 1982) often command the immediate attention of economists working in a developing country. In the second section of this paper, we address these issues. Among the topics covered are shadow pricing of inputs, weighting of benefits and costs to reflect decision makers' preferences regarding income distribution, and estimating external (or downstream) benefits of resource conservation.

A project or any other effort intended to improve environmental quality must be analyzed by taking into account the general institutional regime affecting resource management. In the third section, the implications of this observation for the evaluation of environmental policy and natural resource development projects are discussed. Special attention is paid to the relationship between land tenure and resource use.

Finally, given this overview of project evaluation methodology and institutional issues, we offer suggestions about how to improve the contribution economists can make to the formulation of strategies to deal with environmental degradation in the Third World.

Issues in Project Analysis

Referring to two types of projects frequently proposed for and implemented in developing countries, we discuss in this section some of the issues that arise as one attempts to analyze an investment intended to ease an environmental constraint on economic development or to arrest environmental degradation. First, in a discussion of bioenergy projects, we elaborate the difficulties of determining appropriate opportunity costs (shadow prices) of inputs and social values of outputs in the face of distorted markets. We also discuss the application of distributional weights to reflect equity concerns. Second, the problems of estimating downstream benefits are highlighted in a discussion of watershed management projects.

Bioenergy Projects

Economic analysis of investments can be placed on a continuum of "accounting stances." At one end, one finds private-level analysis utilizing current market or administered prices of inputs and outputs. At the other end is social-level analysis, which can include consideration of both weighted and unweighted income-distributional impacts. In between lie a series of adjustments or shadow-pricing methods to account for opportunity costs of inputs and values of outputs.

Margolis (1969) suggests why private market prices may not reflect full social benefits and costs:

> .... there are many cases where exchange occurs without money passing hands; where exchanges occur but they are not freely entered into; where exchanges are so constrained by institutional rules that it would be dubious to infer that the terms were satisfactory; and where imperfections in the conditions of exchange would lead us to conclude that the price ratios do not reflect appropriate social judgements about values. Each of these cases gives rise to deficiencies in the use of existing price data as the basis for evaluation of inputs or outputs.

Margolis' observation bears directly on evaluation of bioenergy projects. Costs generated from engineering data and future revenues based on current market prices can be misleading, particularly if one is concerned with societal costs and benefits. These "costs" often do not represent full opportunity costs or the highest-use values of all factors of production. Alternatively, financial or market wages may overstate labor costs of a proposed fuelwood plantation in an area of high under-employment or unemployment. In engineering type analysis, some benefits (e.g., external benefits of forestation) are not counted. Other benefits will be understated simply by multiplying project output by prevailing prices if the local currency is overvalued. The same method will lead to overestimation of other benefits if demand for project outputs is highly inelastic.

Economists frequently use shadow exchange rates to adjust for overvaluation of local currencies and the Bruno Criterion can be used to evaluate the foreign exchange saved or earned by alternative energy projects (Gittinger, 1982). The latter is particularly relevant in evaluating renewable energy options in many developing countries. Frequently these countries are heavily dependent on export earnings or foreign exchange from food, fiber and forestry crops which may compete with bioenergy crops for land.

Major factors increasing elasticity of demand for bioenergy and other end products include the availability of good substitutes, large numbers of uses, high price of the commodity relative to consumers' incomes, and whether the price established is toward the upper (elastic) or lower (inelastic) end of the demand curve (Leftwich, 1966). If a particular bioenergy product or by-product has no close substitutes or few end uses, current market prices based on a relatively small output of the product will probably grossly overstate the revenues from future expansions of output.

Gittinger (1982) identifies other bases for distinguishing between private and social-level analysis, which he labels financial and economic analysis, respectively. In the former, taxes are treated as a cost and subsidies as a return. Interest paid to outside suppliers of money or capital is a cost, while any inputed interest on equity capital is a part of the return to equity capital. By contrast, Gittinger sees economic analysis as concerned with net economic returns to the whole society, frequently based on shadow prices to adjust for market or administered price imperfections. In social-level analysis, taxes and subsidies are treated as transfer payments; that is, taxes are part of the total benefit of a project to society and subsidies are a societal cost.

Both private and social-level analysis are essential for project evaluation. Private-level analysis provides information on the profitability of a given enterprise (e.g., combustion of crop residues for energy) to individual entrepreneurs or investors, and thus gives an indication of incentive structures and/or potential adoption rates. Social cost-benefit analysis attempts to determine net social welfare generated by the project, taking into consideration externalities, pricing of under-employed or unemployed factors, over-valuation of the domestic currency, and other distortions. Once all cost and benefit streams have been given their appropriate prices or shadow values, one must decide on an appropriate rate of discount (or time value) and criteria for net social welfare generated by the project. Because the discount rate measures returns on scarce financial capital, while at the same time indicating society's time preferences, there is always controversy about the proper rate to use when evaluating a project (Baumol, 1969). The alternative efficiency criteria include: (1) the ratio of benefits to costs, (2) net present value (benefits less costs), (3) the internal rate of return, and (4) the payout period. Several authors, including Dasgupta and Pearce (1978) and Gittinger (1982), point out that making choices among projects is affected by decisions regarding which of the four efficiency criteria to use. Whether or not a project passes the "efficiency test" (as indicated, for example, by exceeding a minimum net present value or internal rate of return) depends among other things on: (1) the nature of future benefit and cost streams, e.g., "bunching" of benefits or costs early or late in the time horizon, (2) the ratio of future operating costs to initial capital outlay, and (3) the nature of the capital or budget constraint (e.g., user charges to cover future operating costs and capital outlay).

Analysts should also be concerned with the equity impacts of alternative energy strategies. An ongoing debate in Brazil involves the use of sugarcane or cassava for the production of ethanol for mixing with gasoline. Sugarcane is grown primarily on large plantations, whereas cassava is grown on small farms in more economically depressed areas. Promotion of one crop over the other will have important income distribution impacts that need to be estimated and reported to decisionmakers.

Economists use several alternative methods for handling income distribution impacts, including: (1) explicit weighting of net benefits by income class, group or region, (2) provision of alternative weighting functions and their distributional consequences to decisionmakers, (3) estimation of non-weighted net benefits by income class, group or region, and (4) a constrained optimization approach in which economic efficiency is maximized subject to restrictions on the distribution of benefits and costs created by the project.

Eckstein (1958) first suggested explicit weighting of net benefits by income class based on past resource allocation and tax decisions. Haveman (1965) developed one of the first applications of Eckstein's approach by utilizing the marginal effective tax rates on personal income as an estimate of the value (or marginal utility) of a dollar of net benefits to various income groups affected by a U.S. Army Corps of Engineers water project. Weisbrod (1968) applied the other

Table 6-1. Accounting Stance on Project Evaluation

	Private-Level	Social-Level
Focus:	Net returns to equity capital	Net returns to society
Prices:	Market or administered prices (may assume that markets are perfect or that administered prices have compensated for imperfections)	May require "shadow prices" to compensate for monopolies, externalities, unemployment, or over-valued currency
Taxes:	Cost of production	Part of total societal benefits
Subsidies:	Source of revenue	Part of total societal cost
Purpose(s):	Measure of profitability to individual investors	Measure net social welfare
	Indicate whether individuals will follow project guidelines	Determine if government investment is justified on economic efficiency basis

half of Eckstein's approach by utilizing past expenditure data on Corps of Engineers water resource projects to solve for the implicit weights given to net benefits received by different income classes. Using his simultaneous equations methodology, Weisbrod showed that projects with lower benefit-cost ratios were mounted primarily because of equity concerns.

An early example of providing alternative net benefit weighting functions and their distribution consequences was developed by McGuire (1969). The alternative functions are essentially estimates of the marginal utility of a dollar of net benefits to various income groups affected by a given project or program. Value judgements are required to formulate the alternative functions, but the decision of which function to choose is left to the decision maker(s). Estimation of non-weighted net benefits by income class (approach 3) eliminates the need for the analyst to make any value judgement on distribution weights.

The alternative of constrained optimization usually involves establishing a minimum acceptable distribution of net benefits to a designated low income class or group which must be met by any project or program in the choice set. For example, one might include fuelwood projects in a choice set for further evaluation only if at least one-half of each project's benefits accrue to the poorest one-third of the residents in the target area. The task is then to pick the most efficient project or rank the projects (meeting the minimum distribution

Table 6-2. Income Distribution Analysis

Approaches	Advantages	Disadvantages
Explicit weighting by class or group	Income distribution and efficiency analysis can be combined in what Weisbrod calls "Grand Efficiency"	Difficulty of determining what weights to use
		Past governmental decisions may not reflect current preferences on distribution
		Complicated computations
Provision of alternative weighting functions	Do not have to select a single set of distribution weights	Higher computation costs
	Can help decisionmakers identify their distribution preferences	Must still define a choice set of alternative weighting functions
Non-weighted net benefits by class or group	Frees the analyst from making value judgements on distribution weights	Distribution weights may not be made explicit by decisionmakers
	Presents separate distribution account	
Constrained optimization	Less demanding data requirements	Requires monitoring of projects to stay on target

constraint) on the basis of their economic efficiency, i.e., benefit-cost ratio or internal rate of return.

Summarized in Table 6-2 are some of the advantages and disadvantages of alternative approaches for handling income distribution in the analysis of various projects or programs, including bio-, and other, energy options. Key considerations in selecting an approach include (1) data availability on income by income class with and without the project, (2) existence of reliable data about expenditure decisions and personal income tax rates from which to derive equity weights, and (3) the ability to specify and conform to distribution constraints when planning and executing projects.

Watershed Management

Reservoir construction, which had always been essential for planned expansions in irrigated agriculture, received a major impetus during the energy crisis. As petroleum prices rose, public utilities in developing countries, which previously had relied heavily on oil-burning thermal plants to generate electricity, came under strong economic pressure to exploit alternative sources of energy. Complementing these market forces, the World Bank and regional development banks initiated lending campaigns designed to encourage development of what looked to be the most attractive energy option for many countries: hydroelectricity.

Experience at a number of dam sites yielded two lessons. First, a large share of the benefits of hydroelectric development can be lost because of reservoir sedimentation. Second, sedimentation can be effectively controlled only by limiting soil erosion in upstream areas (Allen, 1974). Unfortunately, though the general concept of watershed management was endorsed in proposals to construct dams (hydroelectric and otherwise), rarely were watershed management projects initiated before a major reservoir sedimentation problem had arisen. Typically, it was after such a problem had manifested itself that a team of specialists was asked to study a proposed erosion control project.

It is essential for the evaluation team to perform economic analysis using two accounting stances: private and social. By indicating which groups of watershed inhabitants would gain and which would lose by complying with the project's soil resource management guidelines, private-level analysis helps project planners and administrators anticipate needs for subsidies and other public sector initiatives to foster erosion control. Social-level analysis is undertaken to determine whether or not the project satisfies efficiency criteria (a positive net present value, a benefit/cost ratio greater than one, etc.).

Private-level project analysis involves comparison of net revenues to be earned by farmers and other rural land users in the watershed if no change in resource management is made with net revenues those individuals could earn by complying with project guidelines. Generally, when the present value of the latter exceeds the present value of the former, the project can be said to be beneficial from the individual's standpoint. Unfortunately, data needed to estimate net revenues for either the with-project case or the without-project case are rarely highly reliable. Research being conducted at international centers in the Third World is yielding information needed to estimate the economic returns associated with agroforestry and other farming systems that conserve soil. However, it is unusual to have good information about the base against which those returns need to be compared: status quo (or without-project) net revenues. This is because hill lands and other areas where soil erosion is high are populated primarily by poor, small farmers, a group that usually receives scant attention from the research and extension establishment in the typical developing country.

As with the costs to rural land users of improved soil resource management, it is a challenge to quantify the downstream benefits of improved watershed management. Gregersen and Brooks (1980) have presented a two-step procedure for estimating those benefits. In the first step, a model of sediment movement within a watershed, river system, and, where appropriate, reservoir is used to simulate the downstream physical impacts of reducing erosion rates in upland regions. In the second step, values are attached to those impacts in order to perform economic analysis of the erosion control project.

Economists are far better prepared to contribute to the second step of the Gregersen-Brooks procedure. Their comparative advantage lies in the estimation of the scarcity values of increased electricity or irrigation water made available because reservoir sedimentation has been reduced. We will not comment here on the estimation of those scarcity values. Instead, we discuss the difficulties of performing the first step of the Gregersen-Brooks procedure. We briefly consider, in order, (a) estimating erosion rates, (b) modelling sediment transport through a watershed to the head of a reservoir, and (c) modelling sediment movement within a reservoir. This discussion of the complexities of sediment transport is intended to encourage economists who estimate off-site benefits of watershed management projects to design sensitivity analyses that compensate for unreliable estimates of the downstream physical impacts of erosion control.

The best possible information on erosion rates under different land uses and soil management techniques is obtained from local research conducted over several years. Rarely are the results of such research available to a team evaluating a watershed management project, however. Accordingly, erosion rates usually must be estimated using some general equation, the most commonly employed being the Universal Soil Loss Equation, or USLE (Wischmeier, 1976). The USLE, which is best suited to the estimation of sheet and rill erosion on an individual field, can furnish useful information about the relative severity of erosion problems in different areas. However, it is an imprecise tool for estimating actual soil loss rates at the watershed or sub-watershed level. The analyst obliged to use the USLE must accept that important sources of erosion (e.g., poor road construction, streambank scour, and gullying) are not reflected in USLE estimates.

Just as the best possible evidence on erosion rates is obtained from local research conducted for several years, so too are the best models of sediment transport within a watershed based on several years' observations of the local phenomenon. Unfortunately, just as data limitations usually oblige one to use the USLE or some other general model to estimate soil loss rates in a third world watershed, so too are analysts usually forced to adapt statistical models developed for other watersheds (hopefully with similar geology and climate) to estimate sediment delivery ratios (SDRs) under "normal" conditions. A sediment delivery ratio is the portion of eroded materials carried out of some given region. One limitation of this approach, which was utilized by Veloz et al. (1985), is particularly crucial for economic analysis of erosion/sedimentation control. Sediment transport models based on SDRs give little insight into the major movement of eroded materials held in "intermediate storage" at various points in watersheds (e.g., in stream beds) that occur during large storms. The expected costs of major sediment movements are difficult to estimate, since the timing of large storms is an unknown.

Finally, in order to estimate the off-site impacts of erosion control, information on deposition and movement of sediments in a reservoir is required. Especially when sedimentation problems are severe in a reservoir, reliable data of this type are often available and can be combined with evidence on dredging costs, lost hydroelectric production, reduced irrigation water withdrawals, and increased depreciation of turbines and other equipment to yield estimates of major costs of sedimentation (Southgate and Veloz, 1985).

To summarize, evaluation of a third world watershed management project, like evaluation of any other developing country natural resource development project, is challenging in several ways. The confidence intervals for estimates of external benefits of erosion control are usually quite large, given that it is extremely difficult to model sediment transport. The base of information needed to estimate on-site costs of improved resource management is also inadequate. In addition, as we point out in the next section, those costs need to be estimated taking into account the institutional regimes faced by those living in regions where the natural environment is being threatened.

Institutional Issues

Bromley (1983) suggests that the disappointing performance of many Third-World environmental projects is explained by the fact that those projects usually do little to alter the incentives existing under prevailing institutional regimes to manage resources in a depletive fashion. If, for example, a price mechanism or a system of use rights to encourage efficient utilization of irrigation water does not exist, soil salinization and waterlogging problems are bound to be observed. Investing in more canals to open up new areas to irrigation does not constitute a long-term solution to those problems. Barring institutional reform, newly opened irrigated lands will eventually become degraded as well.

Failure to appreciate the institutional roots of environmental problems results in faulty private-level project analysis. An example of this is private-level analysis of third world soil conservation projects performed using a microeconomic model best suited to institutional conditions found in affluent countries. In such an analysis, traditional third world agriculture is compared to less erosive activities in much the same way that an individual in the United States decides how to use a parcel of land in which he has a fee simple interest.

This approach yields inaccurate predictions about how individuals with limited property rights in land manage resources. A farmer holding a fee simple interest in land will generally try to maximize the present value of net returns obtained from that land. By contrast, a tenant farmer who perceives that it is possible to lose a leasehold is less willing to absorb costs in the short run for the purpose of enhancing the future productivity of farm land. Similarly, when an individual holds only use rights in a parcel, he has a relatively weak incentive to conserve the resources found on that parcel. For him, conservation strategies featuring periods when land lies fallow are risky. For example, the government owns all land in Burma but recognizes agricultural use rights. Before a Burmese farmer holding use rights forgoes cultivation so that soil quality can improve, he must consider the possibility that he will forfeit those rights (and, implicitly, the rents gained from using land, whether in a conserving or in a depletive fashion).

In the case of LDCs, one must consider not only resource management under a stable institutional environment, but also must assess how change in property institutions affects conservation/depletion decisions. In many parts of the Third World (e.g., in the Amazon Basin), soil erosion and other forms of environmental degradation result as a national government attempts to promote agricultural colonization in areas formerly inhabited exclusively by indigenous peoples. Because national governments typically do not recognize those peoples' communal tenure regimes, those regimes which facilitate the practice of ecologically stable shifting cultivation tend to be abandoned (MacDonald, 1981).

In addition to the abandonment of shifting cultivation along with indigenous tenure regimes, expansion of the dominant society's agricultural frontier usually causes resource depletion because settlers in newly opened land can establish only use rights to that land. In many countries, including those trying to encourage agricultural colonization of the Amazon Basin, land titles can be obtained only by deforesting and then continuously farming or ranching land. Elsewhere, because formal titles to newly opened land are difficult to obtain, settlers develop informal use rights systems. This is often the case in erosive, hilly areas being settled by the rural poor.

There are several reasons why erosive land management decisions are made in a region where agricultural use rights are being established. Clearly, the manner of asserting private rights in heretofore unoccupied land--clearing and farming it--causes significant environmental damage. In addition, the option to settle unoccupied land affects the management of land in which private rights have already been established. Inputs used to reduce the rate at which soil is lost from land already in a farmer's possession carry a high opportunity cost. Those inputs could be used to clear land and thus capture the returns associated with an increased endowment of land. Finally, the private cost of exhausting soils at one location is a function of the costs of clearing land elsewhere and of differences between the accessibility and productivity of newly cleared land and the accessibility and productivity of land being abandoned. If clearing costs are low and if comparable yields can be obtained on unoccupied land located close to exhausted agricultural land, then the cost to farmers of soil depletion is low.

The Contribution of Economics to Environmental Policy and Environmental Projects

Environmental problems arise through the interactions of a variety of factors—social, technical, economic, and institutional. Effective natural resource development policy comprises a strategy for realigning those factors so that environmentally sound economic development can occur. As Bromley (1983) has pointed out, pursuing a policy of integrated management of renewable resources inevitably raises more political controversy than does making an investment to ameliorate a symptom of environmental degradation:

> Investments are politically safe both for the donor (agencies) and the host countries, while management programs are not. Investments have the aura of Pareto safety (i.e., not harming anyone's interest); management programs imply a redistribution of advantage within a fixed resource base. To wait for the payoff from an adjustment in current (resource) use rates is often considered too costly. How much more appealing to install physical infrastructure--ditches, trees, tubewells, fences, and range grasses--and ignore the institutional arrangements that will ensure their long-run viability.

Taking into account Bromley's critique of the emphasis of most current natural resource development projects, we argue that economists invited to analyze investments undertaken to ameliorate symptoms of environmental degradation should use the broadest possible scope of inquiry. Issues that arise whenever an attempt to apply standard benefit-cost methodology in a third-world setting, issues that are well within an economist's range of expertise, must of course be addressed. In addition, though, economists must conduct the applied institutional analysis needed to understand why third world natural resources are being managed in a depletive way and what would be the consequences of proposed changes in environmental policy. Careful delineation of resource users' institutional environments is an essential prerequisite for private-level project analysis (Noronha and Lethem, 1983). Furthermore, only by understanding the incentives to conserve or deplete natural resources that exist under current institutional regimes can effective resource management strategies, in particular, and strategies for sustainable economic development, in general, be identified. By broadening the scope of inquiry in this way, economists can contribute to the formulation of natural resource management strategies that promote environmentally sustainable economic development.

References

Allen, R.N. 1974. "The Anchicaya Hydroelectric Project in Colombia: Design and Sedimentation Problems." In: *The Careless Technology*, J. Milton (ed.), Natural History Press, Garden City, New York.

Baumol, W.J. 1969. On the discount rate for public projects. In: *The Analysis and Evaluation of Public Expenditures: The PPB System* (Vol. I), Washington, DC, U.S. Government Printing Office, pp. 489-504.

Bromley, D.W. 1983. Land and water resources: A new perspective on economic development. In: *Issues in Third World Development*, K.C. Nobe and R.K. Sampath (eds.). Westview Press, Boulder, Colorado.

Dasgupta, A.K., and D.W. Pearce. 1978. *Cost-Benefit Analysis: Theory and Practice*. MacMillan Press, Ltd., London.

Eckstein, Otto. 1958. *Water Resource Development: The Economics of Project Evaluation*. Harvard University Press, Cambridge.

Gittinger, J.P. 1982. *Economic Analysis of Agricultural Projects* (2nd ed.), Johns Hopkins University Press, Baltimore, Maryland.

Gregersen, H., and K. Brooks. 1980. Economic analysis of watershed projects: Special problems and examples. Forestry Paper No. 17, U.N. Food and Agriculture Organization, Rome, Italy.

Haveman, R. 1965. *Water Resource Investment and the Public Interest*, Vanderbilt University Press, Nashville, Tennessee.

Leftwich, R.H. 1966. *The Price System and Resource Allocation*, Holt, Rinehart and Winston, New York.

MacDonald, T. 1981. Indigenous responses to an expanding frontier. In: *Cultural Transformations and Ethnicity in Modern Ecuador*, N. Whitten (ed.). University of Illinois Press, Urbana, Illinois.

Margolis, J. 1969. Shadow prices for incorrect or non-existent market prices. *The Analysis and Evaluation of Public Expenditures: The PBB System* (Vol. I), Washington, DC, U.S. Government Printing Office, pp. 533-546.

McGuire, M. 1969. Program analysis and regional economic objectives. In: *The Analysis and Evaluation of Public Expenditures: The PBB System* (Vol. I), Washington, D.C., U.S. Government Printing Office, pp. 592-610.

Noronha, R., and F.J. Lethem. 1983. Traditional Land Tenures and Land Use Systems in the Design of Agricultural Projects. Staff Working Paper No. 561, World Bank, Washington, DC.

Samuelson, P.A. 1964. *Economics: An Introductory Analysis*. McGraw-Hill, New York.

Southgate, D., and A. Veloz. 1985. The economics of watershed management: Two case studies from Latin America, paper presented at Fourth International Conference on Soil Conservation, Maracay, Venezuela, November.

Veloz, A., D. Southgate, F. Hitzhusen, and R. Macgregor. 1985. The economics of erosion control in a subtropical watershed: A Dominican case. *Land Economics*, Vol. 61, May.

Weisbrod, B. 1968. Income redistribution effects and benefit-cost analysis. *Problems in Public Expenditure Analysis*. Brookings Institution, Washington, DC.

Wischmeier, W.H. 1976. Use and misuse of the universal soil loss equation. *Journal of Soil and Water Conservation*, Vol. 31, January.

7/ The Social Dimension of Natural Resource Management

David O. Hansen
J. Mark Erbaugh

Failures of natural resource conservation and management programs in the Third World often can be traced to the neglect of their social aspects, primarily local values and traditions. Conversely, success is frequently attributable to designing projects consistent with these same factors. In this paper, David Hansen and Mark Erbaugh address social causes of natural resource degradation and the need to create conditions under which conservation projects can and will be successful. A concise case study from the Dominican Republic provides material illustrative of a success story. In summary, they note that social science inputs must be made during the project conceptualization process, rather than during an end-of-project review.

Introduction

Natural resource conservation and management is a high priority issue within the U.S. Agency for International Development (USAID). Many of the previous AID-funded projects in this area have produced less than optimal results; others have resulted in increased resource degradation. These failures, as well as some sterling successes, have been due in large part to the social aspects of the projects. Failures have resulted from a disregard of local values and traditions, including indigenous forms of social organization and process, in project design and implementation. We know what the problems are, but we have yet to establish project design methodologies that adequately consider social phenomena.

In this paper, we address several important aspects of the social organization of natural resource management projects. Our remarks are referenced primarily to soil conservation and management because of our previous work in this area. Specifically, they address social causes of natural resource degradation and important aspects of project design, including the need to create conditions under which the introduction of conservation projects will be successful. The latter will be illustrated with data from a field study conducted in the Dominican Republic.

Development as a Point of Departure

An overview of the components of development provides insights into necessary components of projects. AID defines several general objectives for rural development. The first is to stimulate the self-satisfaction of basic needs through increased production, consumption and trade; the second is to assure that self-satisfaction occurs through widespread participation which facilitates more equitable access to economic, social and political opportunities. Put in generic terms, economic growth is important, but it must be complemented with more equal sharing in the fruits of growth.

Past history has demonstrated that these two objectives often do not complement one another very well. In many cases, the growth objective has received priority over the equity objective in rural development projects. As noted by Moris (1981):

> The paradox we see repeated in program after program is that in order to meet ambitious production goals, new projects exclude themselves from the very organizational frameworks they are claiming to influence. It is time to admit that almost anywhere in the tropics, provided one has a cereal grain crop, plenty of money, a few proven managers, and freedom to work outside of the local administrative system, it is possible to show dramatic production increases in the short-run. But such success is not evidence that the long-run capability of the indigenous system has been changed, or that a large number of peasants have genuinely benefited.

Short-run solutions to national problems such as balance of payments may occur, but lasting rural development, premised on local participation and greater equality of distribution of increased production, will not. It is necessary that development planners find ways to incorporate both growth and equity considerations into project design.

Natural resource management projects are viewed by some as not fitting well with either of these objectives. Conservation measures often imply reduced production in the short-run. Newly planted fruit trees may reduce soil erosion, but they may also take several years to enter into production. A second dilemma is that it is the small, marginal farmers, or the poor rural inhabitants, that are often targeted by natural resource management projects because they occupy steep slopes and/or because they depend on the exploitation of marginal lands for their livelihood. They suffer short-run declines in production because they have no alternatives. Their wealthier counterparts often are not drawn into these projects, or when they are, they have alternative resources from which to gain a livelihood.

The tensions and sometimes contradictions which exist between production and equity goals and between production and conservation goals define an overarching framework for assessing the social dimension of rural development projects, including those concentrating on natural resource management. Several important questions related to social impacts should be incorporated into project design and implementation. What organizational innovations exist to minimize reductions in production implied by some resource conservation measures? How can projects that will increase aggregate productivity be made more equitable, through increasing the breadth of participation? Can factors which induce greater participation in conservation projects be identified, and can ways be found to incorporate them into project design and implementation?

The Problem of Natural Resource Degradation

Addressed from a global perspective, there is another major reason why development projects, and in particular agricultural production projects, should incorporate greater mass participation. Most developing countries still have the majority of their populations living in rural areas and totally dependent on exploitation of the natural resource base for their livelihood. These populations are growing more rapidly than others, thus exacerbating pressures on the land. Urban development, including the creation of new industries, can incorporate small percentages of population increase. However, in most developing countries, rural-to-urban migration signifies a decline in standard of living rather than an improvement, not to mention its deleterious effects on quality of life. Thus, population pressure on the land is likely to increase; as it does, pressures on increasingly marginal, fragile lands will increase. These poor, marginal farmers will have to learn how to farm in ways that maximize conservation if they are to continue to sustain themselves over time.

The Current Situation

The Global 2000 Report (Barney, 1980) emphasized the rapid deterioration of the world's natural resource base. Mismanagement of basic renewable resources is pervasive in many developing countries. We all know the more obvious cases, but they are worth mentioning because they have a bearing on what social scientists can do in this area. Deforestation is occurring at an alarming rate as trees are being cut down more rapidly than they are being planted for fuel as well as to put new lands under cultivation. In the tropics, this has had important negative secondary consequences as soil erosion has increased on hillsides and shallow forest soils have become leached and hardened. Inadequate resource management has also impacted directly on the ability to sustain large capital investment projects. Irrigation, which is so strategic to green revolution technology packages, has produced waterlogging and soil salinization in many countries, and has resulted in much prime land being taken out of production. In Africa, the use of deep, pump-operated wells has encouraged the concentration of livestock in surrounding areas. Overgrazing by these herds has greatly damaged the capacity of land surrounding the wells to sustain human and animal populations.

While it is not possible to foresee all negative consequences of production technologies introduced in developing countries, serious analyses of the aftermath of their introduction in the past can help us avoid them in the future. Case studies are an important tool for overall design and implementation of natural resource management projects.

Social Causes of Natural Resource Degradation

Several general social causes of natural resource degradation have been argued in the literature. None is sufficient in itself and many would argue that they simultaneously impact on the degradation process. They should all be considered in the design of conservation and management projects.

Maldistribution

One of the more popular arguments about why resource degradation occurs centers on the maldistribution of natural resources. The more favored classes have access to more abundant resources which are less prone to degradation. For example, large farmers tend to own land in the valleys, which is less prone to erosion than hillside lands. Furthermore, because of their more favored economic position, they have alternative sources of employment and income should their land be used to introduce conservation practices. Hillside farmers and landless poor, on the other hand, generally have no option, other than to continue farming or otherwise exploiting marginal resource bases. The argument is that until natural resources, decent occupations and income are more equitably distributed, the poor will have no choice other than to continue to exploit marginal resource bases. The obvious solution to this problem is some form of agrarian reform which results in a more equitable distribution of resources.

Tenure

Others argue that individuals will tend not to conserve natural resources if they do not have clear ownership of them. Insecure land tenure can be an important disincentive to reforestation because farmers are not willing to make upfront investments from which they will not reap future benefits (Clark University, 1978). In some cultures, community ownership of reforested lands may be a viable alternative. Soil conservation projects may also fail if the techniques introduced are costly and complicated and are introduced on farms to which the owners have insecure tenure (USAID, 1981). The underlying principle is that farmers will be unwilling to make conservation investments if they feel that they may not reap the benefits of them. In Western cultures, this normally implies that individuals should be given title to their land. In non-Western cultures, it may imply that projects should be based on community or other collective control of resource bases. In any case, there is an urgent need to devise appropriate legal frameworks to fit alternative social and political systems prior to introducing new technologies and systems to manage resources (Carruthers and Stoner, 1981).

Inappropriate Technologies

Another explanation of why natural resource degradation occurs is that technologies introduced to improve conservation and management are inappropriate or inadequate. The need for these technologies is most forcefully argued in the Global 2000 Report (Barney, 1980). Populations of third world countries are increasing, and will continue to increase, at rapid rates. The production of food to sustain them will require the introduction of new technologies to increase the yield per unit of land because arable lands that still have not been brought under cultivation are fast disappearing. Bringing marginal lands under cultivation only exacerbates the resource degradation problem.

However, these new technologies may not be compatible with existing traditional systems of managing natural resources. Their introduction may actually lead to increased degradation by causing breakdowns in traditional management strategies (Lawry, 1983). Social anthropologists have documented many elaborate rituals and management systems used in different cultures to accommodate rapid population growth under conditions of limited natural resource bases (Boserup, 1965; Wilkinson, 1972). The generation of alternative resource management systems which build on existing customs have a greater chance of successful incorporation by third world cultures.

The problem is that the new technologies, in many cases, may be overly sophisticated, or may require new forms of control over the use of impacted resources. For example, irrigation schemes also require adequate attention to drainage in order to avoid waterlogging and salinization. Many communities in the Third World may be either unable or unwilling to sustain the cost of introducing and maintaining adequate drainage systems. Similarly, the introduction of deep wells in arid pastoral lands requires that new forms of regulation of feeding of livestock herds be simultaneously introduced in order to preserve the carrying capacity of grazing lands surrounding them.

Political Instability

A final general argument as to why natural resource degradation occurs is the existence of different types of political instability. In some cases, war or other manifestations of civil strife may create circumstances under which farmers prefer to exploit resources under their control to a maximum. Uncertainty about whether they will control their use in the future dampens their concerns about preserving resources and their continued productivity (Murdoch, 1980). In other cases, the consequences of political instability may result in the undermining of existing natural resource management strategies (Eckholm, 1982). This was the case with the imposition of artificial political boundaries in Africa which disrupted pastoral systems that require the extensive migration of grazing herds. In other instances, the political domination of some social collectivities by others disrupted traditional forms of resource conservation.

Aspects of Project Design

Leonard (1985) summarized recent literature concerning the probable consequences of different institutions, laws, incentives and government programs for natural resource conservation projects. He noted that they should (1) facilitate and be sensitive to local inputs and participation, and (2) ensure that those who make major investments in natural resources management and conservation efforts benefit from those investments.

There are several factors that work against local participation and the relationship between investment and reward. The first is the tendency for centralized projects to be directive, regulatory, and patronizing. Many are generated and controlled by national agencies and fulfill political as well as development objectives. A second is that efficiency objectives take precedence over participatory objectives. Projects tend to be evaluated according to how well they meet the efficiency objective, particularly if they are financed by international development agencies.

We will review five critical aspects of project design and implementation. Obviously, for cases that are not oriented towards or do not incorporate local communities, they may be less applicable. However, social forestry, fuelwood, irrigation and water management, and watershed management projects normally involve local populations. Sensitivity to local inputs and local participation should be reflected in several ways.

Building on Indigenous Forms of Social Organization and Process

Social soundness analyses are routinely conducted as part of project development. They are opportunities to assess the extent to which projects build on existing social institutions and to recommend how to improve this facet of project design. Typically, projects focus on the introduction of new technologies. However, project success depends as much on the institutional innovations which may accompany them. It is a general law of social change that the more abrupt the institutional change which accompanies an innovation, the less likely the innovation is to be successfully grafted. This is particularly true for social forestry, fuelwood, and watershed management projects. Ideally, those projects would incorporate local government institutions and farmers associations and/or other formal organizations, as well as expressions of informal organizations. Most third world rural societies have collective forms of work cooperation that can be used to incorporate local labor inputs into projects. This increases local commitment to projects as well as the use of peer control to ensure conformity and participation. For irrigation management projects, which rigidly define the groups to be involved, it may be necessary to create organizations (Simmons et al., 1983; Radosevich, 1975).

Incorporating Economic and Social Incentives

Most resource conservation projects in the U.S. provide substantial economic incentives to participating farmers. Farmers are paid to put their land in soil banks and most input costs of physical inputs to soil conservation projects are paid by the government. Low interest credit and direct subsidies are also important incentives in the Third World to induce farmer participation. Incentives should be compatible with existing customs in rural communities and may be relatively inexpensive (Barry and Thomas, 1983). However, their allocation and distribution should be tied to the size of inputs made by farmers (USAID, 1981).

Noneconomic incentives may be as important as economic incentives. However, incentives should be both long-term and short-term in order to maintain participation by target groups (USAID, 1980). An example of short-term non-economic incentives are in-kind contributions through the World Food Program and Food for Peace. An USAID study of their use in reforestation programs showed that Title XII Food for Work assets, which are used to pay for labor and contributions through the World Food Program, will result in "planting as many as two or three times the number of trees over a four year period than are expected to be planted by USAID in connection with all of the 77 ongoing forestry-related bilateral assistance-funded projects in 37 countries worldwide" (USAID, 1982).

Utilizing collective work traditions of rural communities to introduce resource conservation measures, such as tree planting and soil conservation measures, provides another form of social gratification to participants.

Incorporating Local Inputs into Project Design

Successful implementation of resource conservation projects, as well as their maintenance over time, depends on the identification of local populations with them. This in turn depends in great part on their perceived compatibility with local goals and customs. Without this identification with the project, inputs will not be conceived, much less extended. Different USAID studies have assessed project failures. In one case, decisions about soil conservation practices were made without farmer inputs (USAID, 1983). In another instance, villagers in Niger acted to subvert a reforestation project's goals because they misunderstood those goals (Spears, 1978). This contrasts sharply with the success of another reforestation project in Niger that involved villagers in its formulation (IDRC, 1977).

Local input should be obtained from all segments of the affected population or from representatives of the community rather than of special interests. Lowdermilk et al. (1980) suggest that inputs can be secured directly through involving representatives of the population, or indirectly through surveys and other data gathering techniques. The key is that village needs and interests be represented in the project.

Participation in Project Implementation

There is a need to cultivate processes that spark local populations to formulate their own collective responses to natural resource depletion problems (Barry and Thomas, 1983). This objective transcends the immediate goals of particular projects and is best achieved through involving local people in the project implementation so that they identify with the successes achieved by projects. Hirschman's (1983) "Principle of Conservation and Mutation of Social Energy" is relevant to this issue. There is a need to build on small successes of collaborative problem solving when attempting more ambitious change efforts.

There are major limitations on the extent to which national governments can reverse trends in natural resource degradation. This is especially true for social forestry programs. Leonard (1984) cites a typical case from India which is designed to help approximately 50 million inhabitants of marginal environments:

> Both in theory and practice, the success of social forestry programs requires the participation of the people in planting and protecting trees and in the equitable sharing of benefits. At present, forest departments are the main implementors of social forestry programs.... community-based and intermediary organizations are also needed. Nongovernmental initiatives can generate innovations in participating community organizations, in designing incentive systems and support services, and in popularizing social forestry for the needs of the people (Ford Foundation, n.d.).

Many natural resource conservation projects, particularly fuelwood projects, involve activities typically carried out by women. Many have failed because women's roles were not considered (Hoskins, 1981; USAID, 1983). Projects tended to have objectives which were not consonant with the perceived needs of affected villagers. This reduced their level of commitment to the objectives. Additionally, projects did not take advantage of labor inputs by women in project implementation.

Local Participant Control and Responsibility

Many projects have not obtained their true potential because they focused too heavily on the creation of formal administrative structures that wind up inducing the performance of project activities, rather than facilitating collective decision-making and subsequent performance. In some cases, investments have been capital-intensive and implemented by technicians imported from outside the community when they did not have to be. Several of these projects have been defined as failures (USAID, 1981).

In many third-world countries, government agencies tend to implement projects directly rather than involving local communities in the process, much less in the decision-making which precedes implementation. This may occur in part because of overconcern for efficiency goals, such as obtaining quantifiable outputs within a relatively short time frame. In other cases, it occurs because government agents do not appreciate the considerable resources and decision-making capacity which are found in impacted rural communities. Still more seriously, in other cases it occurs because government bureaucracies operate at a level which effectively separates them from local populations, a situation which precludes effective dialogue.

Lack of involvement and responsibility for project success usually will result in project failure because commitment to maintaining project inputs is lacking. In addition, the exercise of social control by villagers over one another is likely not to occur because of the absence of collective responsibility.

Openness to Change—An Empirical Study

The social dimensions of project design and implementation which have been discussed are of great importance. However, there is another factor which precedes all of them that must be addressed—the predisposition of the affected population to accept the practices involved in the project as well as the institutional changes that accompany them.

The literature on the adoption of agricultural innovations generally assumes that farmers will adopt new technologies because they are economically profitable. It also assumes that farmers with socioeconomically favored positions will tend to adopt new practices more readily than others. Farmers of higher socioeconomic status are better educated, which supposedly makes them more aware of the advantages of new technologies. They have larger farms, which provide those greater economies of scale implied by use of the new technologies. Finally, they have higher incomes, which make it easier for them to acquire the new technologies. These assumptions fit production practices quite well.

The question to be asked is whether or not these assumptions fit technologies or practices designed to conserve natural resources. Most of these practices tend to reduce profits, at least in the short-run. Several authors have argued that these assumptions do not apply (Hooks, 1980; Nowak, 1983; Pampel and Van Es, 1977; Van Es, 1983).

In the U.S., programs have employed incentives, such as paying for innovations introduced on farms or paying farmers to take land out of production, to induce farmers to adopt conservation practices. Whereas this has been the practical motivation, others have argued the importance of generating favorable attitudes towards the care of natural resources. In general, this implies holding a favorable attitude towards change.

Favorable attitudes towards change, particularly as they relate to farming practices and conservation, may be generated through educational programs designed for this purpose, or through the occurrence of natural phenomena. The introduction of major soil conservation programs in the U.S. followed in the wake of the dust bowl of the south-central plains, which increased the awareness of the need for conservation practices.

In 1981, we assessed the relative importance of social-psychological predispositions toward change and socio-economic background in determining the adoption of soil conservation practices in the Ocoa Watershed, Dominican Republic (Erbaugh, 1983). This formed part of a more general social sounding of the region prior to the initiation of the major USAID-funded natural resource management project, discussed in this volume in the chapter by Kemph and Hernandez. The Ocoa Watershed is atypical because of hurricanes it experienced in 1979, which raised the level of awareness of a need for change in farming practices. Hurricanes David and Frederick caused considerable soil erosion and river basin destruction. The area is further atypical because of the presence of an activist priest who has promoted change, including conservation practices, for over a decade.

Sample

A stratified sample was taken of farmers in the region. The sampling base was farmer associations in the region. They are present in all regions of the watershed. Approximately five members of each association were interviewed, along with one non-member living proximate to each association.

Major Concepts

The relationships among major variables in this model were hypothesized to be time-sequenced. The two major input variables, as depicted in Figure 7-1, were socio-economic background and orientation toward change. The major dependent variable was the adoption of soil conservation practices. In addition, we hypothesized several important intervening variables, namely access to extension services, use of agricultural credit, and awareness of the soil erosion problem. The intervening variables were also time-sequenced on the assumption that contact with agricultural support institutions would lead to increased awareness of soil erosion.

Results

The model was tested using path analysis, a technique borrowed from genetic research which builds on multiple regression and analysis of variance. The correlations of all predictor variables with the adoption variable were statistically significant. However, that of socioeconomic background was negative and trivial in size. Furthermore, socio-economic background failed to correlate significantly with any of the intervening variables in the model. Awareness of erosion was a common phenomenon in the watershed, thanks to the hurricanes and community action work mentioned previously. Extension and credit agencies offered their services to all farmers, irrespective of their socioeconomic status. Perhaps of greater significance was that the orientation-to-change variable correlated significantly with all intervening variables and with the adoption variable. Following the hypothesized causal ordering sequence of variables in the model, it

Figure 7-1: Model of the Adoption of Soil Conservation Practices - Ocoa Watershed

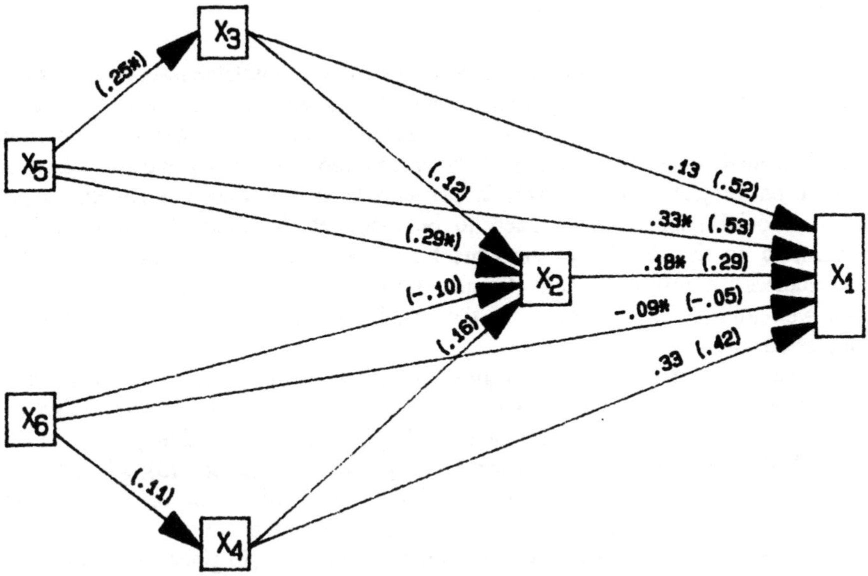

X_1- Adoption of Soil Conservation Practices
X_2- Awareness of Soil Erosion
X_3- Extension Contacts
X_4- Use of Agricultural Credit
X_5- Orientation Toward Change
X_6- Socio-Economic Background

- Stardardized path coefficients (beta weights) in parentheses.
- Correlation coefficients outside parentheses.

* Correlation significant at $p \leq .05$ level.

had a significant direct effect on adoption (p = .52) as well as significant indirect effects through awareness of soil erosion (p = .29 x .18). Orientation-to-change clearly is more important in determining adoption than is socioeconomic background.

Results from this empirical study suggest that orientation to change, including the willingness to change farming practices to conserve soil fertility, is an important predictor of the adoption of conservation practices. In contrast, at least among poor farmers in the Dominican Republic, socio-economic status is of little import. There was little differentiation among farmers by status with respect to the actual adoption of these practices. These results clearly show that the assumptions of the general model of adoption of agricultural practices do not hold well for the adoption of soil conservation practices. Rather, attitudinal variables appear to be of much greater importance than social and economic status in the community. These results provide cross-cultural support for arguments about the limitations of the diffusion model when applied to conservation practices.

Conclusion

There are many facets of project design and implementation that would benefit from interventions by social scientists. Assessing the social impacts of the project and evaluating project success/failure are two instances. However, both are inadequate, if not futile, if the interventions are really meant to have an impact on project success. This is particularly true if they are conducted *post facto*. Social science inputs need to be made at the time of project conceptualization so that its design accounts for social factors which could later harm the chances for project success (Cernea, 1984). These factors are concerned with how well-adjusted the project is to the social and cultural milieu in which it will be carried out.

The most important sociological issues in natural resource management projects revolve about how to engage impacted populations in project design and implementation. This concerns issues of (1) openness to change, particularly technological change; (2) institutional change when required; (3) adaptation of projects to local cultures, including existing forms of social organization and customs; and (4) equitable distribution of project costs and benefits.

Openness to change involves an education process (Engineering Consultants, 1980). For the social engineer, it implies the creation of an environment conducive to change in which innovation is more easily accepted, and long-run as well as short-run benefits of projects are recognized. The inputs of environmental educators to this process are particularly important.

Institutional change may take three forms. First, it may imply the creation of new forms of social organization and process when existing forms are inadequate to achieve project goals that are valued by the population involved. Second, it may involve building on existing forms of social organization and process. And third, it may involve doing away with forms that are inappropriate and that will impede project success.

Equitable distribution of project costs and benefits is essential to collective efforts. Equitable or "fair" should be defined by the project participants. Without this principle of equity, individuals will avoid participation. It is also essential is that the project be designed so that individuals who attempt to reap more than their fair share of the benefits are appropriately sanctioned. This may involve formally structured legal sanctions or harnessing informal processes of group dynamics, such as peer pressure and social control. Finally, social scientists can contribute to the conceptualization of more effective natural resources management projects by highlighting macro causes of natural resource degradation. The critical issue for these inputs is how to construct projects so that they help counteract these forces. In many cases, this will require attention to national policies that impact on the implementation of field projects.

References

Barney, G.O. Study Director. 1980. *The Global 2000 Report to the President: Entering the Twenty-First Century*. Washington DC: U.S. Government Printing Office.

Barry, E., and B. Thomas. 1983. *Natural Resource Management Workshop*. Clark University, Program for International Development, February.

Boserup, E. 1965. *The Conditions of Agricultural Growth: The Economics of Agrarian Change under Population Pressure*. London: Allen and Unwin.

Carruthers, I., and R. Stoner. 1981. Economic Aspects and Policy Issues in Groundwater Development. *World Bank Staff Working Paper* #496, October.

Cernea, M. 1984. Putting People First: The Position of Sociological Knowledge in Planned Rural Development. Keynote Opening Address at the VIth World Congress for Rural Sociology, Manila, Philippines, December.

Clark University. 1978. *Fuelwood and Energy in Eastern Africa: An Assessment of the Environmental Impact of Energy Uses*. Program for International Development.

Eckholm, E.P. 1982. *Down To Earth*. New York: Norton.

Engineering Consultants, Inc. 1980. *Citanduy River Basin Development Project: Panamerican Pilot Watershed Implementation and Evaluation Project*. Denver, Mimeograph.

Erbaugh, J.M. 1983. *Small Farmer Adoption of Soil Conservation Practices in the Ocoa Watershed, Dominican Republic*. The Ohio State University, Unpublished M.S. Thesis.

Ford Foundation. n.d. Precis for a Grant Proposal for Support of the Society for Promotion of Wastelands Development. Request No. DCP-197.

Hirschman, A. 1983. The Principle of Conservation and Mutation of Social Energy. *Grassroots Development*, 7(2):3-9.

Hooks, G. 1980. *The Classical Diffusion Paradigm Reconsidered: An Overview of Criticisms and an Alternative*. The Ohio State University, Unpublished M.S. Thesis.

Hoskins, M. 1981. Women in Forestry for Local Community Development. *Rural Development Participation Review*, 2 (Spring).

International Development Research Centre (IDRC). 1977. *Trees for People*. Ottawa: IDRC.

Lawry, S.W. 1983. Land Tenure, Land Policy and Smallholder Livestock Development in Botswana. *Land Tenure Research Paper* #78, Madison, Wisconsin, March.

Leonard, H.J. 1985. *Divesting Nature's Capital: The Political Economy of Environmental Abuse in the Third World*. New York: Holmes and Meier.

Leonard, H.J. 1984. Socio-Economic Aspects of Natural Resource Management: A Framework for Policy Research. In: *Priorities for Rural Development Research* (M.S. Grindle and S.T. Walker, eds.). Cambridge: Harvard Institute for International development, February.

Lowdermilk, M.K., and W.T. Franklin, et al. 1980. *Development Process for Improving Irrigation Water Management on Farms: Problem Identification Manual*. Colorado State University Technical Report #65.

Moris, J.R. 1981. *Managing Induced Rural Development*. Bloomington: International Development Institute.

Murdoch, W.W. 1980. *The Poverty of Nations: The Political Economy of Hunger and Population*. Baltimore: Johns Hopkins University Press.

Nowak, P. 1983. Adoption and Diffusion of Soil and Water Conservation Practices. *The Rural Sociologist*, 3(2):83-91.

Painter, J.E., et al. 1982. *On-Farm Water Management Project in Pakistan*. USAID: Bureau for Program and Policy Coordination, June.

Pampel, F., and J.C. Van Es. 1977. Environmental Quality and Issues of Adoption Research. *Rural Sociology*, 42(1):57-71.

Radosevich, G.E. 1975. *Water User Organizations for Improving Irrigated Agriculture: Applicability to Pakistan*. Colorado State University, Water Management Technical Report #44.

Simmons, F.F., et al. 1983. *Special Evaluation of the Resources Conservation and Utilization Project*. Arlington: Development Associates, Inc., April.

Spears, J.S. 1978. The Changing Emphasis in World Bank Forestry Lending: A Summary of Recent Experiences and Problems. Special paper presented at the Eighth World Forestry Congress. Jakarta, Indonesia, October 17.

U.S. Agency for International Development (USAID). 1983. *Audit Report on the Resource Conservation and Utilization Project in Nepal*. Office of the Inspector General, July 26.

U.S. Agency for International Development (USAID). 1982. *Proceedings of a Workshop on Energy, Forestry and Environment*. Bureau for Africa, Volume II, Discussion Paper/Case Studies, April.

U.S. Agency for International Development (USAID). 1981. *Assessment of the Second Integrated Rural Development Project: Assumptions and Goals*. Special Evaluation Report, June.

U.S. Agency for International Development (USAID). 1980. *The Socio-Economic Context of Fuelwood Use in Small Rural Communities*. Evaluation Special Study #1.

Van Es, J.C. 1983. The Adoption/Diffusion Tradition Applied to Resource Conservation: Inappropriate Use of Existing Knowledge. *The Rural Sociologist*, 3(2):76-82.

Wilkinson, R.G. 1973. *Poverty and Progress: An Ecological Model of Economic Development*. London: Methuen and Company.

8/ The Economics of Biological Diversity: Apologetics or Theory?

Richard B. Norgaard

Arguing that neoclassical economic models are inadequate to confront issues of biological diversity, Richard Norgaard offers the "coevolutionary development paradigm" as a promising alternative. It poses three questions. First, in what sense is biological diversity important? Second, what are the interrelationships between extinction and the path to development during recent years? Third, what steps must be taken to retain biological diversity for the future? Ultimately, he warns us, the coevolutionary paradigm does not furnish the answers to all questions, but it does offer the possibility of an alternative organization for world views and evidence, questions and answers, and social organization and possible response.

Introduction

During the 1960s, our awareness of global development focused on the rates of increases in population versus food. This Malthusian theme organized the public's general environmental understanding of third world development problems and led academics to juxtapose demographic and economic development theories. The 'green revolution,' complementary resource development, and population programs were subsequently pushed and justified by this Malthusian understanding. During the 1970s, our environmental awareness and concern shifted to problems of pollution and then energy. We began to recognize that the technological path to development was narrow and irreversible. Academic thinking about development began to explore the costs of 'progress' more thoroughly, while technologists sought to widen the path. During the 1980s, the extinction of species has become the environmental theme around which we are focusing our questions about the true costs of development, the range of options, and our ability to choose.

Population, pollution, energy, and extinction have been partial initial framings on the same pastiche of long-standing, widely felt concerns over development. The environmentalists and natural scientists who focus our anxiety have become a part of the political and administrative fabric of Western nations.

A few individuals, notably Paul and Anne Ehrlich, have been effective voices in all three decades and framings. The partial critiques break the media, political, and bureaucratic surface with different framings because communication pathways are unable to convey the whole pastiche or because we are unable to comprehend the full picture. In any case, our response to each framing of the environmental critique also has been piecemeal. We have adopted a technical innovation here, an institutional refinement there, and temporarily increased our sensitivity to a subset of the issues, but we have not significantly changed our overall hopes for or implementation of development.

It is frequently argued that we are unable to comprehend, to convey, and to respond to problems which are especially complex. The models which structure our thinking, communication, social organization, decisions, and actions cannot handle much complexity. The environmental critique covers the full complexity of development, all of the issues of people and their environment. But the response of economists to each new framing of the pastiche suggests yet another hypothesis. We insist on using inappropriate models.

The neoclassical economic model is especially inadequate for inquiry into the problems of biological diversity. The neoclassical paradigm assumes that systems can be divided into parts and shifted to and fro along a continuum of equilibria, denying biological interconnectedness and irreversibility. A coevolutionary paradigm gives a richer explanation of the process of development and species extinction. This paradigm also indicates that significant changes in development philosophy and social organization will be needed to maintain our options. Why we economists use inappropriate models and put so much effort into apologetics instead of into the development of more appropriate theory is the central question.

Conventional Economic Questions, Analyses, and Insights

Economists have responded to the current focus on biological diversity with a plethora of apologetics. Species become extinct because they are common pool resources. Since no one can own and manage them over the long run without others enjoying the gains, all exploit them for immediate profit, frequently to extinction. Thus, species can become extinct because they are public goods. All people can 'freely' enjoy the benefits of knowing a species exists or benefit from the knowledge that might be gained through learning from its biochemical and other ecological adaptations. Since none can be excluded from enjoying species existence or sharing in the knowledge that can be learned, a price cannot be charged and there is no private incentive to protect species. Species also become extinct because their natural rates of increase are less than the market rate of interest. Both rational entrepreneurs and responsible public officials divest the species and invest where earnings are higher. Lastly, extinction is forever, but economic decisions are necessarily made over limited time horizons with incomplete knowledge of the future. The 'trouble' with extinction is that it is irreversible[1].

These arguments are apologetical rather than theoretical. They accept existing economic theory and the conventions that have evolved around it. Existing theory assumes that natural systems have separate components that can be owned and traded in markets. Existing theory assumes that processes are reversible. Existing theory assumes that interest rates are generated in markets where future generations with rights to property—including rights to genetic and environmental system diversity—bargain with current generations. For questions where these atomistic-mechanistic and intergenerational assumptions are especially false, new premises and theory should be developed. Instead, we have explained extinction, developed decision models to optimize extinction, and suggested institutional modifications to rationalize extinction on the basis of somewhat extended, at best, inappropriate theory.

Neoclassical theory is rooted in Newtonian mechanics (Blaug, 1980; Georgescu-Roegen, 1971). Early economists explicitly acknowledged their philosophical debt to Isaac Newton while the early mathematizers of economics—Cournot, Jevons, Pareto, and Walras—formalized economics along the lines of Newton's models.

The neoclassical model is atomistic in its assumption that the services of land, including all aspects of ecological systems as well as the services of labor and capital, can be treated as separate components. These components are like individual atoms which are only combined during the production of goods and services and only related to each other through their relative values determined in exchange. In this view, species are independent of one other except in the market. Of course, when dealing with the economics of biological systems, we modify our models by building in one or two non-market interrelationships for added realism.

The neoclassical model is mechanistic in its assumption that the economic system can operate in equilibrium at any position and move back and forth between positions at will. If more of one of the services of the biological system become available, the economic system adjusts so that more of the goods for which this service is relatively intensive are produced and sold at lower prices, the returns to the biological service fall, and the returns to other inputs increase. If the quantity of this biological service should then decrease to its earlier level, the economy adjusts back again to its earlier levels of outputs, prices, and returns. Atomistic-mechanistic models are characterized by a range of stable equilibria and the reversibility of system changes. Again, of course, when dealing with the problems of extinction, we modify the model by including irreversibility for the particular species modeled.

Modification of the basic assumptions, however, is never extensive. There is a long history to the idea that the test of a science is in its ability to predict (Scriven, 1959). From Bacon on through with minor twists to Popper, this idea has dominated Western epistemology. Prediction requires a tractable model and tractability entails formal symmetry in the relationships within a model. Competitive market relations provide this symmetry for economics much as gravitational forces provided it for Newton. Without the symmetry, the ability to predict and hence to prescribe breaks down. Lipsey and Lancaster (1956) created considerable controversy with their "theory of the second best" simply by pointing out that predictions and prescriptions could not be generally derived if the conventional assumptions of divisibility and competitive markets were violated in more than one instance. The numerous direct and indirect links between people through the environmental system, of course, violate the model's assumptions. While mathematical economists have become much more sophisticated over the past few decades, no significant generalizations have come forth for "second best" worlds (Mittelhammer, Matulich, and Bushaw, 1981). A second tractability furor erupted when environmental economists pointed out the implications of including some irreversibility in the neoclassical model (Fisher, Cicchetti, and Krutilla, 1972; Arrow and Fisher, 1974).

Reality, it seems, is not tractable with respect to the questions of biological diversity on which economists have decided to focus. Yet we find it more 'satisfying' to manipulate inappropriate tractable models than to explore for new models and questions. Thus we have produced numerous investigations into the separate value of inseparable components of the biological system and mechanistic projections of the value of maintaining options in an unforeseeable, evolutionary future. While bewailing the theoretical and empirical challenges the questions of biological diversity pose, we have defended our exercises by arguing that difficult choices must be made with respect to the extent to which biological diversity is to be maintained and that economics, however imperfect, provides the only tractable, rational framework for decision-making.

The neoclassical conception of the social system is also atomistic-mechanistic. Individuals behave independently according to their own values and in their own best interest in markets, politics, and bureaucracies, given the constraints of their individual rights. People respond rationally to new conditions and mechanistically return to their previous behavior when earlier conditions return. As in the case of environmental systems, these basic assumptions are made more realistic in ways most appropriate to the specific question under consideration. But, again, only minimal modifications can be made without losing tractability.

One assumption with respect to the social system should be especially troublesome for economists pondering optimal biological diversity. In economic theory, future generations hold rights to resources including genetic and environmental system diversity. Interest rates reflect offers made by current generations for the use of these resources in exchange for investments in knowledge, capital equipment and facilities, and environmental improvements. In fact, of course, future generations have no such rights and are only provided access to resources through benevolence or default. We deliberately distribute resources to the future through privately and publicly exercised benevolence and leave resources by default because our technology and social organization is inadequate to exploit all resources simultaneously. Models, of course, depend upon simplifying assumptions, and these simplifications can usually be restated as tautologies. Circular reasoning, however, is a little too taut when we pursue how rights to biological diversity should be distributed toward the future with models which assume the distribution is appropriate. This troublesome contradiction between assumptions and reality as well as between model design and use is occasionally noted, but we continue to use efficiency criteria and valuation techniques based on prices, behavior, and 'willingness' rooted in the existing intergenerational distribution of rights to pursue questions concerning intergenerational distribution[2].

Our reliance on economic rationality in a world of science conditioned on atomism-mechanism and 'the proof is in the prediction' is understandable. Given the increasing severity and globalness of the unintended consequences of this breed of science applied beyond the laboratory, however, the vitality of this world view is most perplexing[3]. The parallels between the apologetics for the Christian world view during the rise of Western science and the reason for my selection of the subtitle of this essay should now be emerging.

Coevolutionary Development: An Alternative Paradigm

An ecological-evolutionary world view provides an alternative template for understanding the economics of biological diversity. In this view, economic thought and social prescription are premised on the patterns of complex systems and interactive change. This view highlights how most of the past seven millennia of development since the origins of agricultural technologies and social organization was a process of ecological system transformation and adaptive social system response. Cultural knowledge 'explained' people's relations to their environment and prescribed social organization. The coevolutionary vantage provides needed perspective on how the atomistic-mechanistic world view facilitated technologies to exploit stock resources and rationalized both the capitalist system of individual ownership and markets and centralized social organization with bureaucratic authority. With stock-exploitive development and our collective understanding of systems functionally reduced to the formalities of mechanics, environmental systems began to break down and species to disappear.

To acknowledge that development is an evolutionary process is to acknowledge the conceptual and computational limitations of atomistic- mechanistic thinking. In atomistic-mechanistic systems, change either occurs because an exogenous factor changes and shifts the system to a new equilibrium or because the system has the dynamic property of being in a determinable position, like a rocket on a trajectory, at any point in time. The qualities of the factors, their possibilities for existence in the system, and the relationships between them do not change over time. These assumptions clash with the characterization of evolutionary systems, in which new components and relationships emerge while old ones change or fade away (Popper, 1959; Scriven, 1959). The evolutionary model of systems, while clearly less tractable, is especially descriptive of the process of social and environmental transformation that has resulted in species loss.

Variation, mutation or innovation, and natural selection are the key factors in the evolutionary process. Change occurs as new characteristics prove more fit. In turn, species—or more generally, components in the system—with new characteristics apply new selective pressure on other components. As components change, the relationships between them change. In biological systems, the evolutionary interactions between two species are sometimes so closely intertwined that the evolution of each species is mostly affected by the evolution of the other. Species which "coevolve" in this manner reflect each other. Coevolutionary explanations have been given for the shapes of the beaks of hummingbirds and of the flowers they feed upon, for the behavior of bees and the distribution of flowering plants, and for the biochemical defenses of plants and the immunities of their insect prey (Ehrlich and Raven, 1964; Baker and Hurd, 1968).

The concept of evolution can be broadened to encompass the ongoing feedback processes between social and ecological systems (Norgaard, 1981, 1984a, 1984b). The interactions between social and ecological systems coevolve much faster than biological relations determined over generations through genetic selection. Man's activities modify the ecological system. The ecological system's responses, in turn, provide cause for individual action and social organization. The gains of development arise through the process of positive feedbacks between the systems, through the coevolution of social and ecological systems in a manner favorable to people.

This view of the development process explains the correlations found by cultural ecologists between the characteristics of social and ecological systems (Harris, 1979; Netting, 1977; Rambo, 1983; Rappaport, 1968). Figure 8-1 suggests the complexity of interactions within and between both the social and environmental systems. It also highlights the flows of energy, materials, and information between the systems and from outside the systems. In addition, the interactive processes of selection and adaptation between the two systems are central to the illustration.

Coevolutionary models have proven especially valuable for explaining the past. Anthropologists have generally used coevolutionary models to document the interdependence between traditional cultures and their agricultural ecosystems. Geertz (1963), however, applied the model to help explain agricultural and social transformation into the twentieth century in Indonesia. Economists Boserup (1965 and 1981), Simon (1977), and Wilkinson (1973) have argued that development consists of social reorganization to overcome environmental constraints. Such reorganization, of course, may not succeed in either the short or the long run. I have described the failure of the Brazilian colonization efforts and the success of the Japanese in the Amazon in a coevolutionary framework (Norgaard, 1981 and 1985a).

Coevolutionary development followed unique patterns in each location. Until only several centuries ago, the world was a patchwork quilt of coevolving social and ecological systems. Characteristics of components within the ecological systems were selected in part according to how well they fit the evolving values, knowledge, social organization, and technologies of the local peoples while each of these components of the social system were also continually being selected according to how well they fit the evolving ecological system. Local knowledge, embedded in myths and traditions, was correct, for it had proven fit and become consistent with, through selective evolutionary pressure, the components of the social and ecological systems it explained.

While a patchwork quilt provides a general description, the boundaries of each patch were neither always distinct nor fixed. Myths, values, social organization, technologies, and biological species gradually spilled over the boundaries of the patch within which they initially evolved to become exotics in new patches. Some of these exotics proved fit and thereafter affected the coevolution of

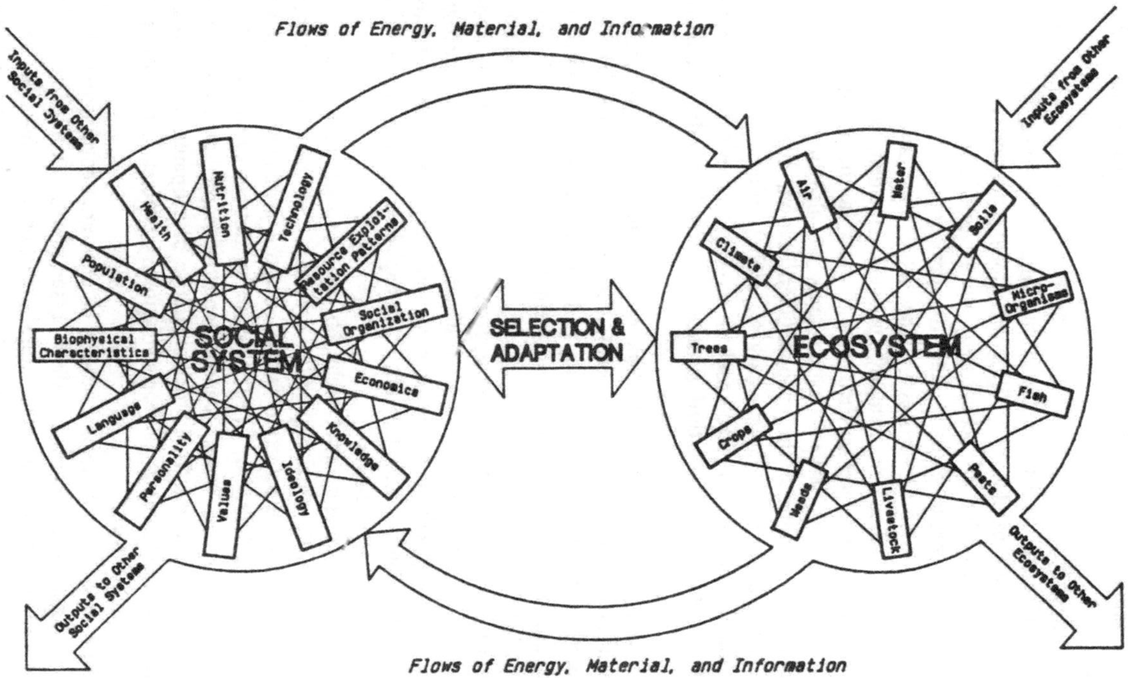

Figure 8-1: Interactions within and between the Social and Environmental Systems. Source: A. Terry Rambo, "Conceptual Approaches to Human Ecology," East-West Environment and Policy Inst. Research Report 14, June 1983, page 26.

system characteristics in their new patches, resetting the dynamics of their growth, or decline, in area and structure. Though spillovers were immensely important, the possible combinations of spillovers and rooting of exotics into different patches was infinite and the pattern of evolution remained patchy, albeit constantly changing.

Development during the past several centuries is markedly different. The mechanistic grid of universal truths developed by Western science has boldly overlayed the coevolutionary patchwork. With the global adoption of Western knowledge and the direct transfer of technologies, social organization and values have also evolved on convergent paths. And the environment has not been immune from this globally unifying process. The urban environments of the rapidly growing third world cities are similarly sprawled, crowded, polluted, and devoid of natural amenities, not unlike their counterparts in the United States and Europe of the same vintage. Rural environments are also merging through the common selective pressure from the cropping, fertilization, and pest control practices of modern agriculture. Global markets, global values, global social organization, and global technologies have resulted in global criteria for environmental fitness. The bold grid of Western science has simplified the elaborate patchwork quilt.

The coevolutionary paradigm highlights how growth during the past century and a half has been stock-exploitive. The potential for this growth was inherent in our ability to discover and adopt technologies and social organization suited to the extraction and use of coal, petroleum, iron, cement, sand, and gravel. But Georgescu-Roegen (1971) has shown that most technological and organizational change simply allows us to exploit low-entropy resources faster and thereby transform the favorable order of the natural world into a homogeneous garbage dump sooner. He correctly critiques increases in well-being that come strictly through higher rates of resource use. Current stock-exploitive growth necessarily comes at the expense of future generations[4].

The coevolutionary paradigm also highlights how social and ecological coevolution has changed with stock-exploitive growth. In the past, social institutions which survived natural selection facilitated more productive and stable interactions with the ecological system. Today, social institutions are designed to facilitate stock exploitation and to reduce concomitant environmental damage and social problems. Coevolution stems from stock-exploitive development rather than results in coevolutionary development. The coevolutionary process is reactive and environmentalists are reactionaries.

Like mechanistic models, evolutionary models of economic development have their own inherent tautologies between their assumptions, predictions, and prescriptions. The random innovation and natural selection that describe evolutionary development become prescriptions much the same as capital accumulation is both the assumption and prescription of the capital accumulation model of growth. Nevertheless, evolutionary views do describe why diversity in both social and ecological systems is necessary, how innovation is important, how natural selection might be hastened and influenced by monitoring and learning systems, and why the productivity of ecosystems should be protected (Norgaard and Dixon, 1986b).

The Coevolutionary Development Paradigm and Biological Diversity

The coevolutionary development paradigm suggests three interrelated questions with respect to biological diversity. First, in what sense is biological diversity important? Second, what are the interrelationships between extinction and the path of development during the past century? Third, what steps need to be taken to retain biological diversity for the future? While these general questions are related to the more specific questions concerning value and optimal decision-making suggested by the neoclassical economic model, the answers and relationships among them prove quite different.

The answer to the first question initially will be stated quite generally, leaving the details to unfold as the subsequent questions are pursued. In short, diversity is intimately linked to coevolutionary development. Diversity is greater because coevolution is a local process, specific to local cultural knowledge and social organization and to the local ecosystem. Coevolutionary development maintains and evolves around the initial characteristics of the local ecosystem. Biological diversity is important because it provides the ingredients for coevolutionary development.

The greater diversity associated with coevolutionary development is, of course, relative to stock-exploitive development. Hence we proceed to our second question. Stock-exploitive development transforms local agroecosystems through the use of common inputs—fertilizers, pesticides, and seed varieties—making initially different systems increasingly alike. Soil is reduced to a medium for fertilizer. Weeds and pests are eliminated. Deprived of the flora with which they coevolved, soil microbes disappear. Beyond agriculture, diversity is reduced through the disruption of ecosystems by mineral extraction, water development and pollution, and urbanization. Ecosystems increasingly reflect the atomistic-mechanistic world view that facilitates stock exploitation.

Both market and centralized social systems under stock-exploitive development support the process of ecosystem simplification. Each local subsistence economy can adapt to and use a large variety of species, and numerous independent subsistence economies support an even broader range of species. Regionally and globally linked industrial economies, on the other hand, demand uniformity. While local populations in the Amazon use numerous tree species in a large variety of ways, only about a dozen of the estimated 500 woody species have market value beyond the region. Likewise, only a few of the 2000 species of fish in the Amazon have commercial value beyond the region, though many species are consumed by the local population. The information, talent, and equipment required for storing, shipping, processing, preparing, and using more than a few species from any region is very costly to maintain in a national, let alone global, economy where other species from other regions also compete for a place in the market.

The global economy, however, puts significant pressure on a few species in each region. In highly diverse ecosystems, this pressure frequently leads to highgrading rather than management. In the Amazon, for example, certain species of trees, turtles, alligators, spotted cats, and more recently certain species of fish have been exploited to extinction or near extinction. These species have been fugitive or 'common property' resources, and the exploitation incentive has almost always been an export market. Highgrading differs from mere exploitation. The process is related to the mix of interdependent species, the areal distributional constraints of the exploited species, and the competition of unexploited species for the niches of the exploited. These relations and people's options for working with and affecting them can be understood in a coevolutionary framework more simply than in a modified atomistic-mechanistic framework.

The coevolutionary perspective suggests that the neoclassical economic argument of specialization, comparative advantage, and the gains from trade has been oversold. Regions cannot develop through coevolutionary processes if they are forever adjusting to the fluctuations of international prices. Local biological and social systems—the culture of agriculture—are destroyed when international markets dictate that corn should be planted one year, wheat the next, and soybeans the third. Both species preservation and the maintenance of cultural knowledge and local technologies and organization need more stability than the integrated world economy has shown during the past several decades. Less, not more, trade is probably in order. This also implies that aid should be through outright grants rather than loans, which on net must be repaid through the sale of products to the lending countries.

Institutional economists have documented how the philosophy of John Locke stems from the atomistic-mechanistic world view and how the idea that each individual can best decide what is good lends support to the Western institution of individual property rights. It appears, however, that no one has elaborated on how the atomistic-mechanistic conception of nature itself seems to have facilitated the idea of property. A world seen as made up of separable components can be divided up and allocated to individuals as private property. In an atomistic-mechanistic world, any particular use of property repeatedly—i.e., mechanically—produces the same outcome. A world view that posits definitive outcomes fosters the idea that there can be an optimum system of property rights (Norgaard, 1986c).

Social systems themselves are becoming more homogeneous. The diversity rooted in the uniquely evolved cultural knowledge of local peoples has been succumbing to the mass, objective knowledge of the West. This reduction in the diversity of world views has made ways of thinking, communicating, organizing, and acting increasingly alike. The selective pressure that people now put on their environments is remarkably similar not only because of shared technology but because of shared social organization and behavior.

Bureaucratic organization has risen along with the rise of Western science. This is not coincidental. Our beliefs in the objectivity, universality, separability, and tractability of scientific knowledge support bureaucratization (Norgaard, 1985b). Atomism, or separability, supports the idea that specific agencies can address specific problems independently. Our belief in the universality of our knowledge supports the centralization of authority over large regions because it is felt that what is known in one place is applicable everywhere. Bureaucratic mandates can be designed rationally, given tractable models of reality. Mandates need not be modified yearly, for the mechanistic relationships of the systems being managed remain stable. Bureaucratization and ecological simplification are coevolutionary in an unfortunate way.

And yet, stock-exploitive development is an apparent success thus far. Through the use of stock resources, we seem to have freed ourselves from the immediate requirements of working with the complexities of specific ecosystems. Western science, stock resources, and global organization have given most individuals access to a greater diversity of goods and opportunities, in spite of species extinction. Our concern with biological diversity is literally hypothetical, moral, and aesthetic. To most people, the probability of reduced material welfare from species loss is less than the likelihood that technologies will evolve to make genetic resources materially less important. Moral and aesthetic arguments typically outweigh the utilitarian. Extapolating the past, the optimists see a rosy future. Simon and Wildavsky (1984) sum up this optimistic position noting, "If genetic extinction doomed mankind, presumably it would have died a billion deaths by now!"

Economic Inquiry Under Clashing World Views: a Summary

The environmental critique of development stems from a system of beliefs that is incongruent with the dominant system that structures social organization and action today. The dominant belief system incorporates an atomistic and mechanistic view of a tractable world. These elements facilitate the belief that people can rationally organize themselves and intervene in the natural world to improve their well-being, and do so with 'fine tuning.' The environmental belief system, on the other hand, indicates cautionary guidelines for development and the rejection of the notion of precise control.

Belief systems are tested by both the unfolding of history and alternative ideas. The role and structure of the state in the West became increasingly rooted in Western science during the past four centuries after having been rooted in Christianity. The transition from a world where people felt obedience to authority to a world where people felt they could control their destiny was revolutionary. For centuries, changes in thought and social organization were self-validating and reinforcing. Such, however, is no longer the case. The evidence is clearly mixed. The existing world view and institutional system once again have defenders engaged in apologetics.

The contending system of beliefs also has many of its roots in Western science. But rather than being rooted in physics and Newton with an understanding of the world as a giant machine, the contenders are rooted in biology and Darwinism with an understanding of the world as a complex, evolving organism. This belief system is notably more humble in its expectations of how effectively people can control their destinies. What few suggestions emerge to guide development conflict with conventional economic wisdom and the existing system of rights to take action.

What should economists do in this time of stress, if not transition? The public debate encourages us to take one side or the other. Whichever side we choose, however, we have to make assumptions about new and broader aspects of reality that can be avoided by continuing to deal with the questions asked within our discipline. Both our participation and our use of critical assumptions will certainly lead to accusations of subjectivity and unscientific behavior by followers of one belief system or another. Our individual desire to advance within the community of economists encourages each of us to defend and use the neoclassical model or, perhaps preferably, to ignore the debate altogether.

One of the objectives of this essay has been to show that one cannot use the neoclassical economic model to explore the questions of biological diversity or other framings of the environmental critique without becoming an apologist for the dominant view. The neoclassical model itself is rooted in the atomistic-mechanistic view, while the concern with biological diversity is rooted in the contending holistic view. But the issues identified by the latter view cannot be explored with a model rooted in the former. A second objective has been to show that economists can work with the contending world view and its general methodological approach. Using ecological-evolutionary models to understand the broad picture of how people relate to their ecological system does not deny the usefulness of the neoclassical model for understanding exchange.

Economists as well as practical people with some of the reins of power might object that the coevolutionary paradigm doesn't answer their questions. This is true, for world views and evidence, questions and answers, and social organization and possible responses are all bundled. The increasing social dissatisfaction stemming from the incongruities between expectations generated by the dominant view and outcomes in reality, however, provides hope for a new template and an alternative grouping with respect to how we relate to our environment.

NOTES

1. For an excellent summary of the economic literature, see Brown, 1985.

2. I am not arguing that there are not issues of efficiency concerning biological diversity. Efficiency issues are still important but cannot be treated independently of the distributive issues. Bromley (1985) develops the argument that much of the distrust of environmental and resource economic analysis stems from our presumption that we are dealing with efficiency problems alone.

3. Numerous enquirers have produced quite a literature on the subject. Boulding (1978, 1981, and 1985) is pursuing development questions in the context of ecological and evolutionary thought applied to both social and natural systems. Institutional economists have long thought in evolutionary terms; the best defense of their position has been developed by a Marxist historian (Thompson, 1978). The recent interest in epistemology within economics is clearly tied to our failure to predict and prescribe (Blaug, 1980; Hahn and Hollis, 1979; Hicks, 1979; Hutchison, 1977; Latsis, 1976; and the reprinting of von Mises, 1981). Philosophers and historians of science have produced an exciting literature (Berman, 1981; Churchman, 1979; Feyerabend, 1974 and 1978; Merchant, 1980; Toulmin, 1982; Ulrich, 1983; Unger, 1975; and Wynne, 1982). Ruckelshaus (1983) vents his perplexity as an environmental administrator. For additional references, see Norgaard (1985b).

4. Georgescu-Roegen (1971) bridged the gap, albeit imperfectly, between economics and thermodynamics but was unable to convince economists of the significance of the second law. Indeed, more

controversy than enlightenment ensued and the bridge is rarely traversed. For a recent exchange, see Daly (1986), Burness and Cummings (1986), and Norgaard (1986a).

REFERENCES

Arrow, K.J., and A.C. Fisher. 1974. Environmental Preservation, Uncertainty, and Irreversibility. *Quarterly Journal of Economics*, 88(2):312-319.

Baker, H.G., and P.D. Hurd. 1968. Intrafloral Ecology. *Annual Review of Entomology*, 13:385-414.

Berman, M. 1981. *The Reenchantment of the World*. Ithaca: Cornell University Press.

Blaug, M. 1980. *The Methodology of Economics*. Cambridge: Cambridge University Press.

Boserup, E. 1965. *The Conditions of Agricultural Growth: The Economics of Agrarian Change under Population Pressure*. Chicago: Aldine.

Boserup, E. 1981. *Population and Technological Change: A Study of Long Term Trends*. Chicago: University of Chicago Press.

Boulding, K.E. 1978. *Ecodynamics: A New Theory of Societal Evolution*. Beverly Hills, CA: Sage Publications.

Boulding, K.E. 1981. *Evolutionary Economics*. Beverly Hills, CA: Sage Publications.

Boulding, K.E. 1985. *The World as a Total System*. Beverly Hills, CA: Sage Publications.

Bromley, D.W. 1985. Resource and Environmental Economics: Knowledge, Discipline and Problems. Paper presented at the Annual Meetings of the American Agricultural Economics Association. Ames, Iowa. August.

Brown, G. Jr. 1985. Valuation of Genetic Resources. Paper presented for the Workshop on Conservation of Genetic Resources. Lake Wilderness, Washington. June 12-16.

Burness, S., and R. Cummings. 1986. Reply (to Daly). *Land Economics*, 62(3). August.

Churchman, C.W. 1979. *The Systems Approach and Its Enemies*. New York: Basic Books.

Daly, H.E. 1986. A Comment on Burness, et al., Thermodynamics and Economic Concepts as Related to Resource-Use Policies. *Land Economics*, 62(3) forthcoming.

Ehrlich, P.R., and P.H. Raven. 1964. Butterflies and Plants, A Study of Coevolution. *Evolution*, 18:586-608.

Feyerabend, P. 1974. *Against Method*. London: New Left Books.

Feyerabend, P. 1978. *Science in a Free Society*. London: New Left Books.

Fisher, A.C., J.V. Krutilla, and C.J. Cicchetti. 1972. The Economics of Environmental Preservation: A Theoretical and Empirical Analysis. *American Economic Review*, 62(4):129-144.

Geertz, C. 1963. *Agricultural Involution: The Process of Ecological Change in Indonesia*. Berkeley: University of California Press.

Georgescu-Roegen, N. 1971. *The Entropy Law and the Economic Process*. Cambridge, MA: Harvard University Press.

Hahn, F., and M. Hollis (eds). 1979. *Philosophy and Economic Theory*. Oxford: Oxford University Press.

Harris, M. 1979. *Cultural Materialism: The Struggle for a Science of Culture*. New York: Random House.

Hicks, J. 1979. *Causality in Economics*. New York: Basic Books.

Hutchison, T.W. 1977. *Knowledge and Ignorance in Economics*. Chicago: University of Chicago Press.

Latsis, S. (ed). 1976. *Method and Appraisal in Economics*. Cambridge: Cambridge University Press.

Lipsey, R., and K. Lancaster. 1956. The General Theory of the Second Best. *Review of Economic Studies*, 24:11-32.

Merchant, C. 1980. *The Death of Nature*. San Francisco: Harper and Row.

Mittelhammer, R.C., S.C. Matulich, and D. Bushaw. 1981. On Implicit Forms of Multiproduct-Multifactor Production Functions. *American Journal of Agricultural Economics*. February, pp. 164-68.

Netting, R. McC. 1977. *Cultural Ecology*. Menlo Park: Cummings.

Norgaard, R.B. 1981. Sociosystem and Ecosystem Coevolution in the Amazon. *Journal of Environmental Economics and Management*, 8(3):238-254.

Norgaard, R.B. 1984a. Coevolutionary Agricultural Development. *Economic Development and Cultural Change*, 32(3):525-546.

Norgaard, R.B. 1984b. Coevolutionary Development Potential. *Land Economics*, 60(2):160-173.

Norgaard, R.B. 1985a. The Bureaucratic Jungle: 'Ordem e Progresso' in the Brazilian Amazon.

Norgaard, R.B. 1985b. Bureaucracy, Systems Management, and the Mythology of Science. Giannini Foundation Working Paper No. 297.

Norgaard, R.B. 1985c. Environmental Economics: An Evolutionary Critique and a Plea for Pluralism. *Journal of Environmental Economics and Management*. December.

Norgaard, R.B. 1986a. Entropy, Economics, and Economists. *Land Economics*, 62(3). August.

Norgaard, R.B., and J.A. Dixon. 1986b. Pluralistic Project Design: An Argument for Combining Economic and Coevolutionary Methodologies. *Policy Sciences*, Forthcoming.

Popper, K.R. 1959. *The Logic of Scientific Discovery*. New York: Basic Books. (Originally published in German in 1934).

Rambo, T.A. 1983. Conceptual Approaches to Human Ecology. Research Report 14. Honolulu: East-West Environment and Policy Institute.

Rappaport, R.A. 1968. *Pigs for the Ancestors: Ritual in the Ecology of a New Guinea People*. New Haven: Yale University Press.

Ruckelshaus, W.D. 1983. Science, Risk, and Public Policy. *Science*, 221:1026-1028.

Scriven, M. 1959. Explanation and Prediction in Evolutionary Theory. *Science*, 130(3374):477-482.

Simon, J.L. 1977. *The Economics of Population Growth*. Princeton: Princeton University Press.

Simon, J.L., and A. Wildavsky. 1984. On Species Loss, The Absence of Data, and Risks to Humanity. In: *The Resourceful Earth: A Response to Global 2000*, J.L. Simon and H. Kahn (eds). Oxford: Blackwell.

Thompson, E.P. 1978. *The Poverty of Theory and Other Essays*. New York: Monthly Review Press.

Toulmin, S. 1982. *The Return to Cosmology: Postmodern Science and the Theology of Nature*. Berkeley: University of California Press.

Ulrich, W. 1983. *Critical Heuristics of Social Planning: A New Approach to Practical Philosophy*. Bern, Switzerland: Paul Haupt Berne.

Unger, R.M. 1975. *Knowledge and Politics*. New York: The Free Press.

von Mises, L. 1981. *Epistemological Problems of Economics*. New York: New York University Press. (First published in German in 1933).

Wilkinson, R.G. 1973. *Poverty and Progress: An Ecological Perspective on Economic Development*. New York: Praeger.

Wynne, B. 1982. *Rationality and Ritual: The Windscale Inquiry and Nuclear Decisions in Britain*. Bucks, England: British Society for the History of Science.

Part III
Case Studies

9/ Evolutionary Conservation Project Planning and Implementation: NARMA in the Dominican Republic

Gary S. Kemph
Abel Hernandez

The Dominican Republic faces a devastating natural resources management problem. Small hillside farmers have destroyed natural perennial groundcover by planting short-cycle crops on slopes which often surpass 100 percent. Attempting to subsist in harsh economic circumstances, they have little alternative but to farm fragile land in an erosive manner. The Dominican government, with assistance from the U.S. Agency for International Development, launched the Natural Resources Management (NARMA) project to identify ecologically sustainable and economically feasible strategies for utilizing the country's resources. Gary Kemph and Abel Hernandez provide a step-by-step account of NARMA's accomplishments and those of preceding projects. Through careful planning and intelligent implementation, NARMA's philosophy, "conservation is production," is being put into practice.

Introduction

The Dominican Republic (DR) is a Caribbean island country which is about 80 percent hilly and mountainous, with elevations from below sea level to over 3000 meters. It was considered 100 percent forested at the turn of the century, a figure which fell to 69 percent in 1946 and then plummeted to 16 percent by 1980.

The DR is now beginning to come to grips with its major natural resource problem: the small hillside farmers who have destroyed natural perennial groundcover and replaced it with short cycle crops on slopes which often surpass 100 percent. The Natural Resources Management (NARMA) project, which began field implementation in mid-1983, had its direct antecedents in the Comprehensive Resource Inventory and Evaluation System (CRIES, known locally as SIEDRA) project of the U.S. Agency for International Development (USAID), the U.S. Department of Agriculture (USDA), and Michigan State University (MSU), which began resource database development in the DR in 1977. One of the early outputs of CRIES was estimates of nationwide erosion rates of 300-1200 tons per hectare per year, which, considering the shallow nature of most of the country's soils, indicate that the DR has approximately 20 years to establish an effective natural resources management program or face human misery of catastrophic proportions.

These startling estimates were confirmed and brought home to the Dominican government (GODR) and USAID decisionmakers during the devastating hurricanes David and Frederick, which hit the DR a week apart in late 1979. USAID's Washington office requested that the DR develop a Country Environmental Profile (CEP) to document natural resource problems, many of which were greatly exacerbated by the hurricanes, and to set tentative priorities before starting project intervention. The CEP was carried out by representatives of about 25 DR public and private sector entities, guided by a team of consultants put together by JRB Associates, and headed by Dr. Gary Hartshorn of the Tropical Science Center in Costa Rica. The enthusiasm and interest generated by the CEP development process, together with the exceptional readability of the document itself, were instrumental in getting NARMA on the drawing boards in 1980 and subsequently has led to additional natural resource-related projects, funded by USAID and GODR, totalling nearly 50 million dollars.

The purpose of this paper is to discuss the major philosophical and conceptual approach which went into the planning of NARMA and has guided its implementation, and to discuss some of the more important institutional, human, and technical problems which have arisen during the project's planning and implementation. First is a section covering the natural resources management philosophy which guided program and project design. Then follows a description of the project components. Next is a discussion of significant implementation problems and successes, followed by a section on some of the lessons learned—lessons which might apply to conservation and natural resource project development in other countries. The final section acts as a small crystal ball of what might be ahead for NARMA.

Program and Project Design Philosophy

The overall conclusion derived from the CEP, based heavily on the soils-climate mapping and corresponding erosion data estimates made under CRIES-SIEDRA, was that the DR only has about 20 years to get an effective nationwide natural resources management program underway. Because of this need for a long term commitment by GODR and USAID, a systematic, problem-oriented and therefore interdisciplinary approach was taken in putting together a portfolio of natural resource projects. The watershed was decided on as the basic management unit because the project is working with biophysical systems whose erosion-sedimentation components are naturally delimited by watershed boundaries. In the DR, each of the four stages of a given watershed (above dam, dam, irrigation canals, on-farm use) is legally in the hands of one or more GODR agencies. Since nearly all of these agencies have long histories of autonomous (i.e., non-cooperative) decision-making, it was decided to put each separate project in the hands of the individual agency with the clearest legal mandate to manage each watershed stage. Basic concepts of "management" and "ecosystems" were explicitly defined and incorporated in program development. A key financial control strategy, learned from USAID results with previous projects, was to put check-writing responsibility directly in the hands of the principal implementor rather than higher up in the bureaucratic hierarchy. Hoping for money to trickle down from "higher up" to the intended implementors before it could be siphoned off to solve endless daily brushfire problems has often proved futile.

Within this overall program portfolio development philosophy, NARMA was the first project to become operational. Its basic premise is that conservation in the DR hill country ("hills" to over 10,000 ft) is a profitmaking activity now, if it is designed and implemented properly (and assuming that it rains a little bit!). Scattered conservation research had shown that yields could often be doubled within a single crop cycle simply through construction of hillside ditches and with no additional production inputs, the increase being due primarily to improved plant water availability. One of the key elements of project planning philosophy was the belief that since small hillside farmers were the principal cause of the erosion/sedimentation problem, they could and should be the primary channel for solving the problem, directly on their own farms. This belief was based on the feeling that farmers would adopt fairly quickly new production practices which would enhance their net income in the short term and at the same time reduce erosion and downstream sedimentation. It was also based on the historical fact that the major theoretical alternative, mountain farmer resettlement to the lowlands, had never been very successful in other countries and that the GODR agrarian reform institute had never demonstrated a capability to handle large resettlement efforts.

Another decision made early during project development was the need to work both from the "top down" and from the "bottom up." Previous Dominican projects which had emphasized either approach exclusively had not been able to institutionalize themselves permanently. NARMA's approach was to initiate work first at the field level in order to demonstrate its ability to control erosion/sedimentation, then quickly to begin educating top decisionmakers as to the need for legal and policy changes to support NARMA-type activities nationwide.

Within the milieu of techno-politico-socioeconomic factors which affect natural resource problems, an attempt was made to concentrate project resources only on those believed to be most critical in affecting erosion and sedimentation. It is worth pointing out that the so-called integrated rural development (IRD) approach was not used in NARMA, simply because it was felt that rural development is more properly viewed as a long-term sector goal rather than a project objective. The thinking was that twenty years hence it will not matter how many schools and medical clinics were built in the name of IRD because everyone will have had to abandon them and move to New York City (currently the "DR's second largest city," with over a half million emigrants), if their means to make a living has washed into the Caribbean Sea. In other words, conservation was viewed as priority number one in the long-term push for rural development.

Another important element of project design was the question of proper, realistic local participation in the project. Here is where the "paratechnician" concept came into play, as did the idea of a formal forum for GODR technical staff and local community leaders to get together periodically and discuss project progress, problems, and future plans. The feeling was that without this counter-balanced forum either the GODR might autonomously isolate itself from local community "felt" needs, or the well-meaning local community leaders might try to use project funds to solve their many day-to-day non-conservation-related problems at the expense of losing the soil base and thus their very livelihood over the longer haul.

During project development it was deemed critical for the GODR to start in one single watershed and demonstrate its ability to organize and integrate the numerous project activities to solve erosion problems in that area before being permitted to spread its personnel and equipment resources to additional watersheds during the project's five-year life.

A final key element of NARMA project design was the use of rudimentary USDA-Soil Conservation Service-type conservation plans as the technical spearhead among the hillside farmers. These were linked to a financial incentives program to assure both initial plan implementation and subsequent maintenance within acceptable technical limits. An evolutionary approach was attempted, starting with the farmer's current land use (erosive short cycle crops and overgrazed forage plants) and management capability, and moving toward gradually longer cycle plants and improved management. This was done in consideration of the often overlooked fact that any technically sound conservation approach (such as replacing shortcycle crops with 20-year-rotation pine trees) which does not permit the farmers to make a living during its implementation cannot possibly work and that the GODR cannot provide that living through subsidies nationwide. The feeling about the incentives was that they should be a one-shot proposition to encourage farmer participation in what quickly would be seen as a profitmaking endeavor (if it rained!) which would become self-financing, rather than a continuous fiscal burden. For the GODR technicians, the primary job performance incentive was to be "short course" and graduate school training both within and outside the DR.

A significant restriction which was placed on the NARMA project and which prevents its being a conceptually complete project is that of its limited emphasis on the forestry subsector. This limitation was due to a 1967 logging ban which made it illegal for farmers to cut trees, whether they had planted them themselves or whether they were part of the natural forest. However, NARMA did plan forestry legislation studies which were intended to lead to changes in the logging ban and open the door for commercial forestry. NARMA also included small agroforestry training and critical area reforestation activities in the hope that, if the logging ban were lifted, these activities could be expanded to more comprehensive forest management activities.

Narma Project Description

NARMA was divided into two components. First was the institutional strengthening component, designed to develop the institutional support channels and procedures base in order to permit the GODR to avoid its 20-year appointment with ecological and socioeconomic suicide. Second was the soil and water conservation component, designed to provide hands-on field experience in several critical watersheds for GODR technicians and local community conservationists during the institutional strengthening process. History has shown that institutional strengthening without relevant field experience can lead to an "ivory tower" disjuncture between a capital city administrative headquarters and its field offices. Conversely, soil and water conservation in a few watersheds without backward linkages to a gradually strengthened institutional support apparatus can lead to the creation of a few green oasis islands in the midst of an everdeepening Dominican grand canyon.

NARMA is composed of 16 distinct but integrated activities involving over a dozen Dominican governmental and private sector entities, and has major technical assistance contracts with five contractors including The Ohio State University, MSU, The University of Kentucky, USDA Office of International Cooperation and Development (OICD), and Teledyne Corporation. The institutional strengthening component has 11 different activities (Table 9-1), designed to support and strengthen NARMA's second component, soil and water conservation, which involves five activities in two watersheds (Table 9-2).

All of these field activities are coordinated by a local field office director who interfaces directly with community leaders through what is referred to as a Watershed Development Committee (WDC). Joint check-signing responsibilities and monthly formal meetings as well as virtually continuous informal communication are shared with local community leaders through this forum.

Total funding for NARMA's five-year life is $21.2 million (US loan and grant, plus GODR counterpart funds), of which about one-third is for institutional strengthening and two-thirds for soil and water conservation.

Project Implementation Problems

During its short life of less than three years, NARMA has had to overcome several difficult institutional, human, and technical problems in achieving its current level of success in implementation.

Institutional Problems

Project implementation was delayed for about a year after the loan agreement was signed because of presidential election politics. Under the Dominican version of the "spoils system," attempts were made by GODR officials to use NARMA resources (vehicles, jobs, and construction and equipment acquisition contracts) to pay off non-project-related campaign promises. The Project Director, a man who had been in government service for over 30 years under the dictator Trujillo and several democratically elected presidents, was politically adroit enough to fend off these attempts at diversion of project resources, but the project could not avoid the loss of an additional year to field implementation. Once begun in

Table 9-1. Institutional Strengthening Activities

Activity	Major Outputs
Information Development:	
Cartography	National aerial photography, watershed thematic mapping, computerized graphical analysis, base map standardization
Monitoring	Soil erosion and water quality monitoring
Zonification	Crosstabs of plant species by ecological units, economic analysis (benefit-cost and linear programming), erosion-sedimentation simulation modelling
Farmer Associations	Studies of farmer and community leader capabilities and attitudes
Marketing	Studies of land use change impacts on local major input and product markets
Planning and Strategy Development:	Four watershed management plans; national strategies for natural resources, forestry, environmental education, and training
Agroforestry:	Training (subsequently expanded to include pre-feasibility studies for two areas to be developed under new forestry project)
Road Construction:	Workshops on conservation engineering
Legislation:	Law cataloging, analysis, and recommendations for improvement
Environmental Education:	Multi-targeted mass media, shortcourse and farmer meeting consciousness-raising; 11 regional conservation demonstration areas
Interagency Coordination:	Seminars, evaluations, office computerization

Table 9-2. Soil and Water Conservation Activities

Activity	Major Outputs
Farm Conservation:	3000 conservation farm plans (prerequisite for incentives participation) implemented on 10,000 hectares
Incentives Package (to support Farm Conservation activity):	Production credit, conservation credit with up to 50 percent subsidy, scholarships to children of para-technicians who most actively support NARMA, limited tree seedlings, small tools
Farming Systems Research:	On-farm research on income increasing/erosion reducing production techniques (primarily reduced and no-tillage farming, hay production for tethered animals, tree cropping)
Critical Area Reforestation:	800 hectare reforestation to protect infrastructure
Soil Survey:	Classification and use interpretation to support farm/watershed planning

early 1983, however, the institutional strengthening activities moved ahead quickly, primarily through bringing in large amounts of short-term technical assistance to overcome the inertia exacerbated by the political campaign. After further election-related delays, fieldwork was initiated about six months later in the first watershed.

Unfortunately, the DR economic situation became extremely precarious, as it did in much of the rest of Latin America, at about the same time that project implementation was begun, and GODR counterpart funds, a prerequisite to USAID disbursement of project funds, were provided at much lower levels than specified in the loan agreement. Also, it was a very dry year (600 mm of rainfall in an area with a 1500 mm average) in the first watershed, so field farming systems research (FSR) results were not representative of those expected over the longer term. This had a doubly negative impact on farmers because of the on-farm, face-to-face approach of FSR. Vehicle, personnel, and equipment acquisition, almost always frustratingly slow under competitive-bidding procedures mandated by the U.S. law, were even slower than normal. Initially, less equipment and fewer vehicles were purchased than planned in order not to give an ostentatious look to

NARMA at a time when the GODR was having to institute emergency fiscal measures just to keep afloat. Government employees, who already had notably low salaries in comparison to their private sector counterparts, were devastated by a forced 10-30 percent pay cut as part of these measures.

A problem which had NARMA stalled for several months was that of eligibility of potential project clients for project-approved credit from the GODR Agricultural Bank (BAGRICOLA). Of the first 25 farm conservation plans submitted to the bank, 20 were rejected because the farmers had bad debts with the bank. During the ensuing discussions between NARMA and BAGRICOLA functionaries, NARMA successfully argued that the large majority of the bad debts were due to natural phenomena (ie., drought) and not to malice by the farmers. Thus these people had to be dealt with since they were the major cause of the country's erosion/sedimentation problems and therefore were the intended NARMA target group. A modified qualification system was instituted by the bank which focussed on eliminating only those farmers who had been irresponsible in handling their debts, not those on whom mother nature had failed to smile satisfactorily.

Another problem with which NARMA has had to deal has been turnover of key administrative personnel, both on the GODR and on the U.S. side. Since the NARMA project development was conceptualized in 1980, NARMA has been directed by four different Secretaries of Agriculture and four different Undersecretaries of Natural Resources, and the GODR has had three different presidents. On the U.S. side, the USAID Mission has had two Directors and three different Agricultural Division Chiefs. In addition, President Reagan replaced President Carter. President Reagan's increasing emphasis on private sector involvement in development, as reflected in the program strategy developed under the new Mission Director in the DR, combined with the Director's personal emphasis on immediate impact projects, has strongly influenced NARMA's evolution. This personnel turnover, with each new administrator arriving with his own distinct background, ideas, and biases, has caused NARMA implementors to spend significant amounts of time not on improving project implementation but on informing these changing administrators of NARMA's conceptual and operational elements. On the positive side, this kind of interaction is, of course, an important and necessary, if difficult, element of the conservation education process.

Human Problems

GODR-community interfacing at the watershed level was problematical in the beginning as each side felt the other out on how they were to interact symbiotically. Local community leaders initially were not very active in project implementation because they were not permitted to co-sign checks as originally planned. After this situation was corrected, the local Watershed Development Committee became an important watchdog over project resource use.

Technical Problems

The only significant technical problem encountered so far is lack of Spanish language capability on the part of many of the more than 100 contractors who have provided technical assistance under NARMA. The result of this communications gap is a significant reduction in the effectiveness of the assistance. At a time when U.S. technical assistance costs have soared to $180,000 per person/year while an experienced GODR technician makes less than $4000 per year, the effectiveness of assistance is under close scrutiny both by GODR and USAID officials. It is a shame that so much high quality technical work is effectively lost due to the inability of U.S. contractors to communicate in the language of those they are hired to help.

A less important technical problem was that of the maintenance of newly constructed hillside ditches before vegetative barriers or other protective groundcover could be established. Several farmers in a small community failed to heed technician admonitions to clean out the sediment which had accumulated in their new ditches after a small thundershower at the onset of the rainy season. A few days later, heavy rains fell on the community and many ditches quickly filled with additional sediment, breaking at weak points along their lower slopes and causing gullies to be formed in the fields. Since that episode, farmers have been very attentive to maintenance needs.

Project Implementation Successes

Institutional Successes

In spite of these problems, NARMA was able to attain nearly 80 percent of its planned first-year outputs with only about 30 percent of the funding planned for. To date, with nearly 60 percent of its planned life behind it, the project cumulatively has achieved about 50 percent of its overall objectives with something less than 40 percent of its planned financial support. This is indicative of the high level of leadership in key positions in the NARMA management structure, leadership which was able to maintain its optimism and employee morale through extremely difficult financial and political times.

Human Successes

Paratechnicians, after initial euphoric bursts through the mountain road system on their new project-provided motorcycles, settled down to specialize in implementation assistance, leaving the farm planning in the hands of the SCS technicians, rather than helping with both as originally planned. This kind of specialization of labor is felt to be healthy, at least for the time being.

The Watershed Development Committee is now working according to original plans as a forum for problem-solving interaction between GODR technicians and local community leaders. Together they constitute a healthy, if not always happy, check-and-balance system on project resource use at the field level.

There is also very encouraging, if preliminary, evidence of project success in convincing hillside farmers to adopt recommended conservation practices. A recent survey of hillside farmers in the project area indicated that 97 percent of them, whether they were actually participating in project activities or not, considered NARMA to be very important to their communities. Many farmers, after seeing their neighbors' success under NARMA, have applied conservation practices themselves without waiting for assistance with farm planning or for credit.

Technical Successes

Preliminary data from the erosion monitoring site indicates that yields can be more than doubled and erosion cut by 90 percent in one crop cycle in comparison with traditional practices, if recommended conservation practices are properly applied and maintained. Net income can be increased significantly in the short run and future income is protected under these circumstances. Proof of the validity of these data would appear to be in the high acceptance rate among farmers of NARMA recommendations.

One final comment on NARMA problems and successes is that from the beginning of project design one of the major questions has been, "Is NARMA too big to be manageable?" The dilemma involved in determining project size is that while the scope and magnitude of the project are increased linearly, project management problems seem to increase at a geometric rate. For each activity added to an integrated project such as NARMA, not only does a vertical linkage have to be established in the chain-of-command, but also horizontal linkages must be established among that activity and each of the other related project activities. If the project is kept small enough to assure manageability, yet turns out to have been too small to create the critical mass necessary to build a permanent commitment to conservation, what have we accomplished? On the other hand, if the project is made large enough to have some assurance that a critical mass can in fact be created yet turns out to have been too unmanageable to have been effective (or too expensive to have been replicated nationwide), then what have we accomplished? The jury is still out on this; it is likely to be debated for years to come.

Generalizable Lessons

Though NARMA is barely halfway through its planned five-year life, a number of lessons have been learned related to the institutional, human, and technical aspects of the project which may have some applicability to other countries.

Institutional Lessons

Probably the most important lesson learned to date in the USAID-GODR portfolio development has been the critical need to put the project financial control directly in the hands of the principal implementing entity. Putting funds at a higher level in the bureaucracy and hoping for them to trickle down to the implementors in the right quantity and with the right timing is not a workable idea during difficult economic circumstances, as the tendency is for the higher level bureaucrats to try to use project funds to solve immediate, non-project-related problems with whatever funds they can get their hands on. Often this is with the sincere intention of reimbursing the funds "just as soon as I get the next disbursement from the national budget office," but those funds are always smaller and later than expected.

A corollary to the first lesson learned is that the local community must be given a voice in project development in order to provide a counterbalancing force against possible government insensitivity to local needs. While local leaders do not necessarily know much about how to deal with conservation problems—which is the proper role of government technicians—and therefore cannot be expected to play a major role in technical planning, they still should be consulted regularly during project planning and given a direct role in control of project implementation.

Next is the lesson that no matter how overwhelming the overall problem to be dealt with and how much political pressure there may be to attack it all at once, starting small geographically with a relatively comprehensive set of activities is much more effective than a geographically dispersed set of more superficial activities. That the tallest mountain is climbed one step at a time is a very relevant analogy here, as is the maxim that you must learn to crawl before you walk, and to do both before you run.

Next is the importance of a resident project advisor who can provide continuity both in the local government agency, as well as with USAID, through the inevitable personnel turnovers that take place during project development and implementation. If there is no one there with an "institutional memory," successive local and USAID bureaucratic leaders (and personnel at *all* levels) may fail to grasp the philosophy, structure, and functions of the project, and they may divert funds to what they see as more pressing problems. This is directly related to the lesson learned pointed out above: the faster the personnel turnover rate, the more critical is the need for resident advisor follow-through.

Human Lessons

The use of paratechnicians allows implementation over a larger area at a lower cost and a faster rate than the use of technicians alone. These paratechnicians also are permanent members of their communities and will be a permanent project benefit lasting well beyond the five-year life of the project. If used properly and realistically, they can bring quick project credibility to local communities and they will defend project interests during the early periods of doubt and uncertainty which are a part of any attempt to change farmers' attitudes and ways of life. They must be complemented with competent technicians to assure proper technology transfer to the farmers.

Another significant finding of NARMA is the importance of mutual reinforcement of project activities. NARMA is not a one-shot proposition for the farmer, relying solely on the paratechnicians to help them through the fears and doubts of conservation innovation. The paratechnician's daily face-to-face contacts with his neighbors are reinforced by periodic visits by soil conservation service, forest service, agricultural bank, environmental education, farming, and systems research technicians, as well as soil surveyors and project administrators and evaluators. This contact results in the farmer not having the lonely feeling of taking a giant leap of faith based only on one man's word, but rather having the feeling that "I wish my neighbors and I had heard about this project sooner from you guys!"

It is worth pointing out that this mutual reinforcement is also important for GODR technicians, particularly the younger ones, for many of the same reasons.

Another lesson learned is that it is important to keep project publicity and public information diffusion consistent with actual achievements. Many a project has let its publicity supercede its achievements, especially during the euphoria and optimism of the early start-up phase, to such an extent that public expectations have far exceeded the project's ability to produce desired results on a timely basis. This results in the project's never quite living up to expectations, no matter what the eventual achievements. This is not easy to gauge, but it is important to keep publicity and public information efforts more in line with "here is what we have done," rather than "here is what we hope to do."

A final lesson learned related to the human element is that of the need to understand the motivations of individuals and learn to mesh them for the overall benefit of the project. This encompasses all types: political, economic, egotistical, altruistic, and so on. For example, instead of simply criticizing politicians and high-level bureaucrats for attempting to divert project resources to non-conservation activities, efforts should be made to teach them that the best way to enhance their political aspirations is to help create and support a "successful project." This is extremely difficult, but unless the diversions are widespread it is usually a much more effective alternative than the complete stopping of project funding disbursements until they "undivert" the resources in question.

Technical Lessons

A very important lesson learned is that of the critical need of emphasizing to *everyone* (farmers, administrators, technicians, politicians) that, as the NARMA slogan says, "*Conservation is production.*" The typical preconceived notion about conservation work by everyone seems to be that conservation is an investment which must be made on faith in the belief that 100 years from now the country might be better off for it. With that uninformed attitude, it is no wonder that politicians and bureaucrats tend to underinvest in conservation work. NARMA and pre-NARMA field evidence, however, indicates that farmers can increase their net income substantially and at the same time significantly reduce erosion and downstream sedimentation if they will apply the simple, labor-intensive conservation practices recommended under NARMA. Government and private sector decisionmakers *must* understand this if they are to make informed decisions on financial resource allocations for the well-being of the country.

Another valuable lesson learned is that, if a rational, documented process is used to think through project design decisions, the project will be much easier to defend during implementation. Had the project not explicitly documented the criteria used for selecting NARMA's first and second watersheds and the activities to implement in them, it is likely that NARMA would have been reoriented both to other areas and to other "rural development" activities. This would have eliminated any possibility of attaining the 20-year goal of a national conservation program.

Finally, is important to distinguish between "integrated rural development" as a project objective and as a long-term program goal. In most developing countries, the milieu of multisectoral development problems is overwhelming. Yet, first aid must be given to those vital functions which form the basis for socio-economic survivability before more comprehensive treatment can be attempted through a long-term hospitalization. The very life blood of an agriculture-based economy is the country's soil and water base. If this base is not stabilized first, the local population will sooner or later have to abandon its other rural development benefits and head for the "city lights."

Future Prospects

NARMA is nearly midway through its five-year project life. It has developed as planned, with few modifications. The few modifications which have taken place have mostly been due to GODR ability to implement more quickly in the second watershed and at lower cost than was originally anticipated. If all continues to go well through the 1986 presidential elections, the GODR is likely to want to develop a second phase of NARMA to cover additional critical watersheds. It is likely that such a second phase would serve to link more closely the existing NARMA, forestry management, and on-farm water management projects. It is also likely that a second phase would touch on additional aspects of natural resources management, such as range management, wildlife management, and fisheries resources, which were not considered as sufficiently high priority to include in NARMA when its development was begun nearly five years ago.

Aside from NARMA, both the on-farm water management and the new forestry projects can expect to be expanded if their implementation is successful. Ideally, due to the limited funds that USAID has for any given type of investment, other international financing agencies, such as World Bank and the Inter-American Development Bank, will come in where the GODR needs financial assistance and build on the solid foundations created by the multifaceted USAID-GODR natural resources management portfolio.

Postscript

In the months that have passed since this paper was originally presented, two major events have taken place which have significantly affected NARMA's continued evolution—the national presidential election campaign and NARMA's second formal evaluation. For a period of about eight months during the election campaign, GODR funds programmed for NARMA (and virtually all other internationally-funded projects) were diverted to "higher priorities." This, in turn, caused USAID to suspend its disbursements until the GODR made good on its project funding commitments. But since the government's coffers were drained during the election campaign, it has not been able to fulfill those commitments. It will now be left to the newly elected government officials to right the fiscal wrongs of their predecessors.

The second project evaluation concluded that, while a substantial human resource base had been created under NARMA, the project was focusing these resources too narrowly on anthropic (manmade, especially by small farmers in this case) erosion while virtually ignoring significant levels of geologic (natural) erosion, and was not emphasizing enough the non-erosion control-related benefits of natural resources development. The evaluators recommended a broader focus on all major erosion/sedimentation sources regardless of farm size, and increased emphasis on improving use of underutilized resources on a sustained yield basis. The evaluation also recommended streamlining of the administrative system in order to better utilize the human resource base, primarily through divestiture of most field implementation activities to the private sector. Whether or not the newly elected government officials will respond to these recommendations will be critical to regaining and maintaining the hard-earned momentum created during the first three years of NARMA implementation.

NOTE

There are a number of other extremely important factors influencing project planning and implementation which are specific to individual countries and projects which were considered too sensitive and controversial to explore in this paper. Among these factors are: (1) personalities, (2) family connections, (3) pervasive corruption, (4) political ideologies, and (5) epidemic incompetence. Their manifestations are widespread, and their dynamic management is a sina qua non to successful project planning and implementation.

Selected NARMA-Related Publications

1985

La Participacion de la AID en el Desarrollo Conservacionista Desde la Epoca de Trujillo. USAID. Invited paper presented at "Seminario Nacional—Conservacion de Suelos y Aguas," Santo Domingo.

Potential for Livestock Production in the Sierra de Baoruco, Dominican Republic. USAID.
Potential for Range and Pasture Development in the Western Dominican Republic. (in process). USAID.
AID's Involvement in Natural Resources Management in the Dominican Republic. Draft submitted to USAID *Front Lines*.
The NARMA Project in the Dominican Republic. Contributed paper presented at annual meeting, Soil Conservation Society of America.
Plan de Manejo de la Cuenca del Rio del Medio. MARENA.

<u>1984</u>

Estrategia Nacional de Manejo de los Recursos Naturales. MARENA. (draft)
Plan de Manejo de la Cuenca del Rio Nizao. MARENA.
On-Farm Water Management. USAID, Project Identification Document.
Estimacion de Produccion Forrajera. USAID.
Forestry Management. USAID, Project Paper.
Forestry Resources Management. USAID, Project Identification Document.
Plan de Manejo de la Cuenca del Rio Las Cuevas. MARENA.

<u>1983</u>

Plan Nacional de Ordenamiento Forestal. MARENA.
El Credito Conservacionista. MARENA.
Management Recommendations for the Forest Fire Area, Valle Nuevo. USAID.
Personal Computer Use in Professional Activities. USAID.
Zonificacion Agrosilvipastoril. MARENA.
Proposal for Range/Pasture Studies-MARENA, Ocoa. MARENA.

<u>1982</u>

Plan de Manejo de la Cuenca del Rio Ocoa. MARENA.
Mission Project Development Cycle Strategy. USAID.
Computing in Outer Mongolia. USAID.
Natural Resources Management Institutions in the Dominican Republic. Peace Corps orientations.
Outline for Converting an Agricultural Sector Assessment into an Agricultural Analysis. USAID.
Country Development Strategy Statement. USAID.

1981

Agricultural Sector Strategy. USAID.
Country Environmental Profile, Dominican Republic. JRB Associates, USAID.
Recommendations for Computerizing USAID. USAID.
Recommendaciones para la Computarizacion de MARENA. MARENA.
Manual de Procedimeientos Administrativos-MARENA. MARENA.
Plan Quinquenal-Fortalecimiento Institucional, MARENA. MARENA.
Plan Operacional-Fortalecimiento Institucional, MARENA. MARENA.
Natural Resources Management. USAID, Project Paper.

1980

Natural Resources Management. USAID, Project Identification Document.
An Agroeconomic Land Resource Assessment for Rice Production in the Central Region of the Dominican Republic. Michigan State University.
CRIES Resident End-of-Tour Report. In CRIES Lessons Learned. Johnson, J. and J. Putman. USDA-ERS.

1979

Project for the Rational Use of the CEA Land Resource Base. USAID.
CRIES Impacts on the Rural Poor. USAID.
Un Estudio Agroeconomico de la Produccion Arrocera en la Region Central (Propuesta). SEA-Depto. Inventario.
Metodologia para la Recoleccion de Datos Agroeconomicos Mediante Entrevistas Regionales. SEA-Depto. Inventario.
Confiabilidad de los Datos Agroeconomicos del Uso Actual de la Tierra. SEA-Depto. Inventario.

1978

The Comprehensive Resource Inventory and Evaluation System (CRIES) in the Dominican Republic. Proceedings of the First International Rangeland Congress.
Sugerencias de Modificaciones del Cuestionario de Analisis Sectorial. SEA-Depto. Inventario.
La Erosion de los Suelos en la Republica Dominicana. SEA-Depto. Inventario.
Enfoque General del Programa SIEDRA. SEA-Depto. Inventario.
Uso Potencial de la Tierra: Evaluacion del Recurso Suelo. Regional Central. SEA-Depto. Inventario.

10/ Environmental Management Education: A Model for Sustainable Natural Resources Development

Robert E. Roth

The primary objective of a conservation strategy for a developing country is to build the institutional frameworks needed to solve conservation problems and facilitate the sustainable development of renewable natural resources. A successful method, Robert Roth suggests, involves the strengthening of environmental education and information dissemination capabilities, with emphasis on public environmental management education and training programs as strategies for the establishment of sound management plans, developmental goals, and an environmental ethic. Field studies from the Dominican Republic and Barbados illustrate the model's success.

Introduction

Global concern about environmental problems, quality of human life, and the impacts of development led to the convening of the United Nations Conference on the Human Environment in Stockholm, Sweden, in June of 1972. Recommendation 96 of the Stockholm Conference called for the establishment of an international program in environmental education that would be interdisciplinary in approach and formal and non-formal in audience, encompassing all levels of education and directed toward the general public (UNESCO, 1976).

Reports of the tenth anniversary of the Stockholm conference also stressed the need for, and role of, environmental education in dealing with global concerns (UNESCO, 1982). Concurrently, the 1975 Belgrade International Workshop on Environmental Education (UNESCO, 1975) and the 1977 Intergovernmental Conference on Environmental Education, held in Tbilisi, Georgia, USSR, explicated the need for "thinking globally, but acting locally" (Stapp, 1982). A projected "Tbilisi +10" international conference, also to be held in the USSR, is expected to continue development of this theme.

In a separate though parallel set of activities, the U.S. Agency for International Development (USAID) initiated a Title XII program that was designed to assist U.S. colleges and universities in the development of faculty expertise to conduct education, research, and public service activities in developing countries, while at the same time improving the quality of education within U.S. institutions. Thus, the historic involvement of the United States with developing countries continued to be supported, but with a clearer recognition of the role of education in confronting the development problems within those countries.

Against this backdrop, the focus on resources, economics, and the abilities of developing countries to cope with escalating problems was increasing. Essential environmental resources of such countries are subjected to stresses of unprecedented magnitude and the health, nutrition, and general well-being of large portions of the population are directly dependent on the integrity and productivity of these resources. Governmental ability to manage resources effectively over time may be the most important prerequisite to the eradication of poverty, the fulfillment of basic human needs, obtaining a quality life and the ultimate achievement of sustained development.

While the natural resources of most developing countries are being rapidly depleted by general deforestation, habitat destruction, desertification, soil erosion, and the pressures of rapid population growth, the abilities of governmental agencies and non-governmental organizations to educate and inform the people about the effective management of natural resources is an important prerequisite to achieving a quality life (Stapp, 1982).

An Environmental Management Education Model

An evolving model for the strengthening of environmental education and information dissemination capabilities within developing countries, for the purpose of building needed institutional frameworks to deal with conservation problems and sustainable development of renewable resources, is presented in Figure 10-1. Examples from the Dominican Republic and Barbados are discussed, stressing public environmental management education and training programs as strategies for the establishment of sound management plans, developmental goals, and an environmental ethic. Further, evaluative approaches to determine program and workshop effectiveness, along with knowledge gain and attitude shift, are discussed.

Environmental Management Education Defined

Environmental management education is concerned with an individual's self-understanding, an understanding of the co-inhabitants of the Earth, and inter-relationships within and among each of these constellations of concern. A major goal is to encourage the individual to develop the ability to make thoughtful decisions which will create an environment that allows one to live a quality life. Specifically, environmental management education is concerned with developing a citizenry that is:

Figure 10-1. A Model for Environmental Management Education (Roth, 1973).

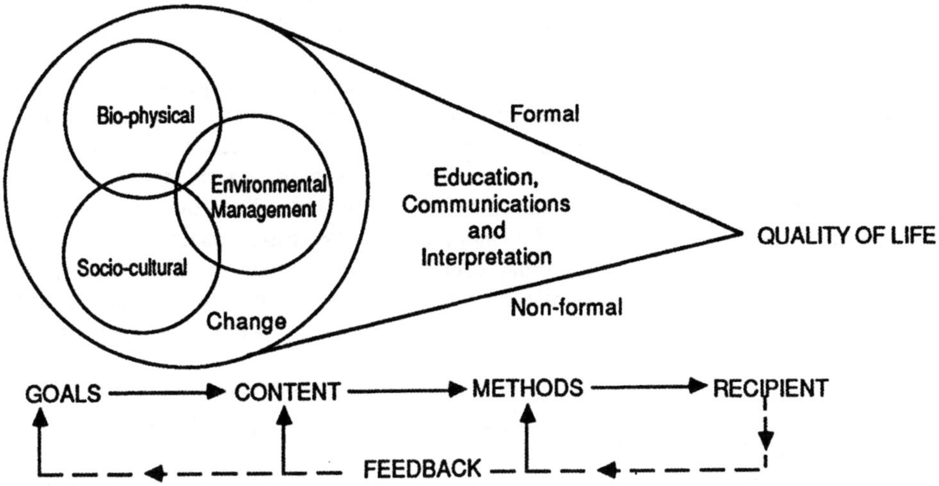

1. knowledgeable about the biophysical and sociocultural environments of which humankind is a part;
2. aware of environmental problems and management alternatives for solving those problems; and
3. motivated to act responsibly in developing diverse environments that are optimum for living a quality life.

(Roth, 1969)

From this definition, it can be seen that environmental management education is concerned with knowledge of the universe, society, and the individual, in that it not only attempts to provide the individual with an understanding of the environment but also views each individual as a potential creative being and encourages acceptance of the responsibility for decision-making.

Another characteristic of environmental management education is that it deals with attitudes—attitudes people hold about themselves, toward other individuals and groups of individuals, and toward their environment. These constellations of ideas greatly affect our level of living and quality of life.

Because environmental management education is not just ecology, resource-use, sociology, art appreciation, philosophy, or management, an interdisciplinary focus is required to embrace the natural sciences, humanities, social sciences, and technology for purposes of developing cognitive understanding, belief and attitude change, and providing motivation for behavioral change and effective action.

A first step towards an agreed-upon body of concepts appropriate for environmental management education was taken when a list of 112 concepts was produced (Roth, 1969). The concepts delineated represented a structure of environmental management concepts.

The list of 112 concepts was subsequently submitted to a panel of experts representing the various disciplines, organized according to topic, and arranged in the order of importance on the basis of a Q-sort analysis. A consensus was reached both as to placement in a major area and as to degree of importance (Bowman, 1972).

The concepts important to know in environmental management education were grouped into four categories: Biophysical, Socio-cultural, Environmental Management, and Change. Each cluster of concepts is viewed as existing on a continuum and the four areas are represented as spheres on the model (Figure 10-1). The four areas are considered to be interrelated. The conceptual core is applied through "Educational and Communication Processes" comprising a range from formal education to nonformal communication strategies. The major goal described on the right side of the model is "Quality of Life," which can also be interpreted as the individual's conception of achieving a workable environmental ethic.

The organization and validity of these environmental management education concepts was found to be appropriate for program development and curriculum organization (Bowman, 1972).

The proposed model has the advantage of being concise, graphic, and logical in its application. It provides an easily visualized guide to the process of program development in both formal and non-formal educational settings regardless of cultural and national context. The program developer is reminded that the identification of appropriate environmental management/education goals, objectives with a behaviorial or measurable orientation, and well-defined and implemented communications or teaching strategies are essential for achieving a "quality life." Feedback of both a formative and summative nature is used in relation to impact on the target audience. Through rigorous evaluation strategies involving pre- and post-testing of concepts and attitudes assessment of skills and performance, and the achievement of anticipated goals in documentable form, it will be possible to demonstrate achievement of intended goals in relation to the improvement of the "Quality of Life."

Townsend (1982) conducted an investigation into the underlying structure of the domain of environmental management education concepts. A refined list of 54 concepts drawn from the works mentioned above was submitted to a randomly selected panel of experts and practitioners in the field for a review of accuracy and validity for environmental management education. The underlying dimensions (factors) of the concepts studied were identified as: (1) Ecology: Interdependence and Living Things; (2) Culture: Interaction with Environmental Considerations; (3) Ethics: Humankind's Moral Responsibility for Environmental Considerations; (4) Natural Resources Management and Use; and (5) Population: Interactions with Environmental Conservation. While differences in perceptions of concept categories between this work and those proposed by Roth (1969) and Bowman (1972) exist, they can be explained by the general nature of the concepts which leaves them open to multiple categorization possibilities.

The series of studies described above was completed in the United States. Current research at The Ohio State University focuses on the applicability of findings in developing countries.

A Dominican Republic Example

The Dominican Republic's natural resource base is deteriorating at an alarming rate. As indicated in the Country Environmental Profile (Hartshorn et al., 1981), annual erosion rates in most of the nation's watersheds are estimated to average 300 metric tons per hectare. Since erosion rates of between 10 and 30 metric tons per hectare are normally considered excessive, the erosion rates in the Dominican Republic are little short of catastrophic.

Massive degradation of watersheds is occurring throughout the country. Every year, millions of tons of soil are washed away as hillside areas are denuded. The color of the rivers are now a bright brown, indicating increased sediment loads in the water. Due to the lack of hillside vegetation cover, the unusually heavy rainfall from 1979's two hurricanes dumping 21 inches of rain in seven days took on calamitous proportions causing major flooding throughout the country. Sedimentation is filling up the nation's reservoirs. The useful lives of multi-million dollar hydroelectric facilities have already been cut to less than half by siltation. In addition, siltation damage to hydroelectric facilities often results in lower-than-planned power output levels and frequent power outages (Hartshorn et al., 1981).

The hillside farmer is at the center of this problem. Often, the only land available to him is in hillside areas which are highly vulnerable to erosion. The agricultural practices the farmer uses are frequently the principal cause of the erosion which results in lower productivity, a major cause of poverty. The hillside farmers are trapped in a vicious cycle which, unless broken, will result in increased destruction and escalating suffering for the hillside poor.

Fortunately, the situation can still be reversed. The degradation of the country's watersheds can be brought under control before the point of irreversible environmental degradation is reached. Time is short, however. It is estimated that within 20 years, the landscape of the Dominican side of the island will resemble that of its neighbor, Haiti.

The Natural Resources Management Project (see chapter by Kemph and Hernandez, in this volume) will assist the Dominican Republic in building an institutional framework to deal with the natural resources conservation problem. This project will form part of a broader USAID strategy which aims to have in place, during the decade, the necessary institutional capacity and field experiences to confront effectively the country's natural resource problems.

A major activity under this component is the strengthening of the Dominican Republic environmental education program. Under this activity, the efforts to generate more public and target group awareness of the natural resource problem and ways to deal with it are being strengthened and expanded. Training workshops are being carried out to teach school teachers, local leaders, technicians, and small farmers to increase local participation in conservation activities. A viable approach to changing hillside farming behavior patterns which can be replicated in other critical watersheds is the goal. It is expected that the project inputs and the spread effects from project activities will cause sufficient numbers of hillside farmers to implement improved conservation practices in order that natural resource degradation can be arrested within a watershed, during the coming decade and in a cost-effective manner.

Objectives of the Environmental Management Education Project in the Dominican Republic include the following:

1. Development of a comprehensive national plan for environmental education.
2. Development and testing of alternative communication techniques to strengthen awareness of resource issues.
3. Training of teachers, leaders, technicians, and farmers in conservation concepts.

Specific inputs include:

1. Short courses for teachers, leaders, technicians, and farmers.
2. A total of 225 one-day workshops for farmers.
3. Purchasing of educational equipment, electrical generators, and buses and other vehicles.
4. Development of a training center at Jimenoa.
5. Providing three person-months of technical assistance.
6. Providing long-term training in environmental education and communications for four staff members of the Subsecretary for Natural Resources (SURENA) from the Ministry of Agriculture.

The Environmental Education component of the project utilizing the proposed model for Environmental Management Education is making significant progress both at the national and watershed levels. Posters, written bulletins, pamphlets, radio programs, T-shirts, bumper stickers, and a video tape of the project have been prepared for the mass media program. Curricula for targeting specific concepts to grades one through six have been designed, although this goes beyond the original project activity. A number of short courses are being designed with different target groups in mind. Construction of a training center at Jimenoa is nearing completion.

Preliminary evaluation of work completed to date reveals that the educational program appears to be the major stimulator of interest in conservation practices (Tinnermeier et al., 1984). Prior to the project, a study by the Dominican Office of Environmental Education revealed that only 40 percent of the campesinos (hillside farmers) used conservation practices. A recent survey indicated more than 80 percent of the campesinos in the target watersheds are now utilizing conservation practices. The program has been very active in organizing courses and in participating in workshops/courses organized by other groups such as the Junta de Desarrollo, a farmers' association in San Jose de Ocoa. Success can be attributed to: (a) use of existing associations and committees to mount courses with farmer groups in different areas; (b) trainers' knowledge of local people and ability to relate positively to their production as well as conservation concerns; (c) preexisting knowledge of conservation methods; (d) availability of transport and adequacy of materials; (e) willingness of personnel from other programs, including military units, to participate; and (f) support from the headquarters staff in Santo Domingo and knowledge of importance of the program.

Initial informal evaluation of farmers' responses to the training programs indicates that there is more interest in specific conservation training than in general exposure to the concepts of environmental protection. Participants are highly receptive to hands-on demonstrations like composting and reforestation. Preliminary evaluation of school students, on the other hand, reveals they are very responsive to more general concepts and to wildlife protection, but not as interested in agricultural conservation practices.

A further advantage of the training effort lies in the ability to relate concern for conservation with concern for production systems. If conservation techniques are treated and presented in isolation, farmers appear to be much less interested in their possible relevance to their situation than when practical exercises like composting or building terraces are utilized as educational activities.

A Barbadan Example

The Caribbean is a region with 15 island nations. Barbados is one of the countries of the Eastern Caribbean with a strong dedication to education and enlightened management of its natural resources. The development of educational approaches has moved from a tentative involvement with innovation stressing concerns like discovery learning, child-oriented instruction, and scientific literacy to a positive Caribbean-controlled thrust involving science and technological education for national development.

A variety of educational models are described by King (1979) as being useful in achieving educational and national development in the Caribbean. The motivation for curriculum development is derived from: (1) the march to independence and other forms of internal self-government sparked by a surge of nationalist feeling and dissatisfaction with colonialism; (2) the attempt to provide a type of education enriched both qualitatively and quantitatively to meet the new demands on society; (3) the need to train manpower, in keeping with the technological demands being made on the system; and (4) the necessity of developing a scientifically literate citizenry.

Emphasis of the Environmental Management Education approach utilized in Barbados was on science teachers in year one of the project, and social studies teachers in the second year. The workshop goal was to utilize the proposed model to portray concepts related to international resources and environmental management education, and to train faculty for international development work.

The project in year two consisted of developing, implementing and evaluating a workshop for secondary social studies teachers in Barbados. Social studies in Barbadian schools is a composite of geography, history, economics, and political science. The interdisciplinary nature of the curriculum lent itself well to providing opportunities to learn about the environment. Environmental education does not appear as a distinct subject in the schools of the island, but an integrated approach through the disciplines has been well accepted.

Coordination of the workshop was accomplished by a representative of the Caribbean Conservation Association, with the assistance of the Barbados Community College and the Ministries of Education, Agriculture, and Housing and Lands. Twenty-seven teachers attended three days of lectures, hands-on activities, development sessions and field trips. As a follow-up, each teacher developed an activity that could be used in his or her current teaching situation, thus applying immediately what was gained from the workshop.

Informal evaluation of the experience revealed that teachers appreciated U.S. involvement in this type of development. Participants left with a new excitement and a wider perspective of what instructional materials and techniques were effective for environmental education.

Evaluation Strategies

Evaluation strategies that would seem to be useful in assessing the effectiveness of the Environmental Management Education model are proposed below.

A determination of appropriate concepts and content is a necessary first step. As indicated previously, the works of Roth (1969), Bowman (1972), and Townsend (1982) provide a basis to identify concepts and provide an organizational structure for their presentation. As the conceptual organization was applied in the Dominican Republic and Barbados, it was possible to speculate on knowledge gained, some attitudes that may have been shifted, and skills that were acquired and employed.

Subjective evaluation is another evolving strategy employed by a team of independent reviewers in the Dominican Republic Environmental Education portion of the Natural Resources Management (NARMA) project (Tinnermeier et al., 1984). Surveys previously conducted and those in progress indicate that conservation practices are being implemented as a result of project activity through the use of video-taped documentaries that provide observation of a visual change in the landscape. In addition, preliminary evidence of concept gain and attitude shift resulting from pre/post assessment of participants in the workshops and mass media campaigns exists and will provide the basis for more detailed and rigorous pre/post studies presently under design.

Fortner (1986) conducted a study to evaluate the environmental education program across the two cultures of Barbados and United States workshop participants by comparing teacher characteristics and adoption potential of existing materials. It was found that both groups had positive attitudes toward teaching and responded enthusiastically to the varied techniques of the workshop activities. School curricular limitations were viewed to be restrictive for adoption in Barbados, but U.S. school curricula were viewed to be more accomodating of materials adoption. The workshops in all cases appeared to achieve the intended objectives and pre/post test evaluations revealed an increased awareness of availability of materials, enhanced techniques, and motivation to adopt activities experienced.

Summary

The proposed model for Environmental Management Education has been utilized in both the Spanish- and English-speaking Caribbean for the implementation of training and education programs. Concepts appropriate for the development and implementation of both conservation and environmental management education appear to be relevant. The variety of methodologies employed for the formal and non-formal education settings appear to be effective. The established goals and objectives of the program examples are being achieved, as evidenced by the various preliminary evaluative strategies. It is suggested that the model for Environmental Management Education be utilized as a guide for the development of either formal or non-formal environmental management education programs in developing, as well as developed, countries.

References

Bowman, M.L. 1972. *The Development and Field Validation of An Instrument to Assess College Students' Attitudes Toward the Determinants of Environmental Issues*. Unpublished Ph.D. Dissertation, The Ohio State University, Columbus.

Fortner, R.W. 1986. Environmental education adoption potential of inservice workshop participants in developed countries. In: *Monograph 3, International Aspects of Environmental Education* (J.H. Perkins, ed.) Troy, OH: North American Association for Environmental Education.

Hartshorn, G., et al. 1981. *The Dominican Republic Country Environmental Profile*. JRB Associates, McLean, Virginia. AID Contract No. AID/SOD/PDC-C-0247.

King, W. 1979. *Patterns of Science Curriculum Development in the Caribbean*, a paper presented at the International Symposium on World Trends in Science Education, Halifax, Canada.

Roth, R.E. 1969. *Fundamental Concepts for Environmental Management Education (K-16)*. Unpublished Ph.D. Dissertation, University of Wisconsin, Madison.

Roth, R.E. 1970. *Environmental Management Concepts - A List.* Technical Report No. 126, Wisconsin Research and Development Center for Cognitive Learning, Madison.

Roth, R.E. 1973. A Model for Environmental Education. *The Journal of Environmental Education.* 5(2):38-39.

Stapp, W.B. 1982. Status and analysis of UNESCO's effort to further environmental education internationally—Toward a national strategy for environmental education. In *Environmental Education in Action-V: International Case Studies in Environmental Education* (M.E. Cowan and W.B. Stapp, eds.) Columbus: ERIC Clearinghouse for Science, Mathematics, and Environmental Education.

Tinnermeier, R., et al. 1984. First Evaluation Report of the Dominican Republic Natural Resources Management Project - NARMA. Santo Domingo, Dominican Republic.

Townsend, R.D. 1982. *An Investigation into the Underlying Structure of the Domain of Environmental Education Concepts.* Unpublished Ph.D. Dissertation, The Ohio State University, Columbus.

UNESCO. 1975. *The International Workshop on Environmental Education*, Belgrade, Yugoslavia, 13-22 October, Final Report. Paris: The International Environmental Education Programme, UNESCO-UNEP, ED-76/WS/95.

UNESCO. 1976. *Connect*, Volume 1, Number 1. Paris.

UNESCO. 1982. *Connect*, Volume 7, Number 1. Paris.

11/ Implementing the World Conservation Strategy: Success Stories from Central America and Colombia

James R. Barborak
Gina C. Green

The institutionalized integration of conservation with economic development is the ambitious goal of the World Conservation Strategy (WCS). The International Union for the Conservation of Nature and Natural Resources (IUCN), the World Wildlife Fund (WWF), and UNESCO are among the agencies and organizations that support numerous third world projects in concert with WCS precepts—specifically, the maintenance of essential ecological processes, the preservation of genetic diversity, and the sustainable utilization of species and ecosystems. James Barborak and Gina Green document four Latin American activities which have been able to develop and sustain local support, stabilize land use and tenure around protected areas, overcome budgetary constraints sufficiently well to function effectively, and deal appropriately with institutional frameworks, in part by helping strengthen them. Focus of these accounts is directed toward the significant roles played by non-governmental organizations in the accomplishment of the WCS goal.

Introduction

Recently, much press coverage has been given to natural resource degradation occurring throughout the tropical world. This degradation is caused by complex natural, social, and economic processes, including rapid population growth and accelerated development to produce foreign exchange. These processes are characterized by deforestation, soil erosion, degradation of coastal environments, and simultaneous over-exploitation and under-utilization of natural resources.

In response to growing worldwide concern about resource degradation, the International Union for the Conservation of Nature and Natural Resources (IUCN), the World Wildlife Fund (WWF), the United Nations Educational, Scientific and Cultural Organization (UNESCO) and many other national and international organizations are supporting pilot conservation projects in Central America and Colombia. These projects, implemented by local government agencies and private conservation groups, are designed to support the objectives of the *World Conservation Strategy*, which aims to integrate conservation and economic development.

The *World Conservation Strategy*, since its publication in 1980, has served conservation practitioners throughout the world as a guide for action to meet three primary objectives: 1) to maintain essential ecological processes; 2) to preserve genetic diversity; and 3) to utilize species and ecosystems in a sustainable environment (IUCN, 1980). The strategy outlines priority actions needed to achieve these objectives, including the preparation and implementation of national and sub-national conservation strategies; integration of conservation concerns in national and regional project development plans; the improvement of conservation legislation and resource management agency administration; the training of conservation practitioners; increased investigation of resource values, uses, and management alternatives; increased environmental education efforts directed toward all segments of national populations; public participation in conservation issues; and conservation-based rural development.

In Latin America, many conservation efforts have failed due to a lack of local support, insufficient efforts to stabilize land use and tenure around protected areas, inadequate budgets, and deficient institutional frameworks. Among the governmental and private sectors there is a general resistance to considering wildland conservation as an integral component of broad-based rural development. However, this paper documents four projects that have managed to overcome these problems: the Wildlands Program of the Tropical Agricultural Research and Training Center (CATIE), Costa Rica; the La Planada Ecodevelopment Project, Colombia; the Kuna Indians Wildlands Project, Panama; and the Costa Rican Park System. They follow the guidelines for action outlined in the *World Conservation Strategy* and provide models for additional projects in Central America, Colombia, and other regions.

This paper also discusses additional successful conservation projects in Latin America and the key participation of non-governmental organizations in the implementation of the *World Conservation Strategy*.

CATIE's Wildlands Program

CATIE is a non-profit institution, founded in 1973 in Turrialba, Costa Rica. The Center is dedicated to fostering rural development, particularly in Central America and the Dominican Republic, through research and training in agriculture, animal husbandry, and renewable natural resource management. Its Wildlands Program is part of CATIE's Renewable Natural Resources Department, which also includes programs of tropical forest silviculture, agroforestry, and watershed management.

The Wildlands Program carries out projects and activities which form a regional strategy designed to create and manage an integrated regional network of protected areas in which conservation is considered a part of sustainable development. Key elements are technical cooperation, fund-raising assistance, research, short-term and post-graduate training courses, and information documentation services. All activities are interwoven through demonstration projects in the countries of the region. Projects and activities are designed, implemented, and managed jointly with national resource management institutions.

Virtually all of the services described are provided without charge to Central American countries. In certain pilot projects, particularly those involving management of critical wildlands, the Wildlands Program assumes direct responsibility for preparing resource inventories, management plans, and funding proposals through cooperative agreements with national governments of the region and/or international or bilateral aid agencies and conservation organizations. Teams of national professionals are always involved in planning and implementing the Wildlands Program's activities and in-service training is an integral part of such efforts. Recent cooperative projects include the La Amistad-Talamanca Range Biosphere Reserve Resource Inventory and Planning Project in Costa Rica (Morales et al., 1983), development of a methodology for biosphere reserve systems planning and its application to a test in Costa Rica, and advising the planning process for Braulio Carillo National Park, Costa Rica.

The Wildlands Program also acts as an ex-officio regional liaison office for a number of aid agencies and conservation organizations that lack offices in the region, such as IUCN/WWF-International, WWF-US, UNESCO, the U.S. Fish and Wildlife Service (USFWS), the U.S. National Park Service (USNPS), and UNESCO's Man and the Biosphere Program and the World Heritage Conservation Secretariat.

The Program has been very successful at obtaining small amounts of operations funding, substantial financial support for individual "on-the-ground" projects in each country, and assistance for regional and national training events. Funding sources include IUCN, WWF-International, USAID, DDA (Swiss Development Assistance); FAO; the Fauna and Flora Preservation Society; the Inter-American Foundation; the Bonner, Wildwings, and Kellogg Foundations; the Rockefeller Brothers Fund; Rare Animal Relief Effort (RARE); UNEP; UNESCO (World Heritage and MAB Programs); USFWS; USNPS; and WWF-US.

A major factor contributing to the success of many conservation projects in Central America and Colombia has been the training opportunities, technical assistance, and help in fundraising that projects have received from the Wildlands Program. In each of the following three examples, La Planada, the Kuna Wildlands Project and the Costa Rican Park System, such assistance has played a key role in project success.

The La Planada Ecodevelopment Project, Colombia

One million hectares of Colombian forests are destroyed each year. Deforestation is due to migratory agriculture practiced by landless peasants, land speculation, and expansion of extensive grazing. However, in spite of this trend, several government and private conservation efforts in Colombia have been quite successful, such as the establishment and management of the La Planada Natural Reserve and Ecodevelopment Project.

La Planada is located between 1000-2000 meters above sea level in the Narino Department on the Pacific slope of the Andes. A Colombian biologist, studying needs for future protected areas in the country, visited the site and documented its great ecological diversity and importance as a center of endemism for the Choco biogeographical province, the world's most diverse biome. The biologist and his assistants, whose work was funded by the World Wildlife Fund-US, discovered that loggers were negotiating with the owner of a 2000 hectare tract of forest to remove all valuable timber. They would leave in their wake a network of logging roads which almost certainly would serve as pathways to colonization and complete destruction of the forest within several years.

The concerned researcher relayed the news to WWF-US, indicating that immediate action was needed to save the site. He also enlisted the support of the Colombian Foundation of Higher Education (FES), which has a long history of promoting integrated rural development and also had an expanding environmental education program. Through a cooperative agreement, the Foundation and WWF-US bought the land and sponsored conservation and development of the La Planada region to serve as a pilot project for integrating conservation and rural development.

Since 1983, progress in implementing the project has occurred at a pace unmatched by the majority of similar projects in northern Latin America. WWF-US and FES initiated activities by hiring the biologist who first identified the site as project director, as well as two more Colombian biologists as assistant director and environmental education specialist. With CATIE and WWF-US consultants, they prepared a three-year operational plan outlining all reserve management programs (research, protection, interpretation, training, environmental education, and administration). To promote sustainable development in nearby communities of colonists and Indians, the plan also includes education, agricultural extension, infrastructure, and health services programs. To gain the support of local residents and leaders, FES, WWF-US staff and CATIE consultants met frequently with local representatives from the start of the project. Neighbors of the reserve were hired as wardens and laborers, most materials were purchased locally, and several important donations to the neighboring communities were made, such as the repair of a community school bus, which galvanized local support. A well-organized local opening ceremony for the reserve and an equally important ceremony in Bogota, the nation's capital, succeeded in obtaining both high-level and local support for the project.

Also since 1983, a sizeable yet rustic project headquarters complex has been constructed, including housing for staff and visiting scientists, an environmental education center, and a workshop. Appropriate technology, including solar lighting and fuel-efficient wood stoves and waterheaters, has been installed. Extension work and ecological research have been initiated, as well as a comprehensive environmental education campaign in local schools and communities. The professional staff have been able to do their jobs better due to their participation in CATIE wildlands management and administration training courses. Based on the recommendations of diagnostic studies carried out by specialists to determine priority community development needs, ecodevelopment activities including agriculture and agroforestry extension, and a number of pilot activities to improve health, sanitation, education and public works are now being improved in the region. FES also promotes increased participation of government ministries and other non-governmental organizations to carry out integrated rural development activities in the project area.

The success of La Planada, which is a very young project, is based on a well-designed partnership between a prestigious Colombian foundation and a U.S. conservation NGO, expert assistance in the crucial initial planning stages, early involvement of the local communities and key national figures, strong national and international financial support, and the selection and training of a small, highly motivated professional staff. La Planada can serve as a model, adapted to local environmental and social conditions, that should be tested elsewhere in Latin America. Many wildland conservation efforts are failing throughout the region due to lack of local support, inadequate efforts to stabilize land use and ownership around protected areas, inadequate budgets and management, and a general failure to consider wildland conservation as an integral component of broad based rural development efforts. But La Planada is succeeding.

The Kuna Wildlands Project, Panama

Throughout Latin America, and particularly Central America, indigenous cultures and tribal lands are under threat due to population growth, inroads by landless peasants, and land speculation by non-Indians. The deculturalization of indigenous peoples has increased because of the opening of access roads to formerly remote areas, and because of discovery and/or increased value of renewable and non-renewable natural resources on Indian lands.

On the northeast coast of Panama, 30,000 Kuna Indians inhabit a 350,000—hectare "comarca" (reserve) which they secured through a war for autonomy with the Panamanian government early in this century. The Kuna Comarca includes the San Blas archipelago of more than 300 small islands, where most of the Kuna live, in addition to the adjacent narrow coastal plains and the steep San Blas Range of mountains, rising up to 950 meters. The Comarca, called Kuna Yala by the Indians, has an annual rainfall ranging between 2.5 and 3.5 meters, and contains numerous marine, coastal, and upland ecosystems containing many unique and endangered species of flora and fauna.

The Kuna live in densely populated villages. For their livelihood, they fish, grow and sell coconuts, raise pigs and chickens, and farm coastal plains. Hunting and gathering of products from the forest play major roles in their subsistence lifestyles. A recent study of just one small part of the reserve identified 72 agroforestry combinations, utilizing 48 trees and 16 crops (Beer, 1985). They use 36 species for building boats, 32 for fuelwood, 40 for home construction, and scores more for medicine, handicrafts, and utensils.

The Kuna are unique among Central American indigenous peoples because of their strong social cohesion, autonomy, education level, and self-reliance. In addition, they successfully integrate economic and technical innovations into their culture. Although the Kuna reserve has been isolated traditionally from Panamanian society, the situation has changed due to the construction in the 1970s of a rural access road to the region sponsored by USAID. In just a few years, non-Indian peasants practicing slash-and-burn agriculture have reached the limits of the reserve and have destroyed huge areas of adjacent forests.

The Kuna actively supported the road initially, but later grew alarmed at the increasing threats it posed to the integrity of their land and culture. After the failure of a Kuna agricultural project, which began in 1974 to demonstrate Kuna control along the reserve border, the Kunas sought advice on alternatives for conservation and management of their land. The Wildlands staff of CATIE was enlisted for technical advice and suggested the creation of a Kuna-managed 60,000-hectare forest park. Technical and financial support to hire staff and manage the area was obtained from CATIE, USAID, the Inter-American Foundation, the University of Panama, WWF-US, the Tropical Science Center, and the Smithsonian Tropical Research Institute.

The objectives of the forest park are to protect the boundaries of the Kuna reserve, to promote scientific research and natural history tourism to the area, to generate income for the Kuna, and to assert ownership and use of the Kuna reserve. A Kuna ranger force is now in place and a CATIE-trained and advised Kuna planning team is now completing the management plan for the reserve, which will be proposed to UNESCO for inclusion in the international network of biosphere reserves. The project has the full support of the Kuna leadership, and a large part of the financial support comes from Kuna organizations. CATIE is also providing technical advice to the Kuna on the improvement of traditional agroforestry systems in order to increase agricultural production and sales to distant markets via the new roads.

Costa Rican National Park System

Since its inception in 1970, Costa Rica's National Park System (CRNPS) has grown to become a model for small, ecologically diverse, tropical countries. The Park System now includes 23 protected areas (national parks, biological reserves, and national monuments) encompassing more than eight percent of the country's territory. Not all ecosystems are represented, yet the overall ecological coverage in the system is very high and includes coral reefs, oceanic islands, coastal mangroves and wetlands, seasonally dry Pacific slope forests, and moist-to-wet lowland, mid-altitude and high-altitude forests and paramo (MacFarland et al., 1983; Boza and Mendoza, 1981).

The park system is not by any means perfect. Pressure on the parks by peasant farmers, loggers, poachers, archaeological site looters, and miners is increasing. The Park Service staff has not increased in seven years, while the number of parks and the total protected area have more than doubled. The Park Service operating budget has been greatly reduced, special sources of revenue have been eliminated, and living conditions for field staff remain quite primitive.

The CRNPS is tackling its financial problems, however, through the private Costa Rican National Parks Foundation. Established with strong support from the

Park Service and conservation groups such as the Nature Conservancy and WWF-US, it has raised several million dollars over the past few years for consolidating the park system. Its priorities include buying private holdings in existing parks, improving infrastructure and equipment, providing bonuses, scholarships and other incentives to park service employees, and establishing parks which represent those ecosystems not found in existing protected ares.

Unlike its counterparts in many other developing countries, the Costa Rica National Park System does not exist merely on paper. In recent years, it has produced a veritable boom in ecological research. Thousands of national and foreign researchers conduct long- and short-term studies in the parks, and many tropical biology university courses visit the parks as well. The fascinating plant and animal life of the parks also attracts growing numbers of natural history tourists from North America and Europe, which provides increased foreign exchange earnings and business opportunities for tour operators, hotels, restaurants, and artisans in a period of economic crisis in Costa Rica.

Now almost all sectors of the Costa Rican population recognize that the protected areas are vital to national development. The parks and reserves protect the fragile headwaters of streams that account for over 90 percent of the country's hydroelectricity generation and irrigation potential and a majority of its potable water surface sources, as well as many aquifer recharge areas. The protection of coastal wetlands is vital to sustain the country's fishing industry. Additional recognition of the importance of the parks is due to the fact that almost all of Costa Rica's natural forests outside protected areas are expected to be cut within the next eight years.

A combination of factors, including public and political support for the parks based on their proven economic importance, strong financial and technical support from the international conservation community, comprehensive training of staff at all levels, and strong leadership by a core of highly trained and motivated Costa Rican conservationists, have enabled the Park Service to achieve so much in so little time.

Although not all of the above factors are present in other Latin American nations that are striving to emulate Costa Rica's example, many of the experiences of the CNRPS can be used as models for nearby countries.

Other Successful Examples of the WCS Strategy

The four conservation cases reviewed in this paper are not only "success stories" in Central America and Colombia, but also indicate what is possible to achieve in spite of the major limitations confronting Latin American conservation professionals. A study to review the status of all conservation projects in Central America, to determine general guidelines for project success, and to complete detailed case studies of key pilot projects and the factors which have contributed to their failure or success, is now underway (Green, 1985). Examples of other successful conservation projects identified to date follow.

The Cauca Valley Corporation (CVC), Colombia

This agency, modeled after the Tennessee Valley Authority (TVA), provides one of the best examples of integrated watershed management on a large scale in Latin America, and also demonstrates the importance of the internalization of costs of production of hydroelectricity, potable water, and irrigation water. The CVC has implemented an ambitious resource conservation and land recovery program in the upper Cauca River Valley, an area of approximately two million hectares.

CVC's conservation measures, including reforestation of degraded watersheds, soil conservation practices, management of protected areas, and environmental education, are financed through property taxes levied on large landowners and a fixed percentage of the revenue derived from corporation-operated hydroelectric dams. This financial autonomy, apolitical charter, broad mandate, and strong local support of the CVC have helped it to realize its objectives effectively.

The Gandoca-Manzanillo Ecodevelopment Project, Costa Rica

This project, spearheaded by local community councils and the New Alchemy Association of Costa Rica, includes a number of programs aimed at improving land use and living standards in a 10,000 hectare area located along the southern Atlantic coast of Costa Rica, just north of the Panama border. Project activities include community nurseries to produce perennial crops, fruit, firewood, and timber trees, environmental education, identification and legal designation of a national wildlife refuge in the project area, promotion of nature-based tourism, promotion of agroforestry, and programs to secure land titles for all families living in the area. Secure land tenure will prevent squatter invasions and enable local farmers to obtain access to financial credit, which will encourage long-term investment in forest land management.

The Merenberg Forest Reserve and Foundation, Colombia

The Merenberg Foundation is a group of concerned Colombians and foreigners promoting the conservation and management of Colombia's remaining tropical forest. The Foundation's programs and activities are implemented at the Merenberg Forest Reserve, which is located in the east-central Colombian Andes, between 2,000 and 2,500 meters above sea level.

The Merenberg Reserve was established in 1932, when a family of German immigrants homesteaded the now-protected forest area. They cleared small pasture areas on nonerosive lands and left protective vegetation along the headwaters of streams as a forest reserve. The owners of Merenberg have kept the forests and pastures productive for fifty years without deterioration of the resource. However, each year the conflicts between the German family and landless peasant farmers intensify over the use of the land.

The Merenberg Foundation was established in 1981 to help protect the forest reserve and resolve the conflicts between the owners and local residents. To address the problem, the Foundation initiated programs of seed collection and propagation of native and exotic species for use in reforestation, woodlots, agroforestry, and silvipastoral activities.

The Foundation's objectives are to manage the reserve as a model conservation project and to educate the local residents to recognize and to realize the potential of the forest in order to raise their own standard of living.

Non-Governmental Conservation Organizations (NGOs)

During the past few years, the growing number, size, and influence of non-governmental conservation groups have played an important role in conservation progress in Central America and Colombia. For example, the government of Belize has entrusted management of protected areas to the Belize Audubon Society (BAS). In Guatemala, the Conservation Studies Center of the University of San Carlos (CECON) has gained government support to manage a successful network of biological reserves called biotopes. These biotopes are among the best managed and protected wildland areas in Central America.

The Honduran Ecological Association (AHE) has promoted environmental education efforts and plays a pivotal role in efforts to improve the country's fledgling conservation programs. The Costa Rican Association for Nature Conservation (ASCONA) has led successful campaigns to create several key protected areas, to fight pesticide abuse, and to promote environmental reviews of development projects that could damage the environment.

In addition, the National Parks Foundations of Panama and Costa Rica and the FES in Colombia are involved in channeling financial resources to conservation projects. All of these operations have benefited from the technical and financial support of bilateral aid agencies (particularly USAID) and privately funded conservation groups such as WWF-US, the Nature Conservancy, the New York Zoological Society, the Audubon Alliance, the Wildwings Foundation, IUCN, and World Wildlife Fund-International.

IUCN's Support to Integrating Conservation and Development

The International Union for the Conservation of Nature and Natural Resources (IUCN) plays a key role through its assistance to government agencies and NGOs in their efforts to integrate conservation objectives and activities within development projects in order to minimize possible environment degradation.

Through its Conservation for Development Center, IUCN is currently supporting projects in Central America including environmental impact reviews for road and irrigation projects in Costa Rica and for pulp mills in Guatemala, seminars for government and non-government decision-makers in Honduras and Nicaragua to increase their understanding of how conservation programs contribute to sustainable development, and preparation of conservation strategies for Belize and the Panamanian province of Bocas del Toro.

Biosphere Reserves and World Heritage Sites

Biosphere reserves are globally significant ecological areas managed for scientific investigation and monitoring, environmental education and training, protection of representative ecosystems, and pilot efforts to improve the inter-relationships between man and his environment, such as allowing indigenous communities to exist within all three Central American biosphere reserves. They are created through the framework provided by UNESCO's Man and the Biosphere Program. While Biosphere Reserve designation implies a management philosophy, World Heritage site designation indicates international recognition of the universal values of the most important natural and cultural heritage sites on earth, through the legal framework of the World Heritage Convention. The majority of the most important protected areas in Central America and Colombia are recognized through these programs. These areas include: the Rio Platano Biosphere Reserve/World Heritage Site (BR/WHS), Honduras; Talamanca Range BR/WHS, Costa Rica; Tikal WHS, Guatemala; Andean Belt BR, Colombia; and Darian BR/WHS, Panama.

UNESCO's Man and the Biosphere Program and the World Heritage Convention provide important technical and financial assistance and training scholarships that enable national agencies to improve the protection and management of these Biosphere Reserves and World Heritage sites.

Summary

In spite of political instability, economic turmoil, civil strife, and population growth in Central America and Colombia, successful conservation projects contributing to sustainable national development can be implemented. There is an important link between the current political and economic difficulties in the region and the degradation of its natural resources; any long-term improvement in the overall political-economic situation will depend on greatly improved natural resource management. Emulation and expansion of the successful projects reviewed here would provide a step towards sustainable development in Central America and Colombia.

Acknowledgments

The authors would like to express appreciation for editorial comments, information, and support provided by Laurel Prevetti, Bob Komives, Roger Morales, and other colleagues.

References

Archibold, G. 1984. PEMASKY: Proyecto de Estudio para el Manajo de Areas Sivestres de Kuna Yala. PEMASKY. Paraiso, Ancon, Panama. 4 p.

Barborak, J., C. MacFarland, and R. Morales. 1983. Training personnel for biosphere reserve and other managed wildlands and watersheds: CATIE's Experience in Central America. Presented at the International Biosphere Reserves Congress, Minsk, USSR, November.

Beer, C. 1985. Personal Communication.

Boza, M., and R. Mendoza. 1981. *The National Parks of Costa Rica*. Madrid: INCAFO. 500 p.

Breslin, P., and M. Chapin. 1984. Conservation Kuna style. *Grassroots Development*, 8(2):26-36.

CATIE (PASC). No date. The Wildlands and Watershed Program of the Tropical Agriculture Research and Training Center. Costa Rica: CATIE. 18 p.

Green, G. 1984. Priorities for land use: A South American example. pp. 185-192. *Commonwealth Forestry Review*, 63(3):185-192.

Green, G. 1985. Project Forest Conservation Projects in Central America: An analysis to determine the factors required for success. World Wildlife Fund - U.S.

Houseal, B., et al. 1985. Indigenous cultures and protected areas in Central America. In: *Proceedings*, World Congress on Cultural Parks, Mesa Verde National Park, Colorado.

International Union for the Conservation of Nature and Natural Resources. 1980. *World Conservation Strategy*. Gland, Switzerland: IUCN.

MacFarland, C., and R. Morales. 1981. Planificacion y Manejo de Los Recursos Silvestres en America Central: Estrategia Para Una Decada Critica. Costa Rica: CATIE. 43 p.

MacFarland, C., R. Morales, and J.R. Barborak. 1983. Establishment, planning and implementing of a National Wildlands System in Costa Rica. In: *National Parks, Conservation and Development*, (J.A. McNeely and R.R. Miller, eds.) Washington DC: Smithsonian Institution Press. pp. 592-600.

MacFarland, C. 1985. Informs: Progreso hasta la fecha y planificacion/programacion futura del Proyecto PEMASKY (Kunas, Panama). CATIE. 15 p.

Morales, R., J.R. Barborak, and C. MacFarland. 1984. Planning and managing a multi-component, multi-category international biosphere reserve: The case of the La Amistad/Talamanca Range/Bocas de Toro Wildlands Complex of Costa Rica and Panama. In: *Conservation, Science and Society: Contributions to the First International Biosphere Reserve Congress*, Minsk, USSR, pp. 168-178.

World Wildlife Fund-U.S. 1983. La Planada is a reality. *Focus*, 5(4):8.

12/ The Strategy of Decentralized Production and Distribution of Improved Charcoal Stoves in Kenya[1]

Eric L. Hyman

As is the case in many developing countries, Kenya's deforestation problems are exacerbated by widespread use of inefficient wood-burning stoves. In this paper, Eric Hyman describes a project to introduce improved stoves in the country. Among factors contributing to the success of the project were the selection of a technology that could be readily adopted by Kenya's stove-making artisans and the diffusion of information about the new stoves through existing cultural channels.

Introduction: Traditional and Improved Stoves

Efforts to replace traditional charcoal stoves with more fuel-efficient stoves have been more successful in Kenya than in many other countries. This paper discusses the strategy of decentralized production and distribution that was responsible for this relative success.

The traditional charcoal stove (jiko) design was introduced into Kenya in the early 1900s by Indian laborers working on construction of the railroad. Within fifty years, through market forces, it had become the predominant type in Kenya.

The jiko is made of scrap metal and assembled by local tinsmiths on a cottage-industry scale. It is shaped like a cylinder and has a door for draft control and ash removal, three-hinged triangular flaps that can hold one cooking pot, three legs to support the round base, a metal grate, and handles. Since the traditional jiko is uninsulated, it radiates heat out to the air as well as to the pot.

The improved stove is an upgraded version of the jiko that incorporates design features from engineering principles and experimentation, as well as from stoves used in other countries. This stove is being adopted faster than was the traditional jiko. The improved stove has a bell-bottom-shaped metal cladding, a ceramic liner with an attached grate, and an insulating layer of cement/vermiculite between the liner and the cladding. These design modifications, which are summarized in Table 12-1, promote fuel efficiency. In addition, the new stove is

Table 12-1. Comparison of Kenyan Traditional and Improved Charcoal Stoves

	Traditional Jiko	**Bell-Bottom Stove**
Retail price in Nairobi ($)	2.50	3.75-5.50
Parts needing replacement	Metal grate	Ceramic liner/grate and insulation
Price of Replacement Parts in Nairobi ($)	0.65	1.90
Frequency of replacement of parts (months)	3	8-12
Expected lifetime at full use (months)	12	24
Efficiency in laboratory tests (%)[a]	20-22	29-32

[a]PHU_2—percent of charcoal's heat utilized in boiling and evaporating 2.0 liters of water for 60 minutes.

Sources: Joseph, Shanahan and Young, 1982; Stewart, 1984; Allen 1985; Kinyanjui, 1985.

relatively easy for informal-sector artisans to manufacture. Because of the latter property, quality control and durability problems which have impeded adoption of fuel-efficient stoves elsewhere were largely avoided (Hyman, 1986).

Information about the improved stove was disseminated through the Kenyan Ministry of Energy's Renewable Energy Development Project (KREDP), which was funded by USAID in 1981. The administrative costs of the stoves component of the KREDP amounted to $230,000, including the costs borne by other organizations. Prorated over the 125,000 improved stoves produced by commercial enterprises mostly in and around Nairobi through mid-1986 (Energy Development International, various dates), the administrative costs were less than $1.84 per stove.

Production and Dissemination Strategy

A limited amount of production assistance was provided to four entrepreneurs for start-up costs and/or construction of a pottery kiln and shed. The project also gave small grants of $31 to $62 to about thirty artisans for partial financing of the costs of tools and materials (Kinyanjui, 1985). The start-up assistance is to be repaid after a commercially viable business has been set up.

There are more than fifteen enterprises now making ceramic liners for the improved stoves. However, most of the liners produced to date have been made by three relatively large enterprises in the Nairobi area. Metal claddings for the bell-bottom stove are made by about 100 informal sector artisans; half of these artisans are located in Nairobi (Opole, 1985). Assembly is done by liner manufacturers as well as by metal artisans.

There is a need to increase production of bell-bottom stoves in other urban areas besides Nairobi. It is inconvenient for users to take improved stoves back to Nairobi for repair; as a result, households either will return to using traditional jikos or will have to buy a new improved jiko prematurely. Also, centralized production of liners might result in large breakage losses in transport. Decentralized production would make it easier for a consumer in other parts of the country to have parts replaced and would also generate additional employment outside Nairobi.

The dissemination strategy of the project was based on three assumptions. First, it was assumed that the efforts of government and NGOs could be most effective if they built on Kenya's strong private sector. Consequently, profit provided the incentive for the production and distribution of goods. The costs were minimized by relying on the informal sector, which has low overhead, pays little or no rent, relies on inexpensive labor, and has access to cheap sources of scrap metal. The project began working with small-scale artisans who already were producing metal products or pottery, because these artisans already possess the basic skills and raw materials needed. Since informal sector artisans can produce stoves competently when given simple designs, the project provided them with some training on the principles of efficient stove design, as well as step-by-step instructions on construction. Some important lessons on how to organize the production of charcoal stoves and train artisans were learned during a field visit to Thailand early in the project.

The private sector also had a critical role to play in convincing households to use the new stoves. It was reasoned that households would be willing to pay the higher price if they could be shown the benefits of doing so. Existing private sector channels of distribution with access to a broad spectrum of urban households were used to demonstrate benefits. Also, it was assumed that households would maintain their same basic cooking practices in judging the improved stoves. Thus, stove designers sought user feedback in the course of the project on how the design could be modified.

The project provided training to artisans, trainers, and managers. The first priority in training was to reach some artisans who already were involved in jiko-making so that production of the improved models could begin. However, the trainees often complained that they could not obtain ceramic liners or sufficient capital. Few had sufficient management or marketing skills. Thus, it might have been better to place more emphasis on the training of entrepreneurs and on the promotion of improved stoves among consumers.

Since charcoal is a purchased fuel (unlike wood in most of Kenya), charcoal users have a strong financial incentive to buy a more efficient stove. Only modest efforts were made at demonstrating improved stoves at public markets or through local institutions. Nevertheless, 125,000 stoves have been sold. Project management was concerned about creating a potential demand that could not be met before production had expanded sufficiently. Although this strategy reflected the initial reality, a stronger demonstration and marketing program is timely now. Promotional efforts now should go beyond influencing the decision to purchase an improved stove, because users must understand the importance of having the stoves repaired properly.

A government loan program to enable consumers to buy improved stoves probably would not be appropriate because there are many other things people would rather buy before stoves and many households are wary of government loans. One large firm had some success arranging for large employers to provide stoves for their employees and recover the cost gradually through payroll deductions. One seller offers a rent-purchase agreement to customers, with rent payments credited to the purchase price.

Lessons from this Experience

The Kenyan experience has considerable replication potential because charcoal use is widespread in urban households and traditional stoves are relatively inefficient in many African countries. Furthermore, the resources needed to carry out an improved charcoal stoves program are relatively modest, provided that indigenous metal-working and pottery industries exist.

Some broader lessons about the factors affecting the design, adoption, and use of appropriate technologies can be gleaned from the Kenyan experience. First, the design work accepted the established technology as a starting point and this helped ensure widespread acceptance by households. Like the traditional jiko, the improved stove is portable. A totally different design would have been unfamiliar to the users and there would have been a greater likelihood that it would not have met their perceived needs. Yet, the fact that there was a readily-observable difference between the traditional and improved stoves (the bell-bottom shape) allowed consumers to recognize the difference between the improved and traditional technologies easily.

The KREDP was timely because it built on the earlier activities of a large number of locals and expatriates. The project also avoided the common pitfalls of inflexibly pushing a single design set in advance of implementation, or spending a lot of time and money trying to change people's cultural preferences for stoves. After lab tests narrowed the range of useful alternative technologies, field tests were conducted to obtain feedback from potential users. Following the field tests, further sorting out of the technologies was left to the natural selection process of consumer purchases.

Many stove projects elsewhere have not been successful because the private sector was not given a role in the design or implementation of the projects. The informal sector lacks the capacity for research and testing, but has the ability to adapt rapidly to introduced designs if they are appropriate. Reliance on existing informal sector artisans avoids the expense of having to establish a whole new infrastructure and to train inexperienced and less committed workers.

Decentralized training and other support can be provided to artisans effectively through non-governmental organizations (NGOs) where these groups have the necessary knowledge, resources, and management ability. These prerequisites are most likely to be met if the activities of various NGOs are well-coordinated and there is a tradition of self-help in the project area.

The Kenyan experience demonstrates the advantages of artisan-built rather than user-built stoves. The informal sector is capable of producing simple consumer goods in large numbers at a relatively low cost and in a way that can maintain a competitive and self-sustaining industry in the long run. Generally, informal sector artisans have a low overhead and can spread the risks of labor-intensive production of a new product across the large number of other products that they make.

Maintaining quality control can be a problem with production by small-scale artisans. In this case, most quality-control problems are with the ceramic liners or cement/vermiculite insulation rather than with the metal cladding. Eventually, competition will drive low-quality producers out of the market or force them to improve their products. In the short-run, however, some consumers could become dissatisfied with the technology as a result of the inferior performance and poor durability of the imitations. To reduce this problem, consumers need to be educated about what to look for in a design and in the fabrication of the good. Quality control stamps on the products or warranties also could be helpful.

Unlike woodstoves, charcoal stoves are used by households that pay cash for cooking fuels; they can save at least 25 percent of their charcoal expenditures by switching to improved stoves. By initially focusing on urban markets, which are more geographically compact and contain a larger proportion of households that purchase fuels, demonstration and distribution may be facilitated.

Private sector distribution of charcoal stoves is usually more cost-effective than government distribution. Nevertheless, the informal sector needs some initial support from public agencies, the media, and/or NGOs in promotion and demonstration of a new technology. An educational program can include demonstrations at exhibitions, markets, churches, schools, and other community organizations, radio and newspaper publicity campaigns, and simple pamphlets that can be retained for future reference.

Government policies affecting the price of charcoal can contribute to deforestation and forest resource degradation and may have slowed the progress of this project. Although the price controls on charcoal are not well-enforced in Kenya, they do have some effect on retail prices and hence reduce the incentives to conserve charcoal.

The Kenyan experience shows that in some cases there is no need for extensive producer or consumer subsidies to disseminate a new technology once it has been developed, tested, and demonstrated. Producer subsidies tend to lead to inefficient production by firms and frequently stifle competition and further innovation. Providing financing to producers at a commercial interest rate is not a subsidy, and may be important in stimulating production.

Where the benefits can be captured by consumers and a technology is affordable, consumer subsidies are unnecessary. In fact, consumer subsidies might slow the project's replication in other locations if consumers defer purchasing the stoves while waiting for a subsidy program to be expanded. Price controls on the products of a new technology can interfere with production goals or can aggravate quality control problems.

In conclusion, publicly financed research and product development are necessary, but the findings should be linked to private-sector production and marketed to satisfy consumer preferences. A wide variety of technologies and approaches may deserve support at first, while leaving selection of the most appropriate ones to the marketplace.

Postscript

Appropriate Technology International (ATI) is providing further technical and financial assistance to build on the achievements of the KREDP and extend commercial dissemination outside Nairobi. To reduce quality control problems in molding the ceramic liners and increase the rate of production, an ATI engineer designed a simple motorized jigger jolly, which is now being disseminated. ATI is also providing liner-making enterprises assistance with equipment for clay crushing and mixing, two other aspects that are critical for quality control. With support from ATI, the Kenya Energy Nongovernmental Organizations Association (KENGO) is carrying out consumer education activities to accelerate the acceptance of the technology.

NOTE

1. Research for this paper was sponsored by Appropriate Technology International (ATI). The viewpoints expressed here are those of the author and not necessarily those of ATI. The author would like to thank the following individuals for their helpful comments: Hugh Allen (Appropriate Technology International); Sam Baldwin (Princeton University): Simon Burne (ITDG); Gerald Chege (KENGO); Ton de Wilde (Appropriate Technology International); Ianto Evans (Aprovecho Institute); Thomas Fricke (Experiment in International Living); Amare Getahun (E/DI); Sandy Hale (E/DI); Philip Hassrick (UNICEF); Keith Openshaw (Energy Initiatives for Africa); Stuart Marwick (Woodburning Stove Group, Eindhoven); Francis Njoroge (Kenyan Ministry of Energy and Regional Development); C. Anthony Pryor (USAID REDSO); and Bill Stewart (University of California at Berkeley, School of Forestry).

References

Allen, H. 1985. Personal communication.

Energy/Development International. Various dates. *Kenya Renewable Energy Development Project, Quarterly Progress Reports*. Nairobi: E/DI.

Hyman, E. 1986. The Economics of Improved Household Charcoal Stoves in Kenya. *Energy Policy*, 14:149-158.

Joseph, S., Y. Shanahan, and P. Young. 1982. *The Comparative Performance of Kenyan Charcoal Stoves*. London: ITDG, Stoves Project Technical Paper No. 1.

Kinyanjui, M. 1985. Personal communication.

Opole, M. 1985. *Review of Programme Cookstove Field Activities*. Nairobi: University of Nairobi, Prepared for E/DI.

Stewart, B. 1984. *Preliminary Testing of a Cast Iron Stove From the Rajamanthri Iron Works, Andra Pradesh, India*. Reading: ITDG.

13/ Sustainable Development of Natural Resources in the Third World: The Human Equation

Sunil K. Roy

Drawing on extensive personal experience, Sunil Roy makes a strong statement supporting his view that social aspects of resource management—patterns of development—demand equivalent attention to technical aspects. The basic issue becomes what kind of development, for whom, and how? Is there enough for everyone's need, if not his/her greed? Achievements proceeding from effective development and management of natural resources have been and are being made in the Third World, but data clearly show that the job is far from done, that the magnitude of the task is growing faster than is institutional capacity for its accomplishment. A complicating factor is the common perception in the Third World that conservation is an elitist pursuit, thus both external to and potentially contrary to the best interests of most people. Also, the outside expert may know the answers only to an incomplete or otherwise inappropriate schedule of questions. Perceived as another form of elitism, the outsider's solutions may create additional problems while compounding the original one.

Frequently, human rather than technical aspects cause difficulties in the management and development of natural resources in the Third World and elsewhere. Many well-conceived projects handled by able administrators and scholars contribute below their potential, require greater inputs, or even founder on individual personalities and local hierarchical sensitivities.

My credentials as an "expert" in the management of natural resources are limited, more instinctive than intellectual, augmented by 30 years of personal experience with the dangers of mining renewable resources, and leading to a total commitment to the concept of sustainable development.

As too often happens, this came about almost too accidentally to be believable. The Imperial policy was to maintain a broad unadministered area below the Indo-Tibetan frontier, with responsibility for it and for the tribal areas of the then North East Frontier Agency carrying over to the post-Independence Ministry of External Affairs. After the 1954 famous but fragile Sino-Indian agreement on the Five Principles of Peaceful Co-Existence, my assignment was to coordinate the extension of the administration right up to the frontier and generally see what was going on across the border in Tibet.

There were no roads and the railhead was in the plains. I had to trek several thousand miles in the upper Himalayas and into Tibet from Ladakh right across to the northeastern corner, where Burma, China and Tibet meet. It was both a formative and inspiring experience. The majesty of the snow peaks, the ecstatic beauty of the valleys, the clarity of the rushing rivers and the wide variety of bird and animal life in magnificent mountain forests enthralled. Yet, even in 1954-57, the deterioration of the Himalayan forests was already evident and its destructive impact on the overall environment was becoming increasingly apparent. The consciousness of impending crisis resulted in my decision then to leave the Foreign Service and to work independently on environmental conservation whenever I had enough to live on. This became possible in 1976-77 when I returned to India to work on what mattered most to me—the conservation of life support systems.

One is forced to raise a basic issue: "What kind of development, for whom, and how?" From this comes the question, *What natural resources?* I think it is generally accepted that the earth's finite resources as presently utilized are not presently able to provide the existing global population with the basics—adequate shelter, nutrition, and potable water. So development in the pattern of the affluent industrialized nations is out of the question for all except a tiny minority in third world countries. Gandhiji summed this up: "There is enough for everyone's need but not for everyone's greed."

In spite of the remarkable achievements of Indian agriculture, about 37 percent of the rural population and 32 percent of the urban population survive on 75 percent of their caloric needs. Further, 7.5 percent of the rural and 5.5 percent of the urban population are unable to obtain even 50 percent of their caloric needs.

Independently, the UNEP World Public Hearing organized in London in 1982 recorded that, globally, every day 5000 children die of starvation.

In other spheres, the changed development picture in India is apparent in the contrast between its position as a subject people in 1947, and today as the world's largest free-wheeling democracy. Then, the only item the freedom movement could boycott was the import of textiles. Now we produce everything indigenously from paper clips to computers to nuclear power stations, and have an Indian satellite in orbit. But is this pattern enough when so many go hungry in India, and are dying of starvation in many third world countries? Let us also note the report in a TV program that 1.5 million children in New York go hungry.

Some insights on attitudes and approaches, current and possible, emerged in deliberations at the World Industry Conference on Environmental Management initiated by the United Nations Environment Program in France in November, 1984. What follows is a summation of some of the interventions.

The industrial view represented by major primary producers and multinationals was concerned with profits, survival and growth, whereas governments viewed development more broadly: employment, income generation, balance of payments, and citizen well-being. An American assessment of the relationship between industry and the environment stated a U.S. industry view:

> While industry has relied on government, both local and national, to provide it with an infrastructure to make its activities possible, government has relied on industry to bring in and create wealth. That relationship was severely jolted in the 1960s and 1970s by the public reaction to the ever-spreading environmental degradation caused by industrial activity in the post World War II boom. Thus, in the early 1970s, the newly created Environmental Protection Agency in the United States, with many lawyers and environmental scientists who had never worked in or for industry, called on industry to meet a whole range of stringent standards on atmosphere and water pollution as contained in the Clean Air and Clean Water Act. The EPA, like comparable agencies elsewhere in the industrialized world, dictated to industry what was expected of it, and not much dialogue took place.

A Japanese spokesman illustrated what could be done through responsible government-industry cooperation. He said that although Japan is only one-and-one-half times larger than Britain or Germany and three-fourths the size of France, its 120 million population is double that of any of these countries. Within this crowded space, Japan in 1982 had achieved a GNP which corresponds to \$13,200,000 per km^2 of habitable area. In response to public criticism of industrial diseases such as Minamata, Yokkaichi asthma, and cadmium poisoning from contaminated rice, mercury levels have been controlled, hydrogen fluoride in Yokkaichi collected, SO_2 emissions reduced to one-eighth of the peak of 0.083 ppm in 1965, and chemical oxygen demand of wastewater reduced by 65 percent in three years.

This was not reflected in the presentations from other industrialized countries, despite data which showed that application of emission control technologies led to savings in energy and raw materials, and in many cases to financial benefits as high as 13 percent of investment costs. This demonstrated the fallacy of the widely held view that conservation means slower growth, and shows that economic development and environmental protection are not only compatible, but mutually reinforcing.

In the same conference, a lone voice challenged the contemporary development approach. Anil Agrawal of the Centre for Science and Environment, New Delhi, spoke for the deprived of the Third World:

> The vast majority of the people of the world—the poor of the Third World—live within a biomass-based subsistence economy. Fundamental needs like food, fuels, building materials, fertilizers, raw materials like bamboos, and various types of grasses for traditional crafts and occupation are all forms of biomass, most of which are collected freely from the immediate environment. For these biomass-dependent people, usually called the poor because they do not benefit

> much from the gross national product, there is another GNP which is far more important, and this is what I call the Gross Nature Product.

The King of Bhutan's comment to economic experts talking about GNP was that he was not interested in GNP, but in GNH, the "Gross National Happiness" of his people. From this I base my emphasis on the human element in sustainable development. Roughly two-thirds of the world population presently outside the mainstream of current development patterns can only survive if there is a change in development thinking. While continuing the process of industrialization, there have to be simultaneous measures introduced for the well-being of these billions. There must be a commitment to the conservation and improvement of the environment on which they are dependent. Mentioned is a perceptive intervention by the French Environment Minister on establishing industries in communities "...which have their own resource needs, climate and culture. The geographical, ecological and human impact must be taken into account to a greater extent than has so far been the case." Much of current development is dislocating essential aspects of the environment, undermining the environmentally sound approaches of people who have survived many millennia under their current circumstances. Their variety is a reflection of the Earth's biological diversity, which we devastate at our peril.

In developing countries environmental conservation has tended to be regarded as an elitist fad to maintain natural beauty and the diversity of wildlife. This is not surprising, because public attention has been concentrated on protecting "endangered species" of a number of glamorous animals. A cartoon response in an Indian paper showed two old farmers sitting smoking their hukkas (hubble bubbles) with the caption, "We wish we were endangered species." This illustrates the sentiments of the majority, including the better-informed people. This is readily understandable where a majority of the population is directly dependent on natural resources for day-to-day living and among whom a substantial percentage live below the poverty line. What needs much greater emphasis is that many of the poor are indeed "endangered," and that the conservation of fauna and flora is vital; their condition is the litmus paper of human survival.

In the context of sustainable development, "essential" is almost a contradiction in terms for third world countries, where natural resources have been so extensively devastated as to be almost in irreversible decline. Considerable variations limit the validity of lumping together a group of countries with vastly different geographic, climatic, socio-cultural, economic, and population conditions. There are common denominators, the most telling of which is the poverty of the majority and the pressure of population on finite resources. The hope of finding a general panacea can only lead to disaster. In a sense, this is related to a schoolboy "howler" in an international exam. A question required a single word answer for "a cure for all ills" and the enterprising answer given: "death"! Perhaps this is symbolic, in the context of our deliberations.

The Sahel famine deaths are not endemic; they have expanded into other parts of Africa. Hundreds of thousands have died of starvation. A Food and Agriculture Organization (FAO) study, *Agriculture Towards 2000*, indicates that even if there is an over 70 percent increase in productivity of the existing cultivated area, an additional 200 million hectares must be cultivated to meet minimum food needs. Experts predict hundreds of millions of deaths as we enter the 21st century and the global population reaches over six billion. This can happen if major people-oriented, environmentally-aware projects are not introduced and urgently implemented. Productivity can be substantially increased in most developing countries. Some "wasted" lands can be brought under cultivation; some marginal land, not really cultivable, can be used for silvi-horticulture, silvi-pastoral, or fuelwood purposes. This requires a reorientation of priorities, the provision of inputs, and the application of improved methods at local levels.

Though population growth is clearly a critical factor, degradation of the natural environment and mass poverty are the real causes. All three are interlinked. A family could well be content with two children, but four becomes the minimum when one family member has to concentrate on finding fuelwood and one on fetching water. The number rises in relation to infant mortality and adult survival to ensure old-age support.

Virtually all third world countries have passed the point where any further pressure on the natural resource base must be preceded by massive regeneration and emergency conservation measures. Development in the traditional pattern touches a very limited segment—industrialists, the urban affluent, and the rich farmers—who now benefit most directly. It threatens the best entrenched because of excessive drawdown in almost every area. Water needs are basic but supply is limited in every urban centre, as is quality. The source in the river Jamuna from which the local waterworks obtains water supplied to about half a million residents in the most affluent areas of Delhi is virtually sullage, a respectable synonym for sewage, contributed by the residents of North Delhi through the formerly prestigious desert river, Sahibi Nadi, now throttled to the Najafgarh Drain. Also called the "ganda nullah" (filthy drain), it carries about 80 percent of the pollutants entering the still sacred river, which receives roughly 200 million litres of human and 20 million litres of industrial waste every day.

A high percentage of the population meets its water needs directly from the river; potable water reaches about one-third of the total population. Eighty percent of all ailments are water-borne diseases. In addition, half the population faces malnutrition. In theory this is a soluble management problem, but it requires an innovative, locally and regionally relevant approach, and a revision of the standard development model. The current model evolved in times of seemingly limitless bounty of the earth, when a handful of imperial countries had uncontrolled access to the natural resources of two-thirds of the world at their own prices.

Those who formulate projects or have occasion to work in developing countries have to adjust their working approach to their target area. This would seem obvious, but the general trend is to apply theory and practice effective elsewhere to entirely different conditions. This comes into play in the personality, attitudes, and family preferences of the individuals involved. The initial approach of visiting experts, foreign or indigenous, must be one of learning more than doing. In addition, there is need for an open-minded attitude toward the views, local knowledge, and sensitivity of the people and officials for whom and with whom the expert will be working. This, in combination with the technological and scientific inputs now available, will do much to ensure the best results for all concerned.

Anyone who has some knowledge of foreign aid programmes in the developing world will know of well-intentioned projects that have not produced the expected results. They have perhaps heard of the negative impact of roads into mountain areas which not only damage the environment but serve little if any meaningful purpose. The enthusiasm of the project source overwhelms local reservations or ignores them or misunderstands local courtesy. The latter is general and becomes linked with project implementation. A polite "yes yes!" too often means "no!" Failure to interpret the nuances can lead to confusion. It is difficult to identify the real need unless there is close liaison with local officials who have developed a sympathetic relationship with people in the project area. Also necessary is the capacity of the project coordinator, national or international, to identify with the local communities and their real needs. I emphasize this because planners are predominantly urban-oriented and remote from project areas. It is in this context that a perceptive Indian comment is offered:

> We need outside help for analysis and understanding of our situation and experience, but not for telling us what we should do. An outsider who comes with ready-made solutions and advice is worse than useless. He must first understand from us what our questions are, and help us articulate the questions better, and then help us find solutions. Outsiders also have to change. He alone is friend who helps us to think about our problems on our own.

This is broadly true in all cases. At a functional level, an African attitude shows practical grass-roots reality and identifies the cause for frequent failures to achieve project objectives. In response to a query from a "white man" on what to plant, a village elder said:

> Neres karites for their fruit, oil and butter, and acacias for the animals in the dry season when there is no more grass....The whites wrote everything down in a notebook, but when they came back they brought eucalyptus trees....Those thin, sickly trunks will not provide more than poles for huts. Furthermore, the wood does not burn well and the leaves are good for nothing. The people from the Department asked a lot of questions but they did not listen.
>
> In the past, the village had asked the agronomist for a grain bank to store their millet at the end of the harvest, some small dikes to prevent the earth from being washed away by the rain, some fencing, and a well to do some market gardening during the dry season.... Nothing ever arrived. The extension agent explained later that none of that was important and that the whites preferred to build a new road and dig wells.

This is where the best of intentions get lost in the dreary desert of dead habit. Patterns of development successful elsewhere are attempted in entirely different socio-economic, cultural, and environmental conditions. Even organizational approaches falter on individual personality and hierarchical misunderstanding. A typical example at the higher echelon is the automatic presumption that once a project has been cleared by the federal authority, the local officials just have to fall in line. This ignores the complex question of state's rights and the individual *amour propres* of the field officials and their superiors, who function in a largely inflexible line of authority. Cordial relations and communication should be maintained at all administrative echelons. This places the onus on the project director to ensure that his colleagues in the field seek, rather than expect, local cooperation because the project has been cleared. There is also an "age factor." Young graduate students have to handle gently their liaison with older field officials, many of whom resent being set aside by "children." Tact and understanding will build a sound working base without which things will not move, or will move only frustratingly slowly. To use a cliche, "People's involvement is the key to success," because it is too often ignored.

In too many projects vast sums have been spent. The implementors will have benefited materially, but little accrues to those for whom it was intended. In sharp contrast, there is a report of implementation of a rural project to control flooding and create storage with local participation. On June 1, 1985 the villagers were provided funds by a Swiss group to build a dam on a nearby stream and were given engineering expertise by Action for Food Production, a non-governmental organization. By July 1, 1985, the villagers had built the dam. Rains were late, but when they came the total storage was roughly 1-1/4 million cubic metres. The cost was about US $7500—which the Swiss field executive had been persuaded to provide without clearance from his headquarters.

There are a large number of similarly effective people-oriented, people-involved, environmentally-aware projects, the best known of which is the *Chipko* ("cling to") movement in the Himalayas. The hill women most directly affected in responding to the impact of destruction of their environment—landslides, floods, non-availability of fuelwood and timber for housing and local industry, and the drying up of village springs through excessive tree felling by contractors—clung to the trees and protected them. Now, no forest department plans in the area are finalized without consulting the people; the Core Group has organized afforestation around its headquarters in the upper catchment of the Alaknanda river.

This can be applied less easily for major projects, but unless there is a dramatic change in approach, considerable national and international funds and effort will be expended with poor or even negative results. A classic case in India is a World Bank project to fell vast areas of mixed deciduous forest in a predominantly tribal area, the Bastar forest, and to plant tropical pine. The project was cleared in New Delhi, but local administrators, aware of the negative impact on tribal populations and the entirely different rainfall and soil conditions, prevaricated and delayed implementation despite pressures, especially from the foresters. The Tribal Affairs departments at the federal and state levels opposed the project. Eventually, after considerable wastage of money, time and effort, it was ruled out by Prime Minister Indira Gandhi.

Much is expected from social forestry projects financed by a multiplicity of international donors, including the World Bank. The most widely distributed seedlings are eucalyptus species; 80 percent is the figure, according to a public statement of a former Inspector General of USAID Forests. The dominance of eucalyptus in USAID-supported social forestry projects has been widely questioned because this imported exotic does little for the fuel and nothing for the fodder needs of the rural majority, for concern about negative impact on the soil, and because the major benefit has gone to big farmers (four hectares and above). The product goes mainly to industries and urban centres, and the Forest Departments are major beneficiaries in funds and additional personnel.

A USAID forestry officer suggested to me that any tree is better than no tree and that only eucalyptus could survive the pressure from grazing cattle. We agreed to disagree, but I provided him with information from the mid-term report of a World Bank social forestry project in Gujarat and UP (Uttar Pradesh). Gujarat has recruited 26 deputy conservators of forests, 34 additional conservators of forests, 340 regional forest officers, 1125 foresters, and 896 protection assistants. UP has not listed any senior positions, but indicates an increase of 128 rangers, 440 foresters and 770 forest guards.

While admitting that the objects of social forestry are directed toward improvement of the lot of the rural poor, the report acknowledges that "no systematic analysis" has been done of this in Gujarat. It also acknowledges that in UP and Gujarat, big farmers and the paper mills they supply with wood for pulp are the primary beneficiaries. The statistics are revealing. Farm forestry, which serves the interests of the larger farmers and meets the needs of industry, is wrongly equated with social forestry, has overshot its target in UP by 3430 percent, and has fallen short in establishing community self-help wood lots by 92 percent.

The conclusions are disconcerting. First, comparative failure of the wood lot schemes argues for their curtailment, with concentration on farm forestry. This is justified by the fact that strip plantation evidently costs Rs.4200 per hectare and village wood lots Rs.3000 per hectare, and yield a benefit between 12 and 15 percent. On the other hand, farm forestry only costs Rs.1600 per hectare, with a return of 25 to 30 percent.

The rural poor, for whom social forestry is planned and for whom fuelwood and fodder have always been free, do not and will not benefit. Meeting their essential needs means continued despoliation of natural resources. This carries over into most planned-from-the top rural development projects. A World Bank study shows that some 3000 wells costing $12 million went to cooperatives serving 20 to 25 farmers. On village wells, the study indicates that the well would end up as the property of one man, the richest landlord in the village. A foreign expert comment is typical: "I no longer ask who is getting the well. I know what the answer will be and I do not want to hear it: 100 percent of these wells are going to the big boys." The inference is that the increased income is used to buy up small farmers and render them landless.

In India very little of the Plan funds allocated for rural and tribal development reach the target populations, and even that is misapplied through inappropriate priorities. Recent visits to tribal and rural areas by Prime Minister Rajiv Gandhi brought this home to him so forcefully that he acknowledged it in a statement to Parliament. He has emphasized the need for consultation with local communities and for the posting of competent, motivated personnel to work on these projects. As a result, the Integrated Rural Development Programme (IRDP) will be revamped, with creation of new groupings so that the poorest elements will receive more than available so far, instead of former groupings of families together and providing standard amounts for all. An equally important outcome is likely to be the concentration of LPG facilities in towns in and near forest areas, because much of the depletion of forests is the result of tribal and forest-dwelling people carrying headloads for sale to urban centres to meet their immediate food needs. Also, state government and local authorities went to extreme lengths to "paper over" persistent failure, resulting in the report of comment to the Tribal Welfare Minister by the PM: "Don't try to whitewash things, do some solid work;" and to the State Chief Minister: "In future I will have to visit without informing."

Hopefully, this marks a watershed in the scope of the *Garibi hatao* (Removal of Poverty) slogan which contributed to earlier election success, but which lost its way through individual and collective inadequacy and greed. Though related to India, it is equally relevant in most developing countries; it is both the challenge and the promise for the future.

I have barely touched on the state of the environment but two extracts which demonstrate something of the Indian situation with its special dependence on the Himalayas follow. Dr. Parmar, the former Chief Minister of a Himalayan State Himachal Pradesh, summed up the first in a 1977 speech:

> It is a pity that we have not been able to implement our National Forest Policy with a semblance of effectiveness in achieving or maintaining about two-thirds of the area in hills under forest cover to secure the objective prescribed in the Forest Policy...Land-use statistics showing a sizable percentage of area being under forest in Jammu and Kashmir; out of total forest area of 15.9 percent, only about 10.5 percent is wooded. In Himachal Pradesh about 13.5 percent of 38.5 percent forest lands are wooded. In the UP hilly region, the position is identical.

It has deteriorated significantly since then. M.S. Swaminathan highlighted the consequences in a 1975 paper:

> The adverse consequences of indiscriminate deforestation and shifting cultivation are now manifesting themselves in numerous ways like flash-floods, land slides, soil erosion, silting of canals and reservoirs, and albedo effects. The damage to the Himalayan ecosystem through extensive deforestation and land slides promoted by the methods adopted for the construction of roads, mining, etc. has become a matter of global concern. If we do not arrest and reverse this process before the end of this century, the entire future of Indo-Gangetic agriculture may be in danger. Since the Indo-Gangetic belt has the maximum untapped agricultural production reservoir in the

country, our ability to feed 1000 million in another 25 years is inextricably interwined with the restoration of the Himalayan eco-system.

Mention of armament expenditures in the context of demands on natural resources is inescapable. According to Inge Thoresson, Chairperson of the Second UN World Disarmament Conference in a 1982 speech, expenditure in this sphere has reached US $600,000 million, and if it continues to increase as before more than 25 percent of the world's natural resources would be so used by the turn of the century. Development planners face greater urgency in evolving more innovative local and regionally meaningful projects. Much can still be achieved, but only with better conceived and implemented strategies designed to meet the essential needs of the majority.

Agencies involved in projects for developing countries with substantial financial inputs must look beyond the technologic development aspect to socio-political priorities and consequences. This applies equally to national governments. In India, development planning has resulted in some improvement in the condition of about 50 percent of the population (no mean achievement) and in considerable prosperity for about 10 percent, with a segment living at levels of opulence comparable to the most affluent elements anywhere in the world. This has not carried over to the rural majority or to the urban poor. It has also been at the cost of what may be irreversible damage to the natural environment. If there is no change in development attitudes, the deforestation and mismanagement of the land and water resources and the widening gap between the "haves" and "have-nots" threaten our future well-being; it can undermine a delicately balanced political stability.

Internationally, the social upheavals and political dislocations in many developing countries are the result of similar distortions, with consequent fundamental resentments at the continuing and growing deprivation of those on the fringes of the economic system in both urban and rural settings. Recent history has too many examples of the dangers of ignoring this and of the failure of attempts to suppress it violently. At the base is the continuing degradation of life-support systems directly linked to pressures to meet the minimum essential needs of the majority and the demands of industry and the affluent society.

The capacity to plan for the sustainable development of natural resources in the Third, or any other, World depends on readiness to revise the pattern and methodology of development. In John Carroll's words:

> Western industrial society, and American society in particular, has difficulty in avoiding neat but fatally artificial, unrealistic separations and divisions of problems and peoples. Unless "blinders" presently in place are removed, unless conditioned mindsets towards the world and towards other people's conception of life are removed, development, sustained or otherwise, is doomed to failure.

14/ Postscript

Deterioration of renewable natural resources in the Third World has attracted increasing attention during the past few years. Some of the consequences of deforestation, soil erosion, and other environmental ills have been described in this book, with the elements of strategies intended to foster resource conservation.

Stated explicity or inferred implicitly in each of the chapters is the need to design environmental policy and resource development projects in ways that take into account local, human realities. Although there are exceptions, policies and projects are generally designed based on reasonably accurate diagnoses of the physical and biological dimensions of environmental realities. In light of technical diagnoses, proposed "interventions" are rarely invalid. When policies and projects fail, insufficient attention to the social and institutional contexts of environmental concern is frequently the cause.

The efforts of representatives of both worlds, particularly in situations where they have worked together and thus have learned from one another, have led to encouraging results in the Third World. Much has been learned about specific, sometimes unique, local physical environments, dramatically increasing the possibility of technology transfer; more had to be learned, and has been learned, about how to select and adapt technologies within the contexts of given institutional situations. It appears that this particular surface has been significantly scratched, though hardly gouged.

Reports such as those collected in this volume offer much to the practitioner who seeks models of what works, and how; what doesn't, and why. They offer something also to the planner, the researcher, the academic, the student—all of whom seek to identify, perhaps to formulate, paradigms to more effectively guide future efforts focused on the sustainable development of natural resources.

Contributors

James R. Barborak	IUCN and WWF Regional Project Director, Wildlands and Watershed Program, Renewable Natural Resource Development, Centro Agronomico Tropical de Investigacion y Ensenanza, Turrialba, Costa Rica
Leslie R. Cooperband	Doctoral candidate, Department of Agronomy, The Ohio State University, Columbus
J. Mark Erbaugh	Program Assistant, International Programs, College of Agriculture, The Ohio State University, Columbus
Gina C. Green	Program Assistant, IUCN and WWF Regional Project, Wildlands and Watershed Program, Renewable Natural Resource Development, Centro Agronomico Tropical de Investigacion y Ensenanza, Turrialba, Costa Rica
Hans Gregersen	Professor, College of Forestry, University of Minnesota, St. Paul
Lawrence S. Hamilton	Research Associate, East-West Center, Honolulu, Hawaii
David O. Hansen	Associate Professor, Department of Agricultural Economics and Rural Sociology, The Ohio State University, Columbus
Abel Hernandez	Director, Projecto MARENA, Dominican Republic
Frederick J. Hitzhusen	Professor, Department of Agricultural Economics and Rural Sociology, The Ohio State University, Columbus
Eric L. Hyman	Appropriate Technology International, Washington, DC
Gary S. Kemph	U.S. Agency for International Development, Dominican Republic

Clarence F. Kooi	U.S. Agency for International Development, Haiti
Terry J. Logan	Professor, Department of Agronomy, The Ohio State University, Columbus
Stephen E. McGaughey	Chief, Inter-American Development Bank, Washington, DC
Richard B. Norgaard	Associate Professor, Agricultural and Resource Economics, University of California at Berkeley
Andrew J. Pearce	Fellow, East-West Center, Honolulu, Hawaii
Robert E. Roth	Professor, School of Natural Resources, The Ohio State University, Columbus
Sunil K. Roy	National Committee for Environmental Training, New Delhi, India
Douglas D. Southgate	Associate Professor, Department of Agricultural Economics and Rural Sociology, The Ohio State University, Columbus

Index

For Product Safety Concerns and Information please contact our EU representative GPSR@taylorandfrancis.com Taylor & Francis Verlag GmbH, Kaufingerstraße 24, 80331 München, Germany

Batch number: 10732529

Printed by Printforce, the Netherlands